W. F. Butler

The Wild North Land

Being the Story of a Winter Journey, With Dogs, Across Northern... Second Edition

W. F. Butler

The Wild North Land
Being the Story of a Winter Journey, With Dogs, Across Northern... Second Edition

ISBN/EAN: 9783744798426

Printed in Europe, USA, Canada, Australia, Japan

Cover: Foto ©Andreas Hilbeck / pixelio.de

More available books at **www.hansebooks.com**

THE
WILD NORTH LAND:

BEING

THE STORY OF A WINTER JOURNEY, WITH DOGS,

ACROSS NORTHERN NORTH AMERICA.

By Captain W. F. BUTLER, F.R.G.S.,

AUTHOR OF "THE GREAT LONE LAND," &c.

"I cannot rest from travel. I will drink life to the lees."
"I am become a name for always roaming with a hungry heart."

WITH ILLUSTRATIONS AND ROUTE MAP.

SECOND EDITION.

London:
SAMPSON LOW, MARSTON, LOW, & SEARLE,
CROWN BUILDINGS, 188, FLEET STREET.
1874.

LONDON:
GILBERT AND RIVINGTON, PRINTERS,
ST. JOHN'S SQUARE.

PREFACE.

PEOPLE are supposed to have an object in every journey they undertake in this world. A man goes to Africa to look for the Nile, to Rome to see the Coliseum or St. Peter's; and once, I believe, a certain traveller tramped all the way to Jerusalem for the sole purpose of playing ball against the walls of that city.

As this matter of object, then, seems to be a rule with travellers, it may be asked by those who read this book, what object had the writer in undertaking a journey across the snowy wilderness of North America, in winter and alone? I fear there is no answer to be given to the question, save such as may be found in the motto on the title-page, or in the pages of the book itself.

About eighteen months ago I was desirous of entering upon African travel. A great explorer had been lost for years in the vast lake-region of Southern Central Africa, and the British Nation—

which, by the way, becomes singularly attached to a man when he is dead, or supposed to be dead—grew anxious to go out to look for him.

As the British Nation could not all go out at once, or together, it endeavoured to select one or two individuals to carry out its wishes.

It will be only necessary to state here, that the British Nation did not select the writer of this book, who forthwith turned his attention from African tropic zones to American frigid ones, and started out upon a lonely cruise.

Many tracks lay before me in that immense region I call "The Wild North Land." Former wandering had made me familiar with the methods of travel pursued in these countries by the Indian tribes, or far-scattered fur-hunters. Fortunate in recovering possession of an old and long-tried Esquimaux dog—the companion of earlier travel—I started in the autumn of 1872 from the Red River of the North, and, reaching Lake Athabasca, completed half my journey by the first week of March in the following year. From Athabasca I followed the many-winding channel of the frozen Peace River to its great cañon in the Rocky Mountains, and, journeying through this pass—for many reasons the most remarkable one in the whole range of the Rocky Mountains—reached the north of British Columbia in the end of May. From thence, following a trail of 350 miles through the dense forests of New Caledonia, I emerged on the 3rd of June at the frontier station of Quesnelle on the Frazer River, still 400 miles north of Victoria.

In the ensuing pages the story of that long tramp —for it was mostly performed on foot—will be duly set forth. Written by camp fire, or in cañon, or in the little log-house of a northern fur fort, when dogs and men rested for a day or two in the long icy run, that narrative will be found, I fear, to bear many indications of the rough scenes 'mid which it has been penned; but as, on a former occasion, many critics passed in gentle silence over the faults and failings of another story of travel in the Great Lone Land, so now it may be my fortune to tell to as kindly an audience, this record of a winter's walk through more distant wilds—for in truth there has been neither time for revision nor correction.

Fortune, which eighteen months ago denied me African adventure, offers it now with liberal hand.

I reached the Atlantic from the Pacific shore to find an expedition starting from England against Ashantee; and long ere this story finds a reader I hope to be pushing my way through the mangrove swamps which lie between the Gold Coast and Coomassie. To others even must fall the task of correcting proofs, while I assume my part in the correction and revision of King Koffi Kancalli, and the administration to his subjects of that proof of British prowess which it has been deemed desirable to give them.

Meantime, my old friends Chief Kar-ka-konias, Kalder, and Cerf-vola, will be absent from this new field; but, nevertheless, there will be present many companions of former travel, and *one* Chief under whose command I first sought the Great Lone Land as the threshold to remoter regions.

W. F. BUTLER.

LONDON,
September 21*st*, 1873.

CONTENTS.

CHAPTER I.
The Situation at Home—The West again—A Land of Silence . 1

CHAPTER II.
Powder versus Primroses—The American Lounger—"Home, sweet Home" 6

CHAPTER III.
Civilization and Savagery—Fort Garry under new aspects—Social Societies—An old Friend—Pony "the perverse" . . . 10

CHAPTER IV.
The Wilderness—A Sunset Scene—A white Savage—Cerf-Vola the Untiring—Doggerel for a Dog—The Hill of the Wolverine—The Indian Paradise—I plan a Surprise—Biscuits and Water 21

CHAPTER V.
The Forks of the Saskatchewan—A perverse Parallel—Diplomatic Bungling—Its Results 36

CHAPTER VI.
Our Winter Home—A Welcome—I start again—The Hunter's Camp—In quest of Buffalo on the Plains—"Lodge-poling" leads to Love 43

CHAPTER VII.
An Ocean of Grass—The Red Man—Whence comes he?—The Buffalo—Puritans and Pioneers—The Red Man's Friend . 49

CONTENTS.

CHAPTER VIII.

Buffalo Hunts—A Picture once seen long remembered—L'Homme capable—A wonderful Lake—The lost Indian—An Apparition—We return Home 57

CHAPTER IX.

Strange Visitors—At-tistighat the Philosopher—Indian Converts—A Domestic Scene—The Winter Packet—Adam and his Dogs 70

CHAPTER X.

A *tale* of Warfare—Dog-sleds—A Missing Link—The North Sea—"Winterers"—Samuel Hearne 83

CHAPTER XI.

A Dog of no Character—The Green Lake—Lac Ile à la Crosse—A Cold Day—Fort Ile à la Crosse—A long-lost Brother—Lost upon the Lake—Unwelcome Neighbours—Mr. Roderick Macfarlane—"A beautiful Morning"—Marble Features . . 95

CHAPTER XII.

The Clearwater—A bygone Ocean—A Land of Lakes—The Athabasca River—Who is he?—Chipewyan Indians—Echo—Major succumbs at last—Mal de Raquette 118

CHAPTER XIII.

Lake Athabasca — Northern Lights — Chipewyan — The real Workers of the World 137

CHAPTER XIV.

A Hudson's Bay Fort—It comes at last—News from the outside World—Tame and wild Savages—Lac Clair—A treacherous Deed—Harper 143

CHAPTER XV.

The Peace River—Volcanos—M. Jean Batiste St. Cyr—Half a Loaf is better than no Bread—An oasis in the Desert—Tecumseh and Black Hawk 158

CHAPTER XVI.

The Buffalo Hills—A fatal Quarrel—The exiled Beavers—"Attal-loo" deplores his Wives—A Cree Interior—An attractive Camp—I camp alone—Cerf-vola without a Supper—The Recreants return—Dunvegan—A Wolf-hunt 171

CHAPTER XVII.

Alexander Mackenzie—The first Sign of Spring—Spanker the Suspicious—Cerf-vola contemplates Cutlets—An Indian Hunter—"Encumbrances"—Furs and Finery—A "Dead Fall"—The Fur Trade at both Ends—An old Fort—A Night Attack—Wife-lifting—Cerf-vola in Difficulties and Boots—The Rocky Mountains at last 191

CHAPTER XVIII.

The wild Animals of the Peace River—Indian Method of hunting the Moose—Twa-poos—The Beaver—The Bear—Bear's Butter—A Bear's Hug and how it ended—Fort St. John—The River awakes—A Rose without a Thorn—Nigger Dan—A threatening Letter—I issue a Judicial Memorandum—Its Effect is all that could be desired—Working up the Peace River 206

CHAPTER XIX.

Start from St. John's—Crossing the Ice—Batiste le Fleur—Chimeroo—The last Wood-buffalo—A dangerous Weapon—Our Raft collapses—Across the Half-way River 225

CHAPTER XX.

Hudson's Hope—A Lover of Literature—Crossing the Peace—An unskilful Pilot—We are upset—Our Rescue—A strange Variety of Arms—The Buffalo's Head—A glorious View . . 236

CHAPTER XXI.

Jacques, the French Miner—A fearful Abyss—The Great Cañon of the Peace River—We are off on our Western Way—Unfortunate Indians—A burnt Baby—"The Moose that walks" . 247

CHAPTER XXII.

Still Westward—The Dangers of the Ice—We enter the main Range—In the Mountains—A Grizzly—The Death of the Moose—Peace River Pass—Pete Joy—The Ominica—"Travellers" at Home 263

CHAPTER XXIII.

The Black Cañon—An ugly Prospect—The vanished Boat—We struggle on—A forlorn Hope—We fail again—An unhoped-for Meeting and a Feast of Joy—The Black Cañon conquered . 279

CHAPTER XXIV.

The Untiring over-estimates his Powers—He is not particular as to the Nature of his Dinner—Toil and Temper—Farewell to the Ominica—Germansen—The Mining Camp—Celebrities . 294

CHAPTER XXV.

Mr. Rufus Sylvester—The Untiring developes a new Sphere of Usefulness—Mansen—A last Landmark 304

CHAPTER XXVI.

British Columbia—Boundaries again—Juan de Fuça—Carver—The Shining Mountains—Jacob Astor—The Monarch of Salmon—Oregon—"Riding and Tying"—Nation Lake—The Pacific . 310

CHAPTER XXVII.

The Look-out Mountain—A gigantic Tree—The Untiring retires before superior Numbers—Fort St. James—A strange Sight in the Forest—Lake Noola—Quesnelle—Cerf-vola in civilized Life —Old Dog, good-bye! 327

ILLUSTRATIONS.

	PAGE
Frontispiece.	
Cerf-Vola, the Esquimaux Dog	16
View from the Spathanaw Watchi	31
"Our Hut at the Forks of the Saskatchewan"	43
Sunset Scene, with Buffalo	57
Tent in the Great Prairie	69
Dog-Train for the North	85
The Valley of the Peace River	158
Alone in the Wilderness	181
Night into Day	187
The Wolf-Chase	189
Clinging to the Canoe	239
Mount Garnet Wolseley and the Peace River	266
Cutting up the Moose	271
Running stern foremost the Black Cañon	283
"The Look-out Mountain"	327

THE
WILD NORTH LAND.

CHAPTER I.

The Situation at Home.—The West again.—A Land of Silence.

THERE had never been so many armies in England. There was a new army, and there was an old army; there was an army of militia, an army of volunteers, and an army of reserve; there were armies on horse, on foot, and on paper. There was the army of the future—of which great things were predicted—and far away, lost in a haze of history (but still more substantial than all other armed realities, present or future), there lay the great dead army of the past.

It was a time when everybody had something to do with military matters, everybody on the social ladder, from the Prime Minister on the topmost round to the mob-mover on the lowest.

Committees controlled the army, Departments dressed it, Radicals railed at it, Liberals lectured had carried him; when thought re-sought again those vast regions of the earth where Nature has graven her image in characters so colossal, that man seems to move slowly amidst an ocean frozen rigid by lapse of time, frozen into those things we name mountains, rivers, prairies, forests; man a mere speck, powerless so far to mark his presence, in blur of smoke, in noise of city, in clash of crank, or whirl of wheel: when these things came back in pictures touched by the soft colours Memory loves to limn with, there were not wanting dull professional outlooks and dearth of service to turn the footsteps gladly into the old regions again, there to trace new paths through the almost exhaustless waste which lies between the lonely prairies of the Saskatchewan and the icy oceans of the North.

What shall we call this land to those who follow us into its depths?

It has prairies, forests, mountains, barren wastes, and rivers; rivers whose single lengths roll through twice a thousand miles of shoreland; prairies over which a rider can steer for months without resting his gaze on aught save the dim verge of the ever-shifting horizon; mountains rent by rivers, ice-topped, glacier-seared, impassable; forests whose sombre pines darken a region half as large as Europe; sterile, treeless wilds whose 400,000 square miles lie spread in awful desolation. How shall it all be called?

In summer, a land of sound, a land echoing with the voices of birds, the ripple of running water, the mournful music of the waving pine-branch; in winter, a land of silence, a land hushed to its inmost depths by the weight of ice, the thick-falling snow, the intense rigour of a merciless cold—its great rivers glimmering in the moonlight, wrapped in their shrouds of ice; its still forests rising weird and spectral against the Aurora-lighted horizon; its notes of bird or brook hushed as if in death; its nights so still that the moving streamers across the northern skies seem to carry to the ear a sense of sound, so motionless around, above, below, lies all other visible nature.

If then we call this region the land of stillness, that name will convey more justly than any other the impress most strongly stamped upon the winter's scene.

CHAPTER II.

Powder *versus* Primroses.—The American Lounger.—" Home, Sweet Home."

It was just time to leave London. The elm-trees in the parks were beginning to put forth their earliest and greenest leaves; innumerable people were flocking into town because custom ordained that the country must be quitted when the spring is at its finest; as though the odour of primroses had something pestilential about it, and anything in the shape of violets except violet powder was terribly injurious to feminine beauty.

Youthful cosmopolites with waxed moustaches had apparently decided to compromise with the spring, and to atone for their abandonment of the country by making a miniature flower-garden of their button-holes. It was the last day of April, and ere the summer leaves had yellowed along the edge of the great sub-Arctic forest, my winter hut had to be hewn and built from the pine-logs of the far-distant Saskatchewan.

In the saloon or on the after-deck of a Cunard steamship steering west, one sees perhaps more of

America's lounging class than can be met with on any other spot in the world; the class is a limited one, in fact it may be a matter of dispute, whether the pure and simple lounger, as we know him in Piccadilly or Pall Mall, is to be found in the New World; but a three, or six, or twelve months' visit to Europe has sufficiently developed the dormant instincts of the class in the New York or Boston man of business, to give colour to the assumption that Columbia possesses a lounger.

It is possible that he is a lounger only for the moment. That one glimpse of Bunker, one echo of Wall Street, will utterly banish for ever the semblance of lounging; but for the present the Great Pyramid *minus* Bunker's Hill, the Corso *minus* Wall Street, have done something towards stamping him with the air and manner of the idler. For the moment he sips his coffee, or throws his cigar-end overboard, with a half-thoughtful, half-*blasé* air; for the moment he has discovered that the sun does not rise and set exclusively in the United States, and that there were just a few shreds and patches of history in the world prior to the declaration of American independence: still, when the big ship has steamed on into the shallow waters which narrow into Sandy Hook or Plymouth Sound, and the broad panorama twixt Long Island and Staten, or

Plymouth and Nahant opens on the view, the old feeling comes back with the old scenes again.

"Sir, the Bay of New York closely resembles the Bay of Naples." There is not the slightest use in telling him that it is quite as like the Bey of Tunis, or the Hospodar of Bulgaria—so we let it be.

"There, sir, is Bunker's Hill."

"Ah, indeed!" drawled a genuine British lounger, with that superb ignorance only to be attained after generations of study, as he quietly scanned the ridge through his lazily-arranged eyeglass. "Bunker—who was Bunker? and what did he do on his hill?"

Yet, ere we hasten away to the North, another word anent our cousin. These things are, after all, the exception; the temptation to tell a good story, or what we may deem such, must not blind us to the truth; the other side of the question must not be forgotten. An English traveller in America will have so much to thank American travel for that he can well afford to smile at such things.

It was an American who painted for us the last scenes of Moorish history, with a colouring as brilliant as that which the Hall of the Lions could boast of in the old days of Grenada's glory. To-day an American dwelling in Rome recalls for us in marble the fierce voluptuous beauty of the Egyptian Queen. Another catches the colouring of Claude, in his "Twilight in the Wilderness." And if, as I have somewhere heard, it is to the writer of the ballad-song that true poetic fame belongs, that song which is heard at lonely camp-fires, which is sung by sailors at the wheel as the canvas-clouded ship reels on under the midnight gloom through the tumbling seas,—the song which has reached the heart of a nation, and lives for ever in the memory of a people,—then let us remember, when we listen to those wondrous notes on whose wings float the simple words, "Be it ever so humble, there is no place like home;" let us remember the land whose memory called them forth from the heart of an American exile.

And now we must away.

CHAPTER III.

Civilization and Savagery.—Fort Garry under new aspects.—Social Societies.—An Old Friend.—"Pony" the perverse.

THE long, hot, dusty American summer was drawing to a close. The sand-fly had had his time, the black-fly had run his round, the mosquito had nearly bitten himself to death, and during that operation had rendered existence unbearable to several millions of the human race. The quiet tranquil fall-time had followed the fierce wasting summer, and all nature seemed to rest and bask in the mellow radiance of September.

In old tales, written I know not by whom, but read chiefly by youthful eyes, we are told of those who seek through lands infested by goblins and demons, by monstrous and uncouth forms of man and beast, for some fair realm of rest and happiness. He who to-day would seek the great solitudes of North America must pass through a somewhat similar ordeal.

Civilization, or what we term such, rolls with

CIVILIZATION AND SAVAGERY. 11

queer strides across the American continent. Far in advance of the last real city lies a land of terrible savagery, a desolate realm in which ruffianism and rowdyism hold sway. Here, in an expansion which is ever shifting, ever moving west and north-west, stand congregated the *civilizers* of the New World,—the navvy, the gambler, the rowdy, the saloon-keeper, the tramster, the murderer.

To civilize a new land is the easiest of tasks if we but set about it after the American model. Here is the recipe. Given a realm from which the red man has been banished, tricked, shot, or hunted out; from which the bison and elk have been chased; a lonely, tenantless land, with some great river flowing in long winding reaches silently through its vast plains and mountain gorges: here, then, is what you have to do:—

Place on the river a steamboat of the rudest construction. Wherever the banks are easy of ascent, or where a smaller stream seeks the main river, build a drinking-house of rough-hewn logs; let the name of God be used only in blasphemy, and language be a medium for the conveyance of curses. Call a hill a " bluff," a valley a " gulch," a fire-fly a " lighting bug," a man a " cuss," three shanties a " city." Let every man chew when he isn't smoking, and spit when he isn't asleep; and then—when half a dozen persons have come to violent ends—when killing has literally become "no murder"—your new land will be thoroughly civilized.

Poor, wild man of the West! scalper, war-raider, savage dweller in woods and on prairies; believer in manitous and dream-omens, painted and eagle-feathered; crafty, stealthy, and treacherous to foe, utterly hopeless to the man-tamer: this is the state of things which supplants thy savagery. This is civilization as it comes to thee from the East. Whenever thy wandering bands roam in from the great West, this is the sight they see in lands but lately their own.

I know not how it is, but in wild glen or lonely prairie, amidst races whose very names are supposed to be synonymous with all that is wild, lawless, or barbarous, I have known many a bond of sympathy, many a link 'twixt their lives and mine own. Nay, when man has been far distant, and nought but the lone spaces lay around me, and the gaunt pine-tree stretched its arms athwart the icy sky, I have felt companionship and friendship for the very dogs that drew my load; but for this band of civilizers, for these brutal pioneers of Anglo-American freedom, in their many stages between unblackened boots and diamond breastpins, I have felt nothing but loathing and disgust.

It was late in the month of September, 1872, when, after a summer of travel in Canada and the United States, I drew near the banks of the Red River of the North. Two years had worked many changes in scene and society; a railroad had reached the river; a "city" stood on the spot where, during a former visit, a midnight storm had burst upon me in the then untenanted prairie. Three steamboats rolled the muddy tide of the winding river before their bluff, ill-shapen bows. Gambling-houses and drinking-saloons, made of boards and brown paper, crowded the black, mud-soaked streets. A stage-coach ran north to Fort Garry 250 miles, and along the track rowdyism was rampant. Horse-stealing was prevalent, and in the "city" just alluded to two murderers walked quietly at large. In fine, the land which borders the Red River, Minnesota, and Dakota, had been thoroughly *civilized*.

But civilization had worked its way even deeper into the North-west. The place formerly known as Fort Garry had civilized into the shorter denomination of "Garry;" the prairie round the Fort had corner lots which sold for more hundreds of dollars than they possessed frontage-feet; and society was divided in opinion as to whether the sale which called forth these prices was a "bogus" one or not.

Representative institutions had been established in the new province of Manitoba, and an election for members of Parliament had just been concluded. Of this triumph of modern liberty over primeval savagery, it is sufficient to say, that the great principle of freedom of election had been fully vindicated by a large body of upright citizens, who, in the freest and most independent manner, had forcibly possessed themselves of the poll-books, and then fired a volley from revolvers, or, in the language of the land, "emptied their shooting-irons" into another body of equally upright citizens, who had the temerity to differ with them as to the choice of a political representative.

It was gently rumoured that some person or persons were to be arrested for this outburst of constitutional patriotism, but any proceeding so calculated to repress the individual independence of the citizen would have been utterly subversive of all representative institutions.

Civilization had also developed itself in other ways. Several national societies had been founded, and were doing prosperously. There was a St. George's Society and a St. Andrew's Society, and, I think, also a St. Patrick's Society. Indeed the memory of these saints appears to be held in considerable reputation in the New World. According to the prospectus and programme of these societies, charity appears to be the vital principle of each association: sick Scotchmen, emigrating English, and indigent Irish, were all requested to come forward and claim relief at the hands of the wealthier sons of St. Andrew, St. George, and St. Patrick. Charity, which is said to begin at home, and which, alas! too frequently ends there also, having thus had its commencement in the home circle, seemed determined to observe all home-like institutions; and the annual dinner was of necessity a very important item in the transactions of each society. Indeed it would be difficult to find a place where, in the present day, one could witness "fichting for Chairlie," "Scots wha haeing," "Manning for a' that," and those other peculiar customs of the Celtic race, carried out with better effect than in the meeting which annually gathers to do justice to the memory of the Apostle of the Picts in the New World.

Amidst all these changes of scene and society there was one thing still unchanged on the confines of the Red River. Close to the stream, at the place known as the Point of Frogs, an old friend met me with many tokens of recognition. A tried companion was he through many long days of wintry travel. There, as fresh and hearty as when I had parted from him two years before, stood Cerf-vola, the Esquimaux dog who had led my train from Cumberland, on the Lower Saskatchewan, across the ice of the great Lakes. Of the four dogs he alone remained. Two years is a long time in the life of any dog, but still a longer period in that of a hauling-dog; and Cerf-vola's comrades of that date, Muskeymote, Cariboo, and Tigre had gone the way of all earthly things.

To become the owner of this old friend again, and of his new companions Spanker and Pony, was a work of necessity; and I quitted the Point of Frogs by the steamboat "Selkirk" with three hauling-dogs in my possession. Strong and stout as of yore; clean-limbed, long-woolled, deep-chested; with ears pointed forward and tail close curled over his broad back, Cerf-vola still stood the picture of an Esquimaux.

Of the other two dogs, Pony was a half-breed, and Spanker, sharp, keen, and restless, was like his leader, a pure Husky; but, unlike the older dog, his nature was wild and fierce: some malignant guardian of his youth had despoiled him of the greater part of his tail, and by doing so had not a little detracted from his personal appearance.

CERF-VOLA, THE ESQUIMAUX DOG.

[*Page* 16.

As these three animals will be my constant companions during many months, through many long leagues of ice and snow, I have here sketched their outward semblance with some care. Civilization and a steamboat appeared to agree but poorly with my new friends. Spanker, failing in making his teeth emancipate his own neck, turned all his attention towards freeing his companion, and after a deal of toil he succeeded in gnawing Pony loose. This notable instance of canine abnegation (in which supporters of the Darwinian theory will easily recognize the connecting link between the Algerine captives assisting each other to freedom, &c., &c., after the manner of the Middle Ages), resulted in the absconding of the dog Pony, who took advantage of the momentary grounding of the steamer to jump on shore and disappear into the neighbouring forest.

It was a wild, tempestuous night; the storm swept the waters of the Red River until at length the steamboat was forced to seek her moorings against the tree-lined shore. Here was a chance of recovering the lost dog. Unfortunately the boat lay on the Dakota side, and the dog was at large somewhere on the Minnesota shore, while between the stormy water heaved in inky darkness. How was the capture to be effected?

As I stood on the lower deck of the steamboat,

pondering how to cross the dark river, a man paddled a small skiff close to the boat's side. "Will you be good enough to put me across the river?" I asked.

"I've no darned time to lose a night like this," he answered, "but if you want to cross jump in." The lantern which he carried showed the skiff to be half-filled with water, but the chance was too good to be lost. I sprang in, and we shot away over the rough river. Kneeling in the bottom of the boat I held the lantern aloft, while my gruff comrade paddled hard. At last we touched the shore; clambering up the wet, slippery bank, I held the light amidst the forest; there, not twenty paces distant, stood Pony.

"Pony, poor fellow, good dog, come, Pony, cess, cess, poor old boy." Alas! all the alluring dogisms by which we usually attract the animal were now utterly useless, and the more I cried "Here, here," the more the wretch went there, there. Meanwhile my boating friend grew impatient; I could hear him above the storm shouting and cursing at me with great volubility: so I made my way back to the shore, gave him his lantern, and went back into the forest, while he shot out into the darkness of the river.

Every now and again I heard the brute Pony close to me in the brushwood. For some time I wandered on; suddenly a light glimmered through the wet trees: approaching the light I found it to issue from an Indian wigwam, and at my summons two or three half-clad creatures came out. There was a dog lost in the woods, would they get lights and help me to catch him? a dollar would be the reward. The dollar threw a new light upon the matter. Burning brands were instantly brought forth from the wigwam fire, but with little result; the vagabond Pony, now utterly scared out of all semblance of dog wit, sought safety in the deepest recesses of the forest, from whence he poured forth howls into the night. I returned to the river, and with the aid of my wigwam friends regained the steamboat. Half an hour later the man on watch saw a dark object swimming around the boat; it was the lost dog. Cerfvola, tied in the rain as a lure, had continued to howl without intermission, and the vagrant Pony had evidently come to the conclusion that there were worse places on a wet autumnal night than the warm deck of the steamboat " Selkirk."

In the earliest days of October all phases of civilization were passed with little regret; and at the Rat Creek, near the southern shore of Lake Manitoba, I bid good-bye to society. The party was a small one—a member of the Imperial Legislature, well known in Ireland, now *en route* to get a glimpse of the great solitudes ere winter had closed in, his servant, mine own, five horses, and two carts.

CHAPTER IV.

The Wilderness.—A Sunset-Scene.—A white Savage.—Cerfvola the Untiring.—Doggerel for a Dog.—The Hill of the Wolverine.—The Indian Paradise.—I plan a Surprise.—Biscuits and Water.

It was the 4th of October, bright with the warmth of the fading summer—that quiet glow which lingers over the face of nature, like the hectic flush upon a dying beauty, ere the wintry storms come to kill.

Small and insignificant, the Musk-Rat Creek flows on towards Lake Manitoba amidst bordering thickets of oak and elm trees. On each side, a prairie just beginning to yellow under the breath of the cold night wind; behind, towards the east, a few far-scattered log-houses smoke, and a trace of husbandry; the advanced works of that army whose rear-guard reaches to the Vistula; before, towards the west, the sun going down over the great silent wilderness. How difficult to realize it! How feeble are our minds to gauge its depths!

He who rides for months through the vast solitudes sees during the hours of his daily travel an unbroken panorama of distance. The seasons come and go; grass grows and flowers die; the fire leaps with tiger bounds along the earth; the snow lies still and quiet over hill and lake; the rivers rise and fall, but the rigid features of the wilderness rest unchanged. Lonely, silent, and impassive; heedless of man, season, or time, the weight of the Infinite seems to brood over it. Once only in the hours of day and night a moment comes when this impassive veil is drawn from its features, and the eye of the wanderer catches a glimpse of the sunken soul of the wilderness; it is the moment which follows the sunset; then a deeper stillness steals over the earth, colours of wondrous hue rise and spread along the western horizon. In a deep sea of emerald and orange of fifty shades, mingled and interwoven together, rose-coloured isles float anchored to great golden threads; while, far away, seemingly beyond and above all, one broad flash of crimson light, the parting sun's last gift, reddens upwards to the zenith. And then, when every moment brings a change, and the night gathers closer to the earth, and some waveless, nameless lake glimmers in uncertain shore-line and in shadow of inverted hill-top; when a light that seems born of another world (so weirdly distant is it from ours) lingers along the western sky, then hanging like a lamp over the tomb of the sun, the Evening Star gleams out upon the darkening wilderness.

It may be only a fancy, a conceit bred from loneliness and long wandering, but at such times the great solitude has seemed to me to open its soul, and that in its depths I read its secrets.

Ten days dawned and died; the Mauvais Bois, the Sand Ridges, western shore of an older world's immense lake, the Pine Creek, the far-stretching hills of the Little Saskatchewan rose, drew near, and faded behind us. A wild, cold storm swept down from the north, and, raging a day and a night, tore the yellow leaves from the poplar thickets, and scared the wild fowl far southward to a warmer home.

Late on the 10th of October we reached the Hudson's Bay Company's post of Beaver Creek, the western limit to the travels of my friend. Here, after a stay of three days and a feast of roasted beaver, we parted; he to return to Killarney, St. Stephen's, and Denominational Education —a new name for the old feud between those great patriot armies, the *Ins* and the *Outs*; I to seek the lonely lands where, far beyond the distant Saskatchewan, the great Unchagah, parent of a still mightier stream, rolls through remote lakes and whispering pines its waters to the Polar Seas.

With one man, three horses and three dogs, and all those requisites of food, arms, and raiment with which a former journey had familiarized me, I started on the 14th of October bound for the North-west. I was virtually alone; my companion was a half-breed taken at chance from the wigwam at the scene of the dog Pony's midnight escapade on the Red River. Chance had on this occasion proved a failure, and the man had already shown many symptoms of worthlessness. He had served as a soldier in an American corps raised by a certain Hatch, to hold in check the Sioux after the massacre of Minnesota in 1862. A raid made by nine troopers of this corps, against an Indian tent occupied by some dozen women and children, appears to have been the most noteworthy event in the history of Hatch's Battalion. Having surrounded the wigwam in the night, these cowards shot the miserable inmates, then scalping and mutilating their bodies they returned to their comrades, bearing the gory scalp-locks as trophies of their prowess.

Hatch is said to have at once forwarded to Was'ington a despatch, announcing " a decisive v" .ory over the Sioux by the troops under his command." But a darker sequel to the tale must remain in shadow, for, if the story told to a Breton missionary rests on a base of truth, the history of human guilt may be searched in vain for a parallel of atrocity.

I had other companions besides this *ci-devant* trooper, of a far more congenial nature, to share my spare time with. A good dog is so much a nobler beast than an indifferent man that one sometimes gladly exchanges the society of one for that of the other.

A great French writer has told us that animals were put on earth to show us the evil effects of passions run riot and unchecked. But it seems to me that the reverse would be closer to the truth. The humanity which Napoleon deemed a dog taught to man on Bassino's battle-field is not the only virtue we can learn from that lower world which is bound to us by such close ties, and yet lies so strangely apart from us. Be that as it may, a man can seldom feel alone if he has a dog to share his supper, to stretch near him under the starlight, to answer him with tail-wag, or glance of eye, or prick of ear.

Day after day Cerf-vola and his comrades trotted on in all the freedom which summer and autumn give to the great dog family in the north. Now chasing a badger, who invariably popped in his burrow in time to save his skin; now sending a pack of prairie grouse flying from the long grass; now wading breast-deep into a lake where a few wild ducks still lingered, loath to quit their summer nesting-haunts.

Of all the dogs I have known Cerf-vola possessed the largest share of tact. He never fought a pitched battle, yet no dog dared dispute his supremacy. Other dogs had to maintain their leadership by many a deadly conflict, but he quietly assumed it, and invariably his assumption was left unchallenged; nay, even upon his arrival at some Hudson Bay fort, some place wherein he had never before set foot, he was wont to instantly appoint himself director-general of all the Company's dogs, whose days from earliest puppyhood had been passed within the palisades. I have often watched him at this work, and marvelled by what mysterious power he held his sway. I have seen two or three large dogs flee before a couple of bounds merely made by him in their direction, while a certain will-some-one-hold-me-back? kind of look pervaded his face, as though he was only prevented from rending his enemy into small pieces by the restraining influence which the surface of the ground exercised upon his legs.

His great weight no doubt carried respect with

it. At the lazy time of the year he weighed nearly 100 pounds, and his size was in no way diminished by the immense coat of hair and fine fur which enveloped him. Had Sir Boyle Roche known this dog he would not have given to a bird alone the faculty of being in two places at once, for no mortal eye could measure the interval between Cerfvola's demolishment of two pieces of dog-meat, or Pemmican, flung in different directions at the same moment.

Thus we journeyed on. Sometimes when the sheen of a lake suggested the evening camp, while yet the sun was above the horizon, my three friends would accompany me on a ramble through the thicket-lined hills. At such times, had any Indian watched from sedgy shore or bordering willow copse the solitary wanderer who, with dogs following close, treaded the lonely lake shore, he would have probably carried to his brethren a strange story of the " white man's medicine." He would have averred that he had heard a white man talking to a big, bushy-tailed dog, somewhere amidst the Touchwood Hills, and singing to him a " great medicine song " when the sun went down.

And if now we reproduce for the reader the medicine song which the white man strung together for his bushy-tailed dog, we may perhaps forestall some critic's verdict by prefixing to it the singularly appropriate title of

DOGGEREL.

And so, old friend, we are met again, companions still to be,
Across the waves of drifted snow, across the prairie sea.
Again we'll tread the silent lake, the frozen swamp, the fen,
Beneath the snow-crown'd sombre pine we'll build our camp again :
And long before the icy dawn, while hush'd all nature lies,
And weird and wan the white lights flash across the northern skies ;
Thy place, as in past days thou'lt take, the leader of the train,
To steer until the stars die out above the dusky plain ;
Then on, thro' space by wood and hill, until the wintry day
In pale gleams o'er the snow-capped ridge has worn itself away,
And twilight bids us seek the brake, where midst the pines once more
The fire will gleam before us, the stars will glimmer o'er.
There stretch'd upon the snow-drift, before the pine log's glare,
Thy master's couch and supper with welcome thou wilt share,
To rest, unless some prowling wolf should keep thee watchful still,
While louely through the midnight sounds his wail upon the hill.

And when the storm raves around, and thick and blinding snow
Comes whirling in wild eddies around, above, below ;
Still all unmoved thou'lt keep thy pace as manfully as when
Thy matchless mettle first I tried in lone Pasquia's glen.

Thus day by day we'll pierce the wilds where rolls the Arctic
 stream,
Where Athabasca's silent lakes, through whispering pine-trees
 gleam.
Until, where far Unchagah's flood by giant cliffs is crown'd,
Thy bells will feed the echoes, long hungering for a sound.
Old dog, they say thou hast no life beyond this earth of ours,
That toil and truth give thee no place amidst Elysian bowers.
Ah well, e'en so, I look for thee when all our danger's past,
That on some hearth-rug, far at home, thou'lt rest thy limbs at
 last.

A long distance of rolling plain, of hills fringed with thickets, of treeless waste, and lakes spreading into unseen declivities, stretches out between the Qu'Appelle and Saskatchewan rivers. Roamed over by but few bands of Indians, and almost bereft of the larger kind of game, whose bleached bones cover it thickly, this expanse lies in unbroken solitude for more than three hundred miles. Through it the great trail to the north lays its long, winding course; but no other trace of man is to be found; and over lake and thicket, hill and waste, broods the loneliness of the untenanted.

Once it was a famous field of Indian fight, in the old days when Crees and Assineboine strove for mastery. Now it has almost lost the tradition of battle, but now and again a hill-top or a rivercourse, whose French or English name faintly echoes the Indian meaning, tells to the traveller who cares to look below the surface some story of fight in bygone times.

The hill of the Wolverine and the lonely Spathanaw Watchi have witnessed many a deed of Indian daring and Indian perfidy in days not long passed away, but these deeds are now forgotten, for the trader as he unyokes his horses at their base, and kindles his evening fire, little recks of such things, and hails the hill-top only as a landmark on his solitary road.

Alone in a vast waste the Spathanaw Watchi lifts his head, thickets and lakes are at his base, a lonely grave at top, around four hundred miles of horizon, a view so vast that endless space seems for once to find embodiment, and at a single glance the eye is satiated with immensity. There is no mountain range to come up across the sky-line, no river to lay its glistening folds along the middle distance, no dark forest to give shade to foreground or to fringe perspective, no speck of life, no track of man, nothing but the wilderness. Reduced thus to its own nakedness, space stands forth with almost terrible grandeur. One is suddenly brought face to face with that enigma which we try to comprehend by giving to it the names of endless, interminable, measureless; that dark inanity which broods upon a waste of

VIEW FROM THE SPATHANAW WAITCHI.

moorland at dusk, and in which fancy sees the spectral and the shadowy.

Yet in this view from the Spathanaw there is nothing dimly seen; the eye travels to the farthest distance without one effort of vision, and, reaching there, rests untired by its long gaze. As the traveller looks at this wonderful view he stands by the grave of an Indian, and he sees around him for four hundred miles the Indian Paradise. It was from scenes such as this, when the spring had covered them with greensward, and the wild herds darkened them by their myriads, that the shadowy sense of a life beyond the tomb took shape and form in the Red man's mind.

It was the 25th of October when I once more drew near to the South Saskatchewan.

Amidst its high wooded banks the broad river rippled brightly along, as yet showing no trace of that winter now so close at hand. Two years before, all but a few days, I had reached this same river, then shored by dense masses of ice; and now, as I looked from the southern shore, the eye had no little difficulty in tracing through the lingering foliage of the summer the former point of passage, where on the cold November morning my favourite horse had gone down beneath the ice-locked river.

Crossing to the southern shore I turned eastward through a rich undulating land, and riding hard for one day reached the little mission station of Prince Albert, midway between the Red River and the Rocky Mountains.

Those who have followed me through former wanderings may remember a spot where two large rivers unite after many hundred miles of prairie wandering, and form one majestic current on the edge of the Great Northern Forest. To this spot, known as the " Grand Forks of the Saskatchewan," I was now journeying, for there, while the autumn was yet younger, two friends had preceded me to build at the point of confluence a hut for our residence during the early winter.

The evening of the 28th of October found me pushing hastily through a broad belt of firs and pines which crosses the tongue of land between the rivers some ten miles from their junction; beyond this belt of trees the country opened out, but, as it finally narrowed to the point of confluence, the dark pine-clumps, outliers of the dense Northern Forest, again rose into view. With these features a previous visit had made me acquainted; but the night had now closed in ere yet the fir forest had been passed, and the rain, which all day had been ceaseless, settled down with darkness into a still heavier torrent. As we emerged from the pines my baggage-cart suddenly broke down, and there only remained the alternative of camping by the scene of the disaster, or pushing on for the river junction on foot.

Unfortunately the prospect of unexpectedly walking in upon my friends, housed in the depths of the wilderness, amidst the wild rain-storm of the night, proved too strong a temptation; and having secured the cart as best we could against weather and wolves, we set out into the darkness. For more than an hour we walked hard through undulating ground intermixed with swamps and beaver dams, until at length the land began to decline perceptibly.

Descending thus for nearly a mile we came suddenly upon a large, quick-running river, whose waters chafed with sullen noise against boulder-lined shores, and hissed under the wild beating of the rain. With cautious steps we groped our way to the edge and cast a dry branch into the flood; it floated towards the left; the river, then, must be the South Saskatchewan. Was the junction of this river with the northern branch yet distant? or was it close at hand? for if it was near, then my home was near too.

Making our way along the shore we held on for some time, until suddenly there rose before us a steep bank, at the base of which the current ran in whirling eddies. To climb up a high bank on our left, and thus flank this obstacle, next became our toil; soon we found ourselves in a dense wood where innumerable fallen trees lay in endless confusion. For another hour we groped our way through this labyrinth in a vain attempt to reach the upper level, until at last, exhausted by hours of useless toil, wet, hungry, and bruised, I gave the reluctant word to camp.

To camp, what a mockery it seemed without blankets or covering save our rain-soaked clothes, without food save a few biscuits. The cold rain poured down through leafless aspens, and shelter there was none. It was no easy matter to find a dry match, but at length a fire was made, and from the surrounding wood we dragged dead trees to feed the flames. There is no necessity to dwell upon the miserable hours which ensued! All night long the rain hissed down, and the fire was powerless against its drenching torrents. Towards morning we sunk into a deep sleep, lying stretched upon the soaking ground.

At last a streak of dawn broke over the high eastern shore, the light struggled for mastery with the surrounding darkness and finally prevailed, and descending to the river showed the broad current sweeping on to the north-east. Quitting without regret our cheerless bivouac, we climbed with stiff limbs the high overhanging bank, and gained the upper level. Far away the river still held its course to the northeast, deep sunken 300 feet below the prairie level: we were still distant from the Forks.

Retracing our steps through miles of fallen timber we reached the cart, but the morning had worn on to midday before our long-wished-for breakfast smoked in the kettle. Three hours later on, during an evening which had cleared sufficiently to allow the sun to glint through cloud rifts on pine forest and prairie, I reached the lofty ridge which overlooks the Forks of the Saskatchewan.

CHAPTER V.

The Forks of the Saskatchewan.—A perverse Parallel.—
Diplomatic Bungling.—Its results.

Two hundred and fifty feet above water level, the narrow tongue of land rises over the junction of the two Saskatchewan rivers. Bare and level at top, its scarped front descends like a wall to the rivers; but land-slip and the wear of time have carried down to a lower level the loose sand and earth of the plateau, and thickly clustering along the northern face, pines, birch, and poplar shroud the steep descent. It is difficult to imagine a wilder scene than that which lay beneath this projecting point.

From north-west and from south-west two broad rivers roll their waters into one common channel, two rivers deep furrowed below the prairie level, curving in great bends through tree-fringed valleys. One river has travelled through eight hundred miles of rich rolling landscape; the other has run its course of nine hundred through waste and arid solitudes; both have had their sources in mountain summits where the avalanche thundered forth to solitude the tidings of their birth. And here at this point, like two lives, which, coming from a distance, are drawn together by some mysterious sympathy, and blended into one are henceforth to know only the final separation, these rivers roll their currents into one majestic stream, which, sinking into a deep gorge, sweeps eastward through unbroken pine forest. As yet no steamboat furrows the deep water; no whistle breaks the sleeping echoes of these grim scarped shores; the winding stream rests in voiceless solitude, and the summer sun goes down beyond silent river reaches, gleaming upon a virgin land.

Standing at this junction of the two Saskatchewan rivers, the traveller sees to the north and east the dark ranks of the great sub-Arctic forest, while to the south and west begin the endless prairies of the middle continent. It is not a bad position from whence to glance at the vast region known to us as British North America.

When the fatal error at Saratoga had made room for diplomatists of Old and New England, and removed the arbitrament of rebellion from the campaign to the council, those who drew on the part of Great Britain the boundary-lines of her transatlantic empire, bungled even more conspicuously in the treaty-chamber than her generals had failed in the field. Geographical knowledge appears ever to have been deemed superfluous to those whose business it was to shape the destinies of our colonial dominions, and if something more tangible than report be true, it is not many months since the British members at a celebrated conference stared blankly at each other when the free navigation of a river of *more than two thousand miles in length* was mooted at the Council Board. But then, what statesman has leisure to master such trifles as the existence of the great river Yukon, amid the more important brain toil of framing rabbit laws, defining compound householders, and solving other equally momentous questions of our Imperial and Parochial politics? However to our subject. When in 1783 the great quarrel between Britain and her Colonies was finally adjusted, the northern boundary of the United States was to follow the 49th parallel of latitude from the north-west angle of the Lake of the Woods to the river Mississippi, and thence down that river, &c., &c.

Nothing could possibly have been more simple, a child might comprehend it; but unfortunately it fell out in course of time that the 49th parallel was one of very considerable latitude indeed, not at all a parallel of diplomatic respectability, or one that could be depended on, for neither at one end or the other could it be induced to approach the north-west angle of the Lake of the Woods or the river Mississippi. Do all that sextant, or quadrant, or zenith telescope could, the 49th parallel would not come to terms.

Doggedly and determinedly it kept its own course; and, utterly regardless of big-wig or diplomatic fogie, it formed an offensive and defensive alliance with the Sun and the Pole Star (two equally obstinate and big-wig disrespectful bodies), and struck out for itself an independent line.

Beyond the Mississippi there lay a vast region, a region where now millions (soon to be tens of millions) draw from prairie and river flat the long-sleeping richness of the soil. Then it was a great wilderness, over which the dusky bison and his wilder master roamed, in that fierce freedom which civilization ends for ever.

To the big-wigs at the Council Board this region was a myth—a land so far beyond the confines of diplomatic geography that its very existence was questioned. Not so to the shrewd solicitor, admiral, auctioneer, general conveyancer, and Jack-of-all-trades in one, who guided the foreign policy of the United States.

Unencumbered by the trappings of diplomatic

tradition, he saw, vaguely perhaps, but still with prescient knowledge, the empire which it was possible to build in that western wild; and as every shifting scene in the outside world's politics called up some new occasion for boundary rearrangement, or treaty rectification, he grasped eagerly at a fresh foothold, an additional scrap of territory, in that land which was to him an unborn empire, to us a half-begotten wilderness. Louisiana, purchased from Napoleon for a trifle, became in his hands a region larger than European Russia, and the vast water-shed of the Missouri passed into the Empire of the United States.

Cut off from the Mississippi, isolated from the Missouri, the unlucky boundary traversed an arid waste until it terminated at the Rocky Mountains.

Long before a citizen of the United States had crossed the Missouri, Canadian explorers had reached the Rocky Mountains and penetrated through their fastnesses to the Pacific; and British and Canadian fur traders had grown old in their forts across the Continent before Lewis and Clark, the pioneers of American exploration, had passed the Missouri. Discovered by a British sailor, explored by British subjects, it might well have been supposed that the great region along the Pacific slope, known to us as Oregon, belonged indisputably to England; but at some new treaty "rectification," the old story was once more repeated, and the unlucky 49th parallel again selected to carry across the Mountains to the Pacific Ocean, the same record of British bungling and American astuteness which the Atlantic had witnessed sixty years earlier on the rugged estuary of the St. Croix.

For the present our business lies only with that portion of British territory east of the Rocky Mountains, and between them, the Bay of Hudson and the Arctic Ocean.

From the base of the great range of the Rocky Mountains, the Continent of British America slopes towards North and East, until, unbroken by one mountain summit, but in a profound and lasting desolation, it dips its shaggy arms and ice-bound capes into a sea as drear and desolate.

Two great rivers, following of necessity this depression, shed their waters into the Bay of Hudson. One is the Saskatchewan, of which we have already spoken; the other, that river known by various names—"English," because the English traders first entered the country by it; "Beaver," from the numbers of that animal trapped along it in olden time; "Churchill," because a fort of that name stands at its estuary;

and " Missinipi," or " much water," by the wild races who dwell upon it. The first river has a total length of 1700 miles; the last runs its course through worthless forest and primeval rock for 1200 miles.

"OUR HUT AT THE FORKS OF THE SASKATCHEWAN."

[*Page* 43.

CHAPTER VI.

Our Winter Home.—A Welcome.—I start again.—The Hunter's Camp.—In quest of Buffalo on the Plains.—" Lodge-poling " leads to Love.

AT the foot of the high ridge which marks the junction of the two Saskatchewans, deep in pines and poplars, through which vistas had been cut to give glimpses along the converging rivers, stood the winter hut of which I have already spoken. From its chimney blue smoke curled up amongst the trees into the lower atmosphere, and the sound of wood-cutting came ringing from below, a token of labour not yet completed in our wild and secluded resting-place.

I stood for a moment looking down on this scene—a home in the great wilderness—and then a loud shout echoed into the valley to carry tidings of our arrival to the inmates of the hut. In an instant it was answered from below, and the solitudes rang with many a note of welcome, while half a dozen dogs bayed furious defiance at my pack, already become boisterously jubilant on the ridge above. When friends meet thus, after long travel and separation, there are many questions to ask and to answer, and the autumn evening had worn to midnight ere the pine-log fire threw its light upon a silent hut.

The winter season was now at hand; our house was nearly completed, our stores put away, our dogs kennelled; but one most pressing want had yet to be supplied—our winter stock of meat had to be gathered in, and there was no time to lose about obtaining it.

It was the last of October, just one day after my arrival at the Forks, when we turned our faces westward in quest of buffalo. They were said to be a long way off—200 miles nearer to the setting sun—out somewhere on that great motionless ocean, where no tree, no bush breaks the vast expanse of prairie; land to which the wild men of the West and those who lead wild lives there have turned for many an age in search of that food which nature once so generously scattered over the plains of Central North America.

Journeying slowly towards the west—for already the snow had begun to fall in many storms, and the landscape had become wrapt in its winter mantle—we reached in five days one of those curious assemblages of half-breed hunters which are to be found in winter on the borders of the great plains.

Huts promiscuously crowded together; horses, dogs, women, children, all intermixed in a confusion worthy of Donnybrook Fair; half-breed hunters, ribboned, tasselled, and capôted, lazy, idle, and, if there is any spirit in the camp, sure to be intoxicated; remnants and wrecks of buffalo lying everywhere around; robes stretched and drying; meat piled on stages; wolf-skins spread over framework; women drawing water and carrying wood; and at dusk from the little hut the glow of firelight through parchment windows, the sound of fiddle scraped with rough hunter hand, and the quick thud of hunter heel as Louison, or Bâtiste, or Gabriel foot it ceaselessly upon the half-hewn floors.

Unquestionably these French half-breeds are wild birds—hunters, drinkers, rovers, rascals if you will—yet generous and hospitable withal; destined to disappear before the white man's footprint, and ere that time has come owing many of their vices to the pioneer American, whose worst qualities the wild man, or semi-wild man, has been ever too sure to imitate.

After a delay of three days in this hunter's camp, which by some strange anomaly was denominated "la mission," its sole claim to that title being the residence of a French priest in the community, we started on our journey further west.

The winter had now regularly set in; the broad South Saskatchewan was rolling thick masses of ice down its half-closed channel, the snow-covering had deepened on the landscape, the wind blew keenly over the prairie. Many of our horses had been too poor to take upon this journey, and the half-breed whom I had brought from Red River, dreading the exposure of the plains, had taken advantage of the hunter's camp to desert our service; so another man had been engaged, and, with three fresh horses and an urchin attendant in the shape of a little half-breed, designated by our new man as "l'homme capable," and for whose services he demanded only the moderate sum of five shillings per diem, we held our course along the South Saskatchewan towards the Great Prairie.

Xavier Bâtoche was a fair sample of his class. The blood of four nationalities mingled in his veins. His grandfather had been a French Canadian, his grandmother a Crow squaw; English and Cree had contributed to his descent on his mother's side. The ceremony of taking a wife in the early days of the north-west fur trade was not an elaborate performance, or one much encumbered by social or religious preliminaries. If it did not literally fulfil the condition of force implied by the word "taking," it usually developed into a question of barter; a horse, a flint gun, some white cloth and beads, could purchase the hand and heart of the fairest squaw in Prairie land. If she did not love after one of these valuable "presents" had been made to her father, the lodge-poles were always handy to enforce that obedience necessary to domestic happiness—admirable idea, the roof-tree contributed to the peace of the hearth-stone, and jealousy fled before a "lodge-poling." To return to Bâtoche; Crow and Cree, French and English, had contrived to produce a genial, good-humoured, handsome fellow; the previous year had been one of plenty, buffalo had once more appeared in vast herds on the prairies of the Saskatchewan; wolf-skins, robes, and pemmican had fetched high prices, and Bâtoche was rich and prosperous.

Two days' journeying brought us to the edge of the great prairie; silent, vast, and desolate it spread away into unseen space; the snow but scantily covered the yellow grass, and the November wind sighed mournfully through the wrecks of summer vegetation as it sped along its thousand leagues of unmeasured meadow. At the last copse of poplar and willow we halted for a day, to bake bread and cut wood sufficient for a week's food and fuel, and then we launched our ocean ships—horses and sleds—out into the great meadow.

CHAPTER VII.

An Ocean of Grass.—The Red Man.—Whence comes he?—
The Buffalo.—Puritans and Pioneers.—The Red Man's Friend.

THE general term "prairie" comprises many varieties of open landscape. There are the level, alluvial prairies of Illinois, long since settled and colonized; there are the low, fertile prairies of the Red River, where the rich black mould, fallow under five months of snow, puts forth the rank luxuriance of a hot-bed during the half tropic heat of summer; there are the sandy prairies of the Assineboine and Qu' Appelle, intermixed with clusters of aspen and of willow, and broken by lakes and saline ponds : but above each and all—exceeding all other prairies and open spaces—wild, treeless, and ocean-like in everything save motion, there stands forth in dreary grandeur the Great Prairie itself.

What the Irish Sea, the Channel, the Baltic, and the Mediterranean are to the Atlantic, so are these various outlying regions of plain to the vast rigid ocean of the central continent. It is true that on the Red River, or the Qu'Appelle, or along the line I have lately passed, one may frequently "get out of sight of land;" there are spaces where no tree or bush breaks the long monotony of the sky-line; but all these expanses are as nothing compared to the true prairie.

The unending vision of sky and grass, the dim, distant, and ever-shifting horizon; the ridges that seem to be rolled upon one another in motionless torpor; the effect of sunrise and sunset, of night narrowing the vision to nothing, and morning only expanding it to a shapeless blank; the sigh and sough of a breeze that seems an echo in unison with the solitude of which it is the sole voice; and, above all, the sense of lonely, unending distance which comes to the *voyageur* when day after day has gone by, night has closed, and morning dawned upon his onward progress under the same ever-moving horizon of grass and sky.

Only two wild creatures have made this grassy desert their home.

Back, since ages at whose birth we can only guess, but which in all human probability go deeper into the past than the reign of Arab in Yemen, or Kirghis in Turkestan, the wild red man has roamed these wastes: back into that dark night which hangs for ever over all we know or shall know of early America. "The time before the white man came," what a measureless eternity lies hidden under the words! This prairie was here when the stones of the pyramid were unhewn, and the site of Babylon was a river meadow—here as it is to-day, treeless, desolate, and storm-swept. But where and whence came the wild denizens of the waste? Who shall say? Fifty writers have broached their various theories, a hundred solutions have been offered. The missionary claims them as the lost tribes of Israel, one ethnologist finds in them a likeness to the Tartar, another sees the Celtic eye, another the Roman nose, another traces them back to Japan, or China, or Australasia; the old world is scarcely large enough to give them room for their speculations. And what say we? Nothing; or if aught, a conjecture perhaps more vague and shadowy than the rest. It has seemed to us when watching this strange, wild hunter, this keen, untutored scholar of nature, this human creature that sickens beneath our civilization, and dies midst our prosperity—it has seemed to us that he was of a race older and more remote than our own, a stock coeval with a shadowy age—a remnant, perchance, of an earlier creation which has vanished from the earth, preserved here in these wilds—a waif flung by the surge of time to these later ages of our own.

This New World is older than our old one. Its 30,000 feet in depth of Argoic rock tell us of an age when nought of living form moved over the iron earth. And here, probably first of all, the molten sands rose above the boiling floods, and evolved and crusted into a chaotic continent.

These are but idle speculations; still the antiquity of the Indian race rests upon other foundations. Far to the south, where the prairies rise into the lofty plateau of New Mexico, ruined monuments, weed-grown, and hidden beneath ivy and trailing parasites, stand like spectres from the tomb of time. Before these mouldering rock-hewn cities conjecture halts; the past has drawn over them a veil that no research can pierce, no learning solve. Inscrutable as the vestiges of an earlier earth they stand, the lonely, ruined wrecks of the Red man's race.

So much for the earlier existence of the human dweller on the prairie; to us he is but a savage—the impediment to our progress—the human counterpart of forests which have to be felled, mountains which must be tunnelled, rivers whose broad currents are things to conquer; he is an obstacle, and he must be swept away. To us it matters not whether his race dwelt here before a Celt had raised a Druid altar. The self-styled heirs to all the centuries reck little of such things.

And now let us turn for a moment to that other wild creature which has made its dwelling on the Great Prairie.

Over the grassy ocean of the west there has moved from time immemorial a restless tide. Backwards and forwards, now north, now south—now filling the dark gorges of the Rocky Mountains—now trailing into the valleys of the Rio del Norte—now pouring down the wooded slopes of the Saskatchewan, surged millions on millions of dusky bisons.

What led them in their strange migrations no man could tell, but all at once a mighty impulse seemed to seize the myriad herds, and they moved over the broad realm which gave them birth as the waves of the ocean roll before the storm. Nothing stopped them on their march; great rivers stretched before them with steep, overhanging banks, and beds treacherous with quicksand and shifting bar; huge chasms and earth-rents, the work of subterraneous forces, crossed their line of march, but still the countless thousands swept on. Through day and night the earth trembled beneath their tramp, and the air was filled with the deep bellowing of their unnumbered throats.

Crowds of wolves and flocks of vultures dogged and hovered along their way, for many a huge beast, half sunken in quicksand, caught amidst whirling ice flow, or bruised and maimed at the foot of some steep precipice, marked their line of march, like the wrecks lying spread behind a routed army. Nearly two millions of square miles formed their undivided domain; on three sides a forest boundary encircled it, on the fourth a great mountain range loomed up against the western sky. Through this enormous area countless creeks and rivers meandered through the meadows, where the prairie grass grew thick and rank, and the cotton woods spread their serpentine belts. Out in the vast prairie the Missouri, the Platte, the Sweet Water, the Arkansas, the South Saskatchewan, the Bighorn, the Yellowstone, rolled their volumes towards the east, gathering a thousand affluents as they flowed.

Countless ages passed, tribes warred and wandered, but the life of the wilderness lay deep beneath the waves of time, and the roll of the passing centuries disturbed not its slumber.

At last the white man came, and soon from south and north the restless adventurers of Latin Europe pierced the encircling forests, and beheld the mighty meadows of the Central Continent. Spaniards on the south, Frenchmen on the north, no one in the centre; for the prudent Plymouth Puritan was more intent on flogging witches and gathering riches than on penetrating the tangled forest which lay westward of his settlement. No; his was not the work of adventure and discovery. Others might go before and brave the thousand perils of flood and forest; he would follow after, as the Jew pedlar follows the spendthrift, as the sutler dogs the footsteps of the soldier.

What though he be in possession of the wide dominion now, and the names of France and Spain be shrunken into a shapeless dream; *that* only proves what we knew before, that the men who lead the way to a great future are fated never to reap the golden harvest of their dreams.

And ever since that advent of the white man the scene has changed; the long slumber of the wilderness was broken, and hand in hand with the new life death moved amidst the wild denizens of the Prairies. Human life scattered over a vast area, animal life counted by tens of millions, take a long time to destroy; and it is only to-day—370 years after a Portuguese sailor killed and captured a band of harmless Indians, and 350 since a Spanish soldier first beheld a herd of buffaloes beyond the meadows of the Mississippi—that the long, hopeless struggle of the wild dwellers of the wilderness may be said to have reached its closing hour.

In thus classing together the buffalo and the red man as twin dwellers on the Great Prairie, I have but followed the Indian idea.

"What shall we do?" said a young Sioux warrior to an American officer on the Upper Missouri some fifteen years ago. "What shall we do? the buffalo is our only friend. When he goes all is over with the Dacotahs. I speak thus to you because like me you are a Brave."

It was little wonder that he called the buffalo his only friend. Its skin gave him a house, its robe a blanket and a bed, its undressed hide a boat, its short, curved horn a powder-flask, its meat his daily food, its sinew a string for his bow, its leather a lariot for his horse, a saddle, bridle, rein, and bit. Its tail formed an ornament for his tent, its inner skin a book in which to sketch the brave deeds of his life, the "medicine robe" of his history. House, boat, food, bed, and covering, every want from infancy to age, and after life itself had passed, wrapt in his buffalo robe the red man waited for the dawn.

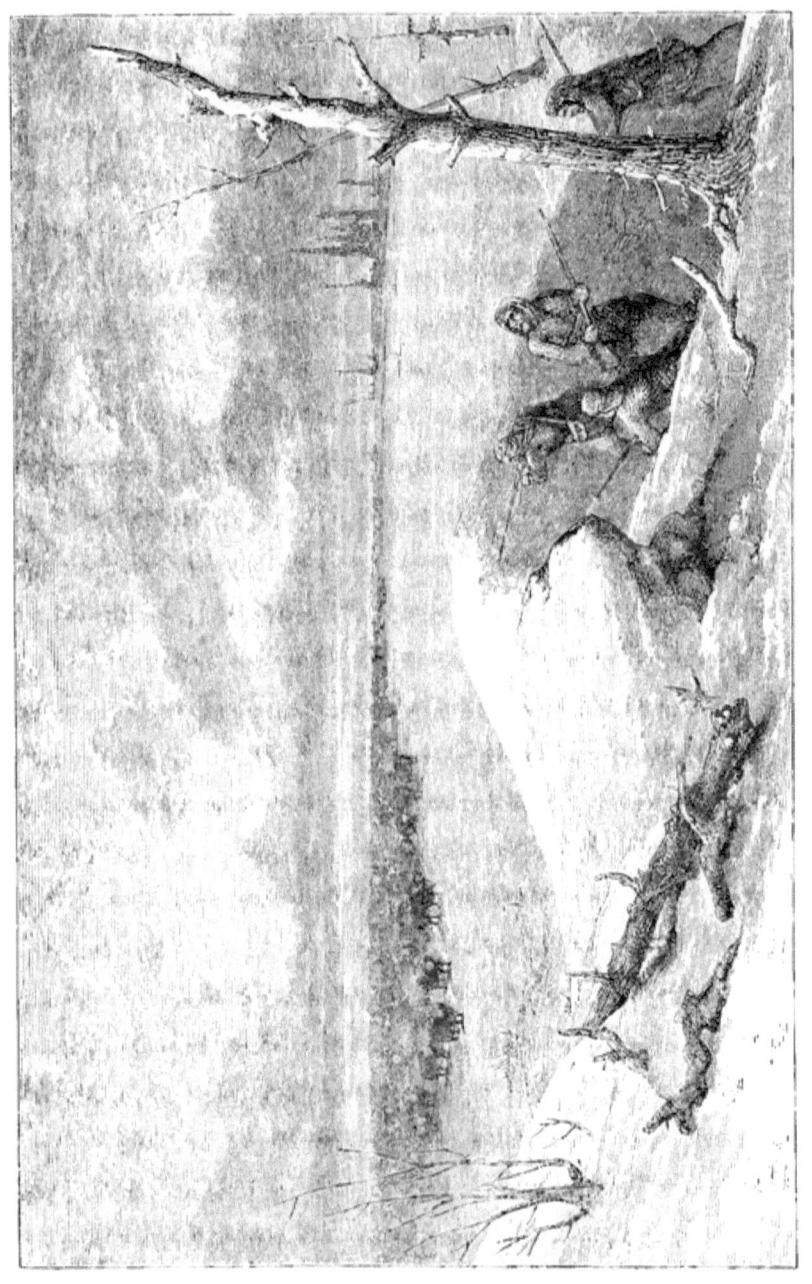

SUNSET SCENE, WITH BUFFALO. [*Page* 57.

CHAPTER VIII.

Buffalo Hunts.—A Picture once seen, long remembered.—
L'Homme capable.—A wonderful Lake.—The lost Indian.—
An Apparition.—We return home.

It was mid-November before we reached the buffalo; the snow had deepened, the cold had become intense, and our horses under the influence of travel, cold, and exposure, had become miserably thin. To hunt the herds on horseback would have been an impossibility; the new-fallen snow hid the murderous badger holes that covered the prairie surface, and to gallop weak horses over such ground must have been certain disaster.

Buffalo hunts on horseback or on foot have frequently been the theme of travellers' story. Ruxton and Palliser, and Mayne Reid and Catlin, have filled many a page with glowing descriptions of charge and counter-charge, stalk and stampede. Washington Irving has lighted with his genius the dull records of western wanderings, and to sketch now the pursuit of that huge beast (so soon to be an extinct giant) would be to repeat a thrice-told tale.

Who has not seen in pencil sketch or pen story the image of the huge, shaggy beast careering madly before an eagle-feathered red man, whose horse decked like its rider with the feathered trophy, launches himself swiftly over the prairie? The full-drawn bow, the deadly arrow, the stricken animal, the wild confusion of the flying herd, the wounded giant turning to bay;—all these have been described a thousand times; so also has the stalk, the stealthy approach under the wolf-skin covering, the careful shot and the stupid stare of the startled animals as they pause a moment to gather consciousness that this thing which they deemed a wolf in the grass is in reality their most deadly enemy, man. All these have found record from pen and pencil; but I much doubt me if it be possible to place before a reader's mental vision anything like a true picture of the sense of solitude, of endless space, of awful desolation which at times comes to the traveller's mind as he looks over some vast prairie and beholds a lonely herd of bisons trailing slowly across that snow-wrapt, endless expanse, into the shadows of the coming night.

Such a sight I have beheld more than once, and its memory returns at times with the sigh of the south wind, or the waving of a pine branch. It is from moments such as these that the wanderer draws the recompence of his toil, and reaps in aftertime the harvest of his hardship. No book has told the story, no picture has caught the colouring of sky and plain, no sound can echo back the music of that untainted breeze, sighing so mournfully through the yellow grass, but all the same the vision returns without one effort of remembrance: the vast plain snow-wrapt, the west ablaze with gold, and green, and saffron, and colours never classed or catalogued, while the horizon circle from north to east and south grows dim and indistinct, and, far off, the bison herd in long, scattered file trails slowly across the blue-white snow into the caverns of the sunset.

We carried with us a leather tent of eight skins, small of its kind, but capable of sheltering the five individuals comprising our party. This tent, pitched in some hollow at sunset, formed the sole speck of life amidst the vast solitude. Ten poles resting on the ground, and locked together at the top, supported the leather covering. An open space at the apex of the tent was supposed to allow the smoke to escape, but the smoke usually seemed to consider itself under no restraint whatever in the dim interior of our lodge, and seldom or never took advantage of the means of freedom so liberally provided for it. Our stock of fuel was very limited, and barely sufficed to boil a kettle and fry a dish of pemmican at the opening or close of each day. When the evening meal was finished, we sat awhile grouped around the small fire in the centre. "L'homme capable" ran round our line of traps, returning with a couple of kit foxes, the fattest of which he skinned and roasted for his supper. Then we gathered the blankets close together, and lying down slept until the dawn came struggling through the open roof, and cold and hungry we sat again around the little fire. Thus we journeyed on.

Scattered over the wide prairie which lies between the South Saskatchewan and the Eagle Hills roamed many herds of buffalo. But their numbers were very far short of those immense herds which, until a few years ago, were wont to cover the treeless regions of the west. Yet they were numerous enough to make the onlooker marvel how they still held their own against the ever-increasing odds arrayed against them.

Around the wide circle of this prairie ocean lay scattered not less than 15,000 wild people, all preying with wasteful vigour upon these scattered herds; but the numbers killed for the consumption of these Indian or half-Indian men formed but a small item in the lists of slaughter. To the north and east the denizens of the remote parts of the great regions locked in savage distance, the land of fur, the land which stretches to the wintry shores of the Bay of Hudson, and the storm-swept capes of the Arctic Ocean, looked for their means of summer transport to these wandering herds in the, to them, far distant Saskatchewan. What food was it that the tired *voyageur* munched so stolidly at nightfall by the camp fire on some long *portage* of the Winnipeg, the Nelson, or the Beaver Rivers, or ate with so much relish ere the morning sun was glinting along the waves of far Lake Athabasca; and his boat, rich laden with precious fur, rocked on the secluded shore of some nameless bay? It was buffalo pemmican from the Saskatchewan. And what food was it that these dozen hungry dogs devoured with such haste by that lonely camp fire in the dark pine forest, when all nature lay in its mid-winter torpor frozen to the soul; when the pine-log flared upon some snow-sheeted lake, or ice-bound river in the great wilderness of the north? It was the same hard mixture of fat and dried buffalo-meat pounded down into a solid mass which the Indians called "pemmican." Small wonder then that the great herds had dwindled down to their present numbers, and that now the once wide domain of the buffalo had shrunken into the limits of the great prairie.

Yet, even still, the numbers annually killed seem

quite incredible; 12,000 are said to fall to the Blackfeet tribes alone; in a single hunt the French half-breeds, whose winter camp we had lately visited, had killed 600 cows. The forts of the Hudson's Bay Company were filled with many thousand bags of pemmican, and to each bag two animals may be counted; while not less than 30,000 robes had already found their way to the Red River, and fully as many more in skins of parchment or in leather had been traded or consumed in the thousand wants of savage life; and all are ruthlessly killed—young and old, calves and cows, it matters little; the Indian and the half-breed know no such quality as forethought. Nor, looking at this annual havoc, and seeing still in spite of all the dusky herds yet roaming over the treeless waste, can we marvel that the Red man should ascribe to agencies other than mortal the seemingly endless numbers of his favourite animal?

South-west from the Eagle Hills, far out in the prairie, there lies a lake whose waters never rest; day and night a ceaseless murmur breaks the silence of the spot.

"See," says the red man, "it is from under that lake that our buffalo comes. You say they are all gone; but look, they come again and again to us. We cannot kill them all—they are there under that lake. Do you hear the noise which never ceases? It is the buffalo fighting with each other far down under the ground, and striving to get out upon the prairie—where else can they come from?"

We may well ask the question where do they come from? for in truth the vast expanse of the great prairie seems too small to save them from their relentless foes.

The creek of the Eagle Hills winds through the prairie in long, lazy bends. The beaver has made his home under its banks; and in some of the serpentine bends the bastard maple lifts its gnarled trunk, and the willow copses grow thickly. It is a favourite ground for the hunter in summer; but now, in mid-November, no sign of man was visible, and we had the little thicket oasis all to ourselves.

It was in this spot, some two years ago, that the following event occurred. In a band of Crees travelling over the plains there happened to be a blind Indian. Following the band one day he lagged behind, and the party dipping over a ridge on the prairie became lost to sound. Becoming suddenly alarmed at having thus lost his friends, he began to run swiftly in hope of overtaking them; but now his judgment was at fault, and the direction of his run was the wrong one—he found himself alone on the immense plains. Tired at last by the speed to which feverish anxiety had urged him, he sat down to think over his chances. It was hopeless to attempt to regain his party; he was far out in the grassy ocean, and south, west, and east, lay hundreds of miles of undulating plain; to the north many days' journey, but still near, in relative distance, lay the forts of the white man, and the trail which led from one to the other. He would steer for the north, and would endeavour to reach one of these forts. It was midsummer; he had no food, but the carcases of lately-killed buffalo were, he knew, numerous in that part of the prairie, and lakes or ponds were to be found at intervals.

He set out, and for three days he journeyed north. "How did he steer?" the reader will ask; "for have you not told us the man was blind?" Nevertheless, he steered with accuracy towards the north. From sunrise he kept the warm glow on his naked right shoulder; six hours later the heat fell full upon his back; towards evening the rays were on his left side; and when the sun had gone, and the damp dew began to fall, he lay down for the night: thus he held a tolerably correct course. At times the soft mud of a lake shore cloyed his feet; but that promised water, and after a drink he resumed his way; the lakelet was rounded and the course pursued. There was no food; for two days he travelled on patiently, until at last he stumbled over the bones of a buffalo. He felt around; it had been killed some time, and the wolves had left scant pickings on ribs or legs, but on the massive head the skin was yet untouched, and his knife enabled him to satisfy his hunger, and to carry away a few scraps of skin and flesh.

Thus recruited he pressed on. It was drawing towards evening on the fifth day of his weary journey when he found himself reduced to starvation, weak from protracted hunger and faint from thirst; the day had been a warm one, and no friendly lake had given him drink. His scanty food had been long exhausted, and there seemed but little hope that he could live to feel the warm sun again. Its rays were growing faint upon his left shoulder, when his feet suddenly sank into soft mud, and the reeds and flags of a swamp brushed against his legs: here was water, he lay down and drank a long, long draught. Then he bethought him, Was it not better to stay here while life lasted? here he had at least water, and of all the pangs that can afflict the lost wanderer that of thirst is the hardest to bear. He lay down midst the reeds, determined to wait for death.

Some few miles distant to the north-east lay the creek of the Eagle Hills. That evening a

F

party of hunters from the distant fort of Â la Corne, had appeared on the wide prairies which surrounded this creek; they were in search of buffalo, it wanted an hour of sunset. The man in charge looked at the sinking sun, and he bethought him of a camping-place. "Go to such and such a bend of the creek," he said to his hunters, "unyoke the horses and make the camp. I will ride to yonder hill and take a look over the plains for buffalo; I will rejoin you at the camp."

The party separated, and their leader pushed on to the hill-top for a better survey of the plains. When he reached the summit of the ridge he cast a look on every side; no buffalo were to be seen, but to his surprise, his men, instead of obeying his orders as to the route, appeared to be steering in a different direction from the one he had indicated, and were already far away to the south. When he again overtook them they were in the act of camping on the borders of a swampy lake, a long way from the place he had intended; they had mistaken the track, they said, and seeing water here had camped at sunset.

It was not a good place, and the officer felt annoyed at their stupidity. While they spoke together thus, a figure suddenly rose from the reeds at the further side of the lake, and called loudly for assistance. For a moment the hunters were amazed at this sudden apparition; they were somewhat startled too, for the Blackfeet bands were said to be on the war-trail. But presently they saw that there was only a solitary stranger, and that he was blind and helpless : it was the lost Cree. He had long before heard the hunters' approach, but not less deadly was the fear of Blackfeet than the dread of death by starvation. Both meant *death;* but one meant scalping, therefore dishonour in addition. It was only when the welcome sounds of the Cree language fell on his ear that he could reveal his presence in the reed-fringed lake.

I have told this story at length just as I heard it from the man who had been in charge of the party of hunters, because it brings home to the mind of the outsider, not only the power of endurance which the Indian displays in the face of physical difficulties, but also the state of society produced by the never-ending wars among the Indian tribes. Of the mistake which caused the hunters to alter their course and pitch their camp in another direction than that intended by their leader I have nothing to say ; chance is a strange *leader* people say. Tables are said to be turned by unseen powers seemingly like the stars in the song, " because they've nothing else to do ;" but for my part I had rather believe that men's footsteps are turned south instead of west under other Guidance than that of chance, when that change of direction, heedless though it be, saves some lost wanderer who has lain down to die.

It was the 3rd of December, when with thin and tired horses, we returned to the Forks of the Saskatchewan. We found our house wholly completed; on the stage in front safe from dogs and wolves the produce of the hunt was piled, the weary horses were turned loose on the ridge above, and with a few books on a shelf over a rude but comfortable bed, I prepared to pass the next two months of winter.

It was full time to reach home; the snow lay deep upon the ground; the cold, which had set in unusually early, had even in mid-November fallen to thirty degrees below zero, and some of our last buffalo stalks had been made under a temperature in which frozen fingers usually followed the handling, with unmittened hands, of rifle stock or gun trigger.

Those who in summer or autumn visit the great prairie of the Saskatchewan can form but a faint idea of its winter fierceness and utter desolation. They are prone to paint the scene as wanting only the settler's hut, the yoke of oxen, the waggon, to become at once the paradise of the husbandman. They little know of what

TENT IN THE GREAT PRAIRIE.

[Page 63.

they speak. Should they really wish to form a true conception of life in these solitudes, let them go out towards the close of November into the treeless waste; *then,* midst fierce storm and biting cold, and snowdrift so dense that earth and heaven seem wrapped together in indistinguishable chaos, they will witness a sight as different from their summer ideal as a mid-Atlantic mid-winter storm varies from a tranquil moonlight on the Ægean Sea.

During the sixteen days in which we traversed the prairie on our return journey, we had not seen one soul, one human being moving over it; the picture of its desolation was complete.

CHAPTER IX.

Strange Visitors.—At-tistighat the Philosopher.—Indian Converts.—A Domestic Scene.—The Winter Packet.—Adam and his Dogs.

DECEMBER passed away, the new year came, the cold became more intense. The snow deepened and the broad rivers lay hushed under their sparkling covering; wide roadways for our dog sleighs. At times there came a day of beautiful clearness, the sun shone brightly, the sky was of the deepest blue, and the earth sparkled in its spotless covering. At night the moon hung over the snow-wrapt river and silent pines with the brilliancy of a fairy scene; but many a day and night of storm and bitter tempest passed, and not unfrequently the thermometer placed against the hut wall marked full 70 degrees of frost.

Towards the end of the year four of our horses died, from the depth and hardness of the snow. The others would have soon followed if left to find their own sustenance, but a timely removal to the Fort à la Corne, twenty miles lower down the river, saved them.

When the year was drawing to its close two Indians pitched their lodge on the opposite side of the North River, and finding our stage pretty well stocked with food they began to starve immediately. In other words, it was easier to come to us for buffalo meat than to hunt deer for themselves: at all hours of the day they were with us, and frequently the whole family, two men, two squaws, and three children, would form a doleful procession to our hut for food. An Indian never knocks at a door; he lifts the latch, enters quietly, shakes hands with every one, and seats himself, without a word, upon the floor. You may be at breakfast, at dinner, or in bed, it doesn't matter. If food be not offered to him, he will wait until the meal is finished, and then say that he has not eaten for so many hours, as the case may be. Our stock of food was not over sufficient, but it was impossible to refuse it to them even though they would not hunt for themselves; and when the three children were paraded—all pretty little things from four to seven years of age—the argument of course became irresistible.

It was useless to tell them that the winter was long, that no more buffalo could be obtained; they seemed to regard starvation as an ordinary event to be calculated upon, that as long as any food was to be obtained it was to be eaten at all times, and that when it was gone—well then the best thing was to do without it.

January drew to a close in very violent storms accompanied by great cold. Early one morning "At-tistighat," or as we called him Bourgout No. 1, arrived with news that his brother had gone away two days before, that he had no blanket, no food; and that, as it had not been his intention to stay out, he concluded that he had perished. "At-tistighat" was a great scoundrel, but nevertheless, as the night had been one of terrible storm, we felt anxious for the safety of his brother, who was really a good Indian. "Go," we said to him, "look for your brother; here is pemmican to feed you during your search." He took the food, but coolly asserted that in all probability his brother had shot himself, and that consequently there was no use whatever in going to look for him; "or," he said, "he is dead of cold, in which case it is useless to find him."

While he spoke a footstep outside announced an arrival, the door opened, and the lost Bourgout No. 2 entered, bearing on his back a heavy load of venison.

At-tistighat's line of argument was quite in keeping with the Indian character, and was laughable in its selfish logic. If the man was alive, he would find his own way home; if dead, there was nothing more to be done in the matter: but in any case pemmican was not to be despised.

But despite their habits of begging, and their frequently unseasonable visits, our Cree neighbours afforded us not a little food for amusement in the long winter evenings. Indian character is worth the study, if we will only take the trouble to divest ourselves of the notion that all men should be like ourselves. There is so much of simplicity and cunning, so much of close reasoning and child-like suspicion; so much natural quickness, sense of humour, credulousness, power of observation, faith and fun and selfishness, mixed up together in the Red man's mental composition; that the person who will find nothing in Indian character worth studying will be likely to start from a base of nullity in his own brain system.

In nearly all the dealings of the white man with the red, except perhaps in those of the fur trade, as conducted by the great fur companies, the mistake of judging and treating Indians by European standards has been made. From the earliest ages of American discovery, down to the present moment, this error has been manifest; and it is this error which has rendered the whole missionary labour, the vast machinery set on foot by the charity and benevolence of the various religious bodies during so many centuries, a practical failure to-day.

When that Christian King Francis the First commissioned Cartier to convert the Indians, they were described in the royal edict as " men without knowledge of God, or use of reason;" and as the speediest mode of giving them one, and bringing them to the other, the Quebec chief savage was at once kidnapped, carried to France, baptized, and within six months was a dead man. We may wonder if his wild subjects had imbibed sufficient "reason" during the absence of the ship to realize during the following season the truth of what they were doubtless told, that it was better to be a dead Christian than a live savage; but no doubt, under the circumstances, they might be excused if they " didn't quite see it." Those who would imagine that the case of Munberton could not now occur in missionary enterprise are deceived.

Munberton, who is said to have been a devout Christian in the early days of Acadie, was duly instructed in the Lord's Prayer; at a certain portion of the prayer he was wont to append a request that "fish and moose meat" might also be added to his daily bread. And previous to his death, which occurred many years after his conversion, he is said to have stoutly demanded that the savage rites of sepulture should be bestowed upon his body, in order that he might be well prepared to make vigorous war upon his enemies in the next world. This is of the past; yet it is not many years since a high dignitary of the Church was not a little horrified by a request made by some recently converted Dog-Rib Chiefs that the rite of Baptism should be bestowed upon three flaming red flannel shirts, of which they had for the first time in their lives become the joint possessors.

But all this is too long to enter upon here; enough that to me at least the Indian character is worth the trouble of close examination. If those, whose dealings religious and political with the red man are numerous, would only take a leaf from Goldsmith's experience when he first essayed to become a teacher of English in France, ("for I found," he writes, "that it was necessary I should previously learn French before I could teach them English,") very much of the ill success which had attended labours projected by benevolence, and prosecuted with zeal and devotion, might perhaps be avoided.

Long before ever a white man touched the American shore a misty idea floated through the red man's brain that from far-off lands a stranger would come as the messenger of peace and plenty, where both were so frequently unknown. In Florida, in Novumbega, in Canada, the right hand of fellowship was the *first* proffered to the new comer; and when Cartier entered the palisaded village where now the stately capital of Canada spreads out along the base of the steep ridge, which he named Royal after that master whose " honour " had long been lost ere on Pavia's field he yielded up all else, the dusky denizens of Hochelaga brought forth their sick and stricken comrades " as though a God had come among them."

Three centuries and a half have passed since then; war, pestilence and famine have followed the white man's track. Whole tribes have vanished even in name from the continent, yet still that strange tradition of a white stranger, kind and beneficent, has outlived the unnumbered cruelties of ages; and to-day the starving camp and the shivering bivouac hears again the hopeful yet hopeless story of " a good time coming."

Besides our Indians we were favoured with but few visitors, silence reigned around our residence; a magpie or a whisky-jack sometimes hopped or chattered about our meat stage; in the morning the sharp-tailed grouse croaked in birch or spruce tree, and at dusk, when every other sound was hushed, the small grey owl hooted his lonely cry. Pleasant was it at night when returning after a long day on snow shoes, or a dog trip to the nearest fort, to reach the crest of the steep ridge that surrounded our valley, and see below the fire-light gleaming through the little window of our hut, and the red sparks flying upward from the chimney like fire-flies amidst the dark pine-trees; nor was it less pleasant when as the night wore on the home letter was penned, or the book read, while the pine-log fire burnt brightly and the dogs slept stretched before it, and the light glared on rifle-barrel or axe-head and showed the skin-hung rafters of our lonely home.

As January drew towards a close, it became necessary to make preparations for a long journey. Hitherto I had limited my wanderings to the prairie region of the Saskatchewan, but these wanderings had only been a preliminary to further travel into the great northern wilds.

To pierce the forest region lying north of the Saskatchewan valley, to see the great lakes of the Athabasca and that vast extent of country which pours its waters into the Frozen Ocean, had long been my desire; and when four months earlier I had left the banks of the Red River and turned away from the last limit of civilization, it was with the hope that ere the winter snow had passed from plain and forest my wanderings would have led me at least 2000 miles into that vast wilderness of the north.

But many preparations had to be made against cold and distance. Dogs had to be fattened, leather clothing got ready, harness and sleds looked to, baggage reduced to the very smallest limit, and some one found willing to engage to drive the second dog sled, and to face the vicissitudes of the long northern road. The distance itself was enough to make a man hesitate ere for hire he embarked on such a journey. The first great stage was 750 miles, the second was as many more, and when 1500 miles had been traversed there still must remain half as much again before, on the river systems of the North Pacific, we could emerge into semi-civilized ways of travel.

Many were the routes which my brain sketched out during the months of autumn, but finally my choice rested between two rivers, the Mackenzie rolling its waters into the Frozen Ocean, the Peace River piercing the great defiles of the Rocky Mountains through the cañons and stupendous gorges of Northern British Columbia. A chance meeting decided my course.

One day at the end of October I had camped during a snow-storm for dinner in the Touchwood Hills. Suddenly through the drift a horseman came in sight. He proved to be an officer of the Hudson's Bay Company from the distant post of Dunvegan on the Peace River: of all men he was the one I most wished to see. Ninety days earlier he had left his station; it was far away, but still with dogs over the ice of frozen rivers and lakes, through the snow of long leagues of forest and musky and prairie, I might hope to reach that post on Upper Peace River in sixty days; twenty days more might carry me through the defiles of the Rocky Mountains to waters which flow south into the Pacific. "Good-bye, *bon voyage*," and we went our different ways; he towards Red River, I for Athabasca and the Peace River.

And now, as I have said, the end of January had come, and it was time to start; all my preparations were completed, Cerf-vola and his companions were fat, strong, and hearty. Dog shoes, copper kettles, a buffalo robe, a thermometer, some three or four dozen rounds of ammunition, a little tobacco and pain-killer, a dial compass, a pedometer, snow shoes, about fifteen pounds of baggage, tea, sugar, a little flour, and lastly, the inevitable pemmican; all were put together, and I only waited the arrival of the winter packet from the south to set out.

Let me see if I can convey to the reader's mind a notion of this winter packet.

Towards the middle of the month of December there is unusual bustle in the office of the Hudson's Bay Company at Fort Garry on the Red River;

the winter packet is being made ready. Two oblong boxes are filled with letters and papers addressed to nine different districts of the northern continent. The limited term district is a singularly unappropriate one: a single instance will suffice. From the post of the Forks of the Athabasca and Clear Water Rivers to the Rocky Mountain Portage is fully 900 miles as a man can travel, yet all that distance lies within the limits of the single Athabasca district, and there are others larger still. From the Fort Resolution on the Slave River to the ramparts on the Upper Yukon, 1100 miles lay their lengths within the limits of the Mackenzie River district.

Just as the days are at their shortest, a dog sled bearing the winter packet starts from Fort Garry; a man walks behind it, another man some distance in advance of the dogs. It holds its way down the Red River to Lake Winnipeg; in about nine days' travel it crosses that lake to the north shore at Norway House; from thence, lessened of its packet of letters for the Bay of Hudson and the distant Churchill, it journeys in twenty days' travel up the Great Saskatchewan River to Carlton House. Here it undergoes a complete readjustment; the Saskatchewan and Lesser Slave Lake letters are detached from it, and about the 1st of February it starts on its long journey to the north.

During the succeeding months it holds steadily along its northern way, sending off at long, long intervals branch dog packets to right and left; finally, just as the sunshine of mid-May is beginning to carry a faint whisper of the coming spring to the valleys of the Upper Yukon, the dog train, last of many, drags the packet, now but a tiny bundle, into the enclosure of La Pierre's House. It has travelled nearly 3000 miles; a score of different dog teams have hauled it, and it has camped for more than a hundred nights in the great northern forest.

The end of January had come, but contrary to the experience of several years had brought no packet from Fort Garry, and many were the surmises afloat as to the cause of this delay. The old Swampy Indian Adam who, for more than a score of years had driven the dog packet, had tumbled into a water-hole in the ice, and his dogs had literally exemplified one portion of the popular saying of following their leader through fire and water; and the packet, Adam, and the dogs, lay at the bottom of the Saskatchewan River. Such was one anticipated cause of this non-appearance.

To many persons the delay was very vexatious, but to me it was something more. Time was a precious article: it is true a northern winter is a long one, but so also was the route I was about to follow, and I hoped to reach the upper regions of the Rocky Mountains while winter yet held with icy grasp the waters of the Peace River Cañon.

The beginning of February came, and I could wait no longer for the missing packet. On the 3rd, at mid-day, I set out on my journey. The day was bright and beautiful, the dogs climbed defiantly the steep high point, and we paused a moment on the summit; beneath lay hut and pine wood and precipitous bank, all sparkling with snow and sunshine; and beyond, standing motionless and silent, rose the Great Sub-Arctic Forest.

CHAPTER X.

A *tale* of warfare.—Dog-sleds.—A missing link.—The North Sea.—" Winterers."—Samuel Hearne.

DURING the three months which had elapsed since his arrival at the Forks, Cerf-vola had led an idle life; he had led his train occasionally to Fort à la Corne, or hauled a light sled along the ice of the frozen rivers, but these were only desultory trips, and his days had usually passed in peace and plenty.

Perhaps I am wrong in saying peace, for the introduction of several strange dogs had occasioned much warfare, and although he had invariably managed to come off victorious, victory was not obtained without some loss. I have before remarked that he possessed a very large bushy tail. In time of war this appendage was carried prominently over his back, something after the manner of the plumes upon casque of knight in olden times, or the more modern helmet of dragoon in the era of the Peninsular War.

One day, while he was engaged in a desperate

struggle with a bumptious new-comer, a large ill-conditioned mongrel which had already been vanquished, seeing his victor fully occupied, deemed it an auspicious moment for revenge, and springing upon the bushy tail proceeded to attack it with might and main. The unusual noise brought me to the door in time to separate the combatants while yet the tail was intact, but so unlooked for had been the assault that it was found upon examination to be considerably injured. With the aid of a needle and thread it was repaired as best we could, Cerf-vola apparently understanding what the surgical operation meant, for although he indulged in plenty of uproar at every stitch no attempt at biting was made by him. He was now however sound in body and in tail, and he tugged away at his load in blissful ignorance that 1500 miles of labour lay before him.

I know not if my readers are acquainted with the manner in which dogs are used as draught animals in the great fur regions of the north. A dog sled is simply two thin oak or birch-wood boards lashed together with deer-skin thongs: turned up in front like a Norwegian snow shoe, it runs when light over hard snow or ice with great ease; its length is about nine feet, its breadth sixteen inches. Along its outer edges runs a leather lashing, through the loops of which a long

DOG TRAIN FOR THE NORTH. [Page 85.

leather line is passed, to hold in its place whatever may be placed upon it. From the front, close to the turned portion, the traces for draught are attached. The dogs, usually four in number, stand in tandem fashion, one before the other, the best dog generally being placed in front, as "fore-goer," the next best in rear as "steady-dog." It is the business of the foregoer to keep the track, however faint it may be on lake or river. The steerdog guides the sled, and prevents it from striking or catching in tree or root. An ordinary load for four dogs weighs from 2 to 400 lbs.; laden with 200 lbs. dogs will travel on anything like a good track, or on hard snow, about thirty or thirty-five miles in each day. In deep or soft snow the pace is of necessity slow, and twenty to twenty-five miles will form a fair day's work.

If any one should ask what length of time dogs will thus travel day after day, I refer them to the following chapters, wherein the fortunes of Cerf-vola and his brethren, starting out to-day on a long journey, are duly set forth.

Some few miles west of the mission station called Prince Albert I parted from my friend Captain M——, who thus far had accompanied me. He was to return to Red River and Canada, *viâ* Cumberland and the lakes; I to hold my way across the frozen continent to the Pacific. For many months each day would place a double day's distance between us, but we still looked forward to another meeting, even though between us and that prospect there lay the breadth of all the savage continent.

A couple of days later I reached the Hudson's Bay Company's fort of Carlton, the great rendezvous of the winter packets between north and south. From north and west several of the leading agents of the fur company had assembled at Carlton to await the coming of the packet bearing news from the outer world. From Fort Simpson on the far Mackenzie, from Fort Chipwyan on the lonely lake Athabasca, from Edmonton on the Upper Saskatchewan, from Isle à la Crosse, dogs had drawn the masters of these remote establishments to the central station on the middle Saskatchewan. But they waited in vain for the arrival of the packet; with singular punctuality had their various trains arrived within a few days of each other from starting-points 2000 miles apart; yet after a few days' detention these officers felt anxious to set out once more on their journey, and many a time the hill-side on which the packet must first appear was scanned by watchers, and all the boasted second sight and conjuring power of haggard squaw and medicine man was set at work to discover the whereabouts of the " missing link " between the realms of civilization and savagery. To me the delay, except for the exigencies of time and distance, was not irksome. I was in the society of gentlemen whose lives had been passed in all portions of the great north, on the frozen shores of Hudson's Bay, in the mountain fastnesses of the Chipwyan range, or midst the savage solitudes that lie where, in long, low-lying capes, and ice-piled promontories, the shore of America stretches out to meet the waves of the Northern Ocean.

There was one present who in the past seven months had travelled by horse and canoe, boat and dog train, full 4000 miles; and another, destined to be my close companion during many weeks, whose matchless determination and power of endurance had carried him in a single winter from the Lower Mackenzie River to the banks of the Mississippi.

Here, while we await the winter packet, let me sketch with hasty and imperfect touch the lives of those who, as the " winterers " of the great company of adventurers trading into Hudson's Bay, have made their homes in the wilderness.

Two hundred and sixty-two years ago, a French adventurer under the banner of Samuel de Champlain wintered with an Indian tribe on the shores of the Upper Ottawa. In the ensuing spring he returned to Montreal, recounted his adventures, and became the hero of an hour. Beyond the country of the Ottawas he described a vast region, and from the uttermost sources of the Ottawa a large river ran towards the north until it ended in the North Sea. He had been there he said, and on the shore lay the ribs of an English vessel wrecked, and the skeletons of English sailors who had been drowned or murdered. His story was a false one, and ere a year had passed he confessed his duplicity; he had not been near the North Sea, nor had he seen aught that he described.

Yet was there even more than a germ of truth in his tale of wreck and disaster, for just one year earlier in this same North Sea, a brave English sailor had been set adrift in an open boat, with half a dozen faithful seamen; and of all the dark mysteries of the merciless ocean, no mystery lies wrapt in deeper shadow than that which hangs over the fate of Hudson.

But the seventeenth century was not an age when wreck or ruin could daunt the spirit of discovery. Here in this lonely North Sea, the palm of adventure belonged not to France alone. Spain might overrun the rich regions of the tropics, Richelieu (prototype of the great German chancellor of to-day) might plant the *fleur-de-lis* along the mighty St. Lawrence, but the north—the frozen north—must be the land of English enterprise and English daring. The years that followed the casting away of the fearless Hudson saw strange vessels coasting the misty shores of that weird sea; at first, to seek through its bergs and ice floes, its dreary cloud-wrapt fiords and inlets, a passage to the land where ceaseless sunshine glinted on the spice-scented shores of fabulous Cathay; and later on, to trade with the savages who clad themselves in skins, which the fairest favourites of Whitehall or the Louvre (by a strange extreme wherein savagery joined hands with civilization) would be proud to wrap round their snowy shoulders.

Prosecuted at first by desultory and chance adventurers, this trade in furs soon took definite form and became a branch of commerce. On the lonely sea-shores wooden buildings rose along the estuaries of rivers flowing from an unknown land. These were honoured by the title of fort or factory, and then the ships sailed back to England ere the autumn ice had closed upon the waters; while behind in Rupert's Fort, York Factory, Churchill, or Albany (names which tell the political history of their day), stayed the agents, or "winterers," whose work it was to face for a long season of hardship, famine, and disease, a climate so rigorous that not unfrequently, when the returning vessel rose upon the distant sea line, scarce half the eyes that had seen her vanish were there to watch her return. And they had other foes to contend with. Over the height of land, away by the great lakes, and along the forest shores of the St. Lawrence, the adventurers of another nation had long been busy at the mingled work of conquest and traffic. The rival Sultans of France and England could, midst the more pressing cares of their respective harems, find time occasionally to scribble " Henri " or " Charles " at the foot of a parchment scroll which gave a continent to a company; it little mattered whether Spaniard, Frenchman, or Briton had first bestowed the gift, the rival claimants might fight for the possession as they pleased. The geography of this New World was uncertain, and where Florida ended or Canada began was not matter of much consequence. But the great cardinal, like the great chancellor, was not likely to err in the matter of boundaries. " If there should be any doubt about the parts, we can take the whole," was probably as good a maxim then as now; and accordingly we find at one sweep the whole northern continent, from Florida to the Arctic Circle, handed over to a company of which the priest-soldier was the moving spirit.

Thus began the long strife between France and

England in North America,—a strife which only ended under the walls of Quebec. The story of their bravery, their endurance, their constancy, their heroism, has been woven into deathless history by a master-hand.[1] To France belongs the glory of the Great West—not the less her glory because the sun has set for ever upon her empire. Nothing remains to her. Promontory or lonely isle, name of sea-washed cape, or silent lake, half mistily tells of her former dominion. In the deep recesses of some north-western lake or river-reach the echoes still waken to the notes of some old French *chanson*, as the half Indian *voyageur*, ignorant of all save the sound, dips his glistening paddle to the cadence of his song. But of all that Cartier and Champlain, De Monts, La Salle, Marquette, Frontenac, and Montcalm lived and died for—nothing more remains.

Poor France! In the New World and in the Old history owes thee much. Yet in both hast thou paid the full measure of thy people's wrong.

But to return. The seventeenth century had not closed ere the sea of Hudson became the theatre of strife, the wooden palisades of the factories were battered or burnt down; and one fine day in August, 1697, a loud cannonade

[1] Francis Parkman.

boomed over the sullen waters, and before the long summer twilight had closed, the "Hampshire," with her fifty-two guns on high poop or lofty forecastle, lay deep beneath the *icy* sea, her consorts the Frenchman's prize. Nor had she gone down before a foe more powerful, but to the single frigate of Le Moyne d'Iberville, a child of Old and New France, the boldest rover that e'er went forth upon the Northern Seas. Some fifteen years later France resigned her claim to these sterile shores. Blenheim, Ramilies, Oudenarde, and Malplaquet had given to England the sole possession of the frozen north.

And now for nigh seventy years the English Company pursued unmolested its trade along the coast. A strong fort, not of wood and lath and stockade, but of hard English brick and native granite hewn by English hands, rose near the estuary of the Churchill River. To this fort the natives came annually along the English river bearing skins gathered far inland, along the shores of the Lake of the Hills, and the borders of the great river of the north.

With these natives wandered back an Englishman named Samuel Hearne; he reached the Lake Athabasca, and on all sides he heard of large rivers, some coming from south and west, others flowing to the remotest north. He wandered on from tribe to tribe, reached a great lake, descended a great river to the north, and saw at last the Arctic Sea.

Slowly did the Fur Company establish itself in the interior. It was easier to let the natives bring down the rich furs to the coast than to seek them in these friendless regions. But at last a subtle rival appeared on the scene; the story of the North-West Fur Company has often been told, and in another place we have painted the effects of that conflict; here it is enough to say that when in 1822 the north-west became merged into the older corporation; posts or forts had been scattered throughout the entire continent, and that henceforth from Oregon to Ungava, from Mingan to the Mackenzie, the countless tribes knew but one lord and master, the company of adventurers from England trading into Hudson's Bay.

What in the meantime was the work of those wintering agents whose homes were made in the wilderness? God knows their lives were hard. They came generally from the remote isles or highlands of Scotland, they left home young, and the mind tires when it thinks upon the remoteness of many of their fur stations. Dreary and monotonous beyond words was their home life, and hardship was its rule. To travel on foot

1000 miles in winter's darkest time, to live upon the coarsest food, to see nought of bread or sugar for long months, to lie down at night under the freezing branches, to feel cold such as Englishmen in England cannot even comprehend, often to starve, always to dwell iu exile from the great world. Such was the routine of their lives. The names of these northern posts tell the story of their toil. "Resolution," "Providence," "Good Hope," "Enterprise," "Reliance," "Confidence;" such were the titles given to these little forts on the distant Mackenzie, or the desolate shores of the great Slave Lake. Who can tell what memories of early days in the far away Scottish isles, or Highland glen, must have come to these men as the tempest swept the stunted pine-forest, and wrack and drift hurled across the frozen lake—when the dawn and the dusk, separated by only a few hours' daylight, closed into the long, dark night. Perchance the savage scene was lost in a dreamy vision of some lonely Scottish loch, some Druid mound in far away Lewis, some vista of a fireside, when storm howled and waves ran high upon the beach of Stornoway.

CHAPTER XI.

A dog of no character.—The Green Lake.—Lac Ile à la Crosse.—A cold day.—Fort Ile à la Crosse.—A long-lost brother.—Lost upon the Lake.—Unwelcome neighbours.—Mr. Roderick Macfarlane.—A beautiful morning.—Marble features.

On the night of the 11th of February, under a brilliant moonlight, we quitted Fort Carlton; crossing the Saskatchewan, we climbed the steep northern bank, and paused a moment to look back. The moon was at its full, not a cloud slept in the vast blue vault of heaven, a great planet burned in the western sky; the river lay beneath in spotless lustre; shore and prairie, ridge and lowland, sparkled in the sheen of snow and moonlight. Then I sprung upon my sled, and followed the others, for the music of their dog-bells was already getting faint.

The two following days saw us journeying on through a rich and fertile land. Clumps of poplar interspersed with pine, dotted the undulating surface of the country. Lakes were numerous, and the yellow grass along their margins still showed above the deep snow.

Six trains of dogs, twenty-three dogs in all, made a goodly show; the northern ones all beaded, belled, and ribboned, were mostly large powerful animals. Cree, French, and English names were curiously intermixed, and as varied were the tongues used to urge the trains to fresh exertions. Sometimes a dog would be abused, vilified, and cursed, in French alone; at others, he would be implored, in Cree, to put forth greater efforts. "Kuskey-tay-o-atim-moos," or the little "black dog" would be appealed to, "for the love of Heaven to haul his traces." He would be solemnly informed that he was a dog of no character; that he was the child of very disreputable parents; that, in fact, his mother had been no better than she should have been. Generally speaking, this information did not appear to have much effect upon Kuskey-tay-o-atim-moos, who was doubtless well satisfied if the abuse hurled at him and his progenitors exhausted the ire of his driver, and saved his back at the expense of his relations.

Four days of rapid travelling carried us far to the north. Early on the third day of travel the open country, with its lakelets and poplar ridges, was left behind, and the forest region entered upon for the first time.

Day had not yet dawned when we quitted a deserted hut which had given us shelter for the night; a succession of steep hills rose before us, and when the highest had been gained, the dawn had broken upon the dull grey landscape. Before us the great Sub-Arctic Forest stretched away to the north, a line of lakes, its rampart of defence against the wasting fires of the prairie region, lay beneath. This was the southern limit of that vast forest whose northern extreme must be sought where the waters of the Mackenzie mingle with the waves of the Arctic Sea.

We entered this forest, and in four days reached the southern end of the Green Lake, a long narrow sheet of water of great depth. The dogs went briskly over the hard snow on the surface of the ice-covered lake, and ere sun set on the 15th of February we were housed in the little Hudson's Bay post, near the northern extremity of the lake. We had run about 150 miles in four days.

A little more than midway between Carlton and Green Lake, the traveller crosses the height of land between the Saskatchewan and Beaver Rivers; its elevation is about 1700 feet above the sea level, but the rise on either side is barely perceptible, and between the wooded hills, a network of lakes linked together by swamps and muskys spreads in every direction. These lakes abound with the finest fish; the woods are fairly stocked with fur-bearing animals, and the country is in many respects fitted to be made the scene of Indian settlement, upon a plan not yet attempted by American or Canadian governments in their dealings with the red man.

On the morning of the 17th February we quitted the Green Lake, and continued on our northern way. Early on the day of departure we struck the Beaver or Upper Churchill river, and followed its winding course for some forty miles. The shores were well wooded with white spruce, juniper, and birch; the banks, some ten or twenty feet above the surface of the ice, sloped easily back; while at every ten or fifteen miles smaller streams sought the main river, and at each accession the bed of the channel nearly doubled in width.

Hitherto I have not spoken of the cold; the snow lay deep upon the ground, but so far the days had been fine, and the nights, though of course cold, were by no means excessively so. The morning of the 19th February found us camped on a pine ridge, between lakes, about fifteen miles south of Lac Ile à la Crosse, by the spot where an ox had perished of starvation during the previous autumn, his bones now furnishing a night-long repast for our hungry dogs. The night had been very cold, and despite of blanket or buffalo robe it was impossible to remain long asleep. It may seem strange to those who live in warm houses, who sleep in cosy rooms from which the draught is carefully excluded, and to whom the notion of seeking one's rest on the ground, under a pine-tree in mid-winter, would appear eminently suicidal; it may seem strange, I say, how in a climate where cold is measured by degrees as much *below* the freezing point as the hottest shade heat of Carnatic or Scindian summer is known to be *above* it, that men should be able at the close of a hard day's march to lie down to rest under the open heavens. Yet so it is.

When the light begins to fade over the frozen solitude, and the first melancholy hoot of the night owl is heard, the traveller in the north looks around him for " a good camping-place." In the forest country he has not long to seek for it; a few dead trees for fuel, a level space for his fire and his blanket, some green young pines to give him " brush " for his bed, and all his requirements are supplied. The camp is soon made, the fire lighted, the kettle filled with snow and set to boil, the supper finished, dogs fed, and the blankets spread out over the pine brush. It is scarcely necessary to say that there is not much time lost in the operation of undressing; under the circumstances one is more likely to reverse the process, and literally (not figuratively as in the case of modern society, preparing for her ball) to *dress* for the night. Then begins the cold; it has been bitterly cold all day, with darkness; the wind has lulled, and the frost has come out of the cold, grey sky with still, silent rigour. If you have a thermometer placed in the snow at your head the spirit will have shrunken back into the twenties and thirties below zero; and just when the dawn is stealing over the eastern pine tops it will not unfrequently be into the forties. Well then, that is cold if you like! You are tired by a thirty-mile march on snow shoes. You have lain down with stiffened limbs and blistered feet, and sleep comes to you by the mere force of your fatigue; but never goes the consciousness of the cold from your waking brain; and as you lie with crossed arms and up-gathered knees beneath your buffalo robe, you welcome as a benefactor any short-haired, shivering dog who may be forced from his lair in the snow to seek a few hours' sleep upon the outside of your blankets.

Yet do not imagine, reader, that all this is next to an impossibility, that men will perish under many nights of it. Men do not perish thus easily. Nay even, when before dawn the fire has been set alight, and the tea swallowed hot and strong, the whole thing is nigh forgotten, not unfrequently forgotten in the anticipations of a cold still more trying in the day's journey which is before you.

Such was the case now. We had slept coldly, and ere daylight the thermometer showed 32 degrees below zero. A strong wind swept through the fir-trees from the north; at daylight the wind lulled, but every one seemed to anticipate a bad day, and leather coats and capôtes were all in use.

We set off at six o'clock. For a time calmness reigned, but at sunrise the north wind sprang up again, and the cold soon became more than one could bear. Before mid-day we reached the southern end of Lac Ile à la Crosse; before us to the north lay nearly thirty miles of shelterless lake, and down this great stretch of ice the wind came with merciless severity.

We made a fire, drank a great deal of hot tea, muffled up as best we could, and put out into the lake. All that day I had been ill, and with no little difficulty had managed to keep up with the party. I do not think that I had, in the experience of many bitter days of travel, ever felt such cold; but I attributed this to illness more than to the day's severity.

We held on; right in our teeth blew the bitter blast, the dogs with low-bent heads tugged steadily onward, the half-breeds and Indians wrapped their blankets round their heads, and bending forward as they ran made their way against the wind. To run was instantly to freeze one's face; to lie on the sled was to chill through the body to the very marrow. It was impossible to face it long, and again we put in to shore, made a fire, and boiled some tea.

At midday the sun shone, and the thermometer stood at 26° below zero; the sun was utterly powerless to make itself felt in the slightest degree; a drift of dry snow flew before the bitter wind. Was this really great cold? I often asked myself. I had not long to wait for an answer. My two fellow-travellers were perhaps of all men in those regions best able to settle a question of cold. One had spent nigh thirty years in many parts of the Continent; the other had dwelt for years within the Arctic Circle, and had travelled the shores of the Arctic Ocean at a time when the Esquimaux keep close within their greasy snow huts. Both were renowned travellers in a land where bad travellers were unknown: the testimony of such men was conclusive, and for years they had not known so cold a day.

"I doubt if I have ever felt greater cold than this, even on the Anderson or the Mackenzie," said the man who was so well acquainted with winter hardship. After that I did not care so much; if *they* felt it cold, if their cheeks grew white and hard in the bitter blast, surely I could afford to freeze half my face and all my fingers to boot.

Yet at the time it was no laughing matter; to look forward to an hour seemed an infinity of pain. One rubbed and rubbed away at solid nose and white cheek, but that only added one's fingers to the list of iced things one had to carry.

At last the sun began to decline to the west, the wind fell with it, the thick, low-lying drift disappeared, and it was possible by running hard to restore the circulation. With dusk came a magnificent Aurora; the sheeted light quivered over the frozen lake like fleecy clouds of many colours blown across the stars. Night had long closed when we reached the warm shelter of the shore, and saw the welcome lights of houses in the gloom. Dogs barked, bolts rattled, men and children issued from the snow-covered huts; and at the door of his house stood my kind fellow-traveller, the chief factor of the district, waiting to welcome me to his fort of Ile à la Crosse.

The fort of Ile à la Crosse is a solitary spot. Behind it spreads a land of worthless forest, a region abounding in swamps and muskys, in front the long arms of the Cruciform Lake. It is not from its shape that the lake bears its name; in the centre, where the four long arms meet, stands an island, on the open shore of which the Indians in bygone times were wont to play their favourite game of la Crosse. The game named the island, and the island in turn gave its name to the lake. The Beaver River enters the lake at the south-east, and leaves it again on the north-west side. The elevation of the lake above the level of Hudson's Bay cannot be less than 1300 feet, so it is little wonder if the wild winds of the north should have full sweep across its frozen surface. The lake is well stocked with excellent white fish, and by the produce of the net the garrison of the fort is kept wholly in food, about 130 large fish being daily consumed in it.

At a short distance from the fort stands the French Mission. One of the earliest established in the north, it has thrown out many branches into more remote solitudes. Four ladies of the order of Grey Nuns have made their home here, and their school already contains some thirty children. If one wants to see what can be made of a very limited space, one should visit this convent at Ile à la Crosse; the entire building is a small wooden structure, yet school, dormitory, oratory, kitchen, and dining-room are all contained therein.

The sisters seemed happy and contented, chatted gaily of the outside world, or of their far-away homes in Lower Canada. Their present house was only a temporary erection. In one fell night fire had destroyed a, larger building, and consumed their library, oratory, everything; and now its ravages were being slowly repaired. Of course it was an event to be long remembered, and the lady who described to us the calamity seemed still to feel the terror of the moment.

My long journey left me no time for delay, and after one day's rest it became necessary to resume the march. The morning of the 21st February found us again in motion.

We now numbered some five sleds; the officer in charge of the Athabasca district, the next to the north, was still to be my fellow-traveller for nearly 400 miles to his post of Fort Chipewyan. All dogs save mine were fresh ones, but Cerf-vola showed not one sign of fatigue, and Spanker was still strong and hearty. Pony was, however, betraying every indication of giving out, and had long proved himself an arrant scoundrel.

Dogs were scarce in the North this year. A distemper had swept over all the forts, and many a trusty hauler had gone to the land where harness is unknown.

Here, at Ile à la Crosse, I obtained an eighth dog. This dog was Major; he was an Esquimaux from Deer's Lake, the birth-place of Cerf-vola, and he bore a very strong resemblance to my leader. It is not unlikely that they were closely related, perhaps brothers, who had thus, after many wanderings, come together; but, be that as it may, Cerf-vola treated his long-lost brother with evident suspicion, and continued to maintain towards all outsiders a dogged demeanour.

Major's resemblance to the Untiring led to a grievous error on the morning of my departure from the fort.

It was two hours before daylight when the dogs were put into harness; it was a morning of bitter cold; a faint old moon hung in the east; over the dim lake, a shadowy Aurora flickered across the stars; it was as wild and cheerless a sight as eye of mortal could look upon; and the work of getting the poor unwilling dogs into their harness was done by the Indians and half-breeds in no amiable mood.

In the haste and darkness the Untiring was placed last in the train which he had so long led, the new-comer, Major, getting the foremost place. Upon my assuming charge of the train, an ominous tendency to growl and fight on the part of my steer-dog told me something was wrong; it was too dark to see plainly, but a touch of the Untiring's nose told me that the right dog was in the wrong place.

The mistake was quickly rectified, but, nevertheless, I fear its memory long rankled in the mind of Cerf-vola, for all that day, and for some days after, he never missed an opportunity of counter-marching suddenly in his harness and prostrating the unoffending Major at his post of steer-dog; the attack was generally made with so much suddenness and vigour that Major instantly capitulated, "turning a turtle" in his traces. This unlooked-for assault was usually accompanied by a flank movement on the part of Spanker, who, whenever there was anything in the shape of fighting lying around, was sure to have a tooth in it on his own account, being never very particular as to whether he attacked the head of the rear dog or the tail of his friend in front.

All this led at times to fearful confusion in my train; they jumped on one another; they tangled traces, and back-bands, and collar-straps into sad knots and interlacings, which baffled my poor frozen fingers to unravel. Often have I seen them in a huge ball rolling over each other in the snow, while the rapid application of my whip only appeared to make matters worse, conveying the idea to Spanker or the Untiring that they were being badly bitten by an unknown belligerent.

Like the lady in Tennyson's "Princess," they "mouthed and mumbled" each other in a very perplexing manner, but, of course, from a cause totally at variance from that which influenced the matron in the poem. These events only occurred, however, when a new dog was added to the train; and, after a day or so, things got smoothed down, and all tugged at the moose-skin collars in peaceful unanimity.

But to return. We started from Ile à la Crosse, and held our way over a chain of lakes and rivers. Rivière Cruise was passed, Lac Clair lay at sundown far stretching to our right into the blue cold north, and when dusk had come, we were halted for the night in a lonely Indian hut which stood on the shores of the Detroit, fully forty miles from our starting-place of the morning.

"A long, hard, cold day; storm, drift, and desolation. We are lost upon the lake."

Such is the entry which meets my eye as I turn to the page of a scanty note-book which records the 22nd of February; and now looking back upon this day, it does not seem to me that the entry exaggerates in its pithy summing up the misery of the day's travel. To recount the events of each day's journey, to give minutely, starting-point, date, distance, and resting-place, is too frequently an error into which travellers are wont to fall. I have read somewhere in a review of a work on African travel, that no literary skill has hitherto been able to enliven the description of how the traveller left a village of dirty negroes in the morning, and struggled through swamps all day, and crossed a river swarming with hippopotami, and approached a wood where there were elephants, and finally got to another village of dirty negroes in the evening. The reviewer is right; the reiterated recital of Arctic cold and hardship, or of African heat and misery, must be as wearisome to the reader as its realization was painful to the writer; but the traveller has one advantage over the reader, the reality of the "storm, drift, and desolation" had the excitement of the very pain which they produced. To be lost in a haze of blinding snow, to have a spur of icy keenness urging one to fresh exertion, to seek with dazed eyes hour after hour for a faint print of snow shoes or mocassin on the solid surface of a large lake, to see the night approaching and to urge the dogs with whip and voice to fresh exertions, to greater efforts to gain some distant landpoint ere night has wrapped the dreary scene in darkness; all this doled out hour by hour in narrative would be dull indeed.

To me the chief excitement lay in the question, Will this trail lead to aught? Will we save daylight to the shore? But to the reader the fact is already patent that the trail did lead to something, and that the night did not find the travellers still lost on the frozen lake.

Neither could the reader enter into the joy with which, after such a day of toil and hardships, the traveller sees in the gloom the haven he has sought so long; it may be only a rude cabin with windows cut from the snow-drift or the moose-skin, it may be only a camp-fire in a pine clump, but nevertheless the lost wanderer hails with a feeling of intense joy the gleam which tells him of a resting-place; and as he stretches his weary limbs on the hut floor or the pine-bush, he laughs and jests over the misfortunes, fatigues, and fears, which but a short hour before were heartsickening enough.

It was with feelings such as this that I beheld the lights of Rivière la Loche station on the night of the 22nd of February; for, through an afternoon of intense cold and blinding drift, we had struggled in vain to keep the track across the Buffalo Lake. The guide had vanished in the drift, and it was only through the exertions of my companion after hours of toil that we were able to regain the track, and reach, late on Saturday evening, the warm shelter of the little post; a small, clean room, a bright fire, a good supper, an entire twenty-four hours of sleep, and rest in prospect. Is it any wonder that with such surroundings the hut at Rivière la Loche seemed a palace?

And now each succeeding day carried us further

into the great wilderness of the north, over lakes whose dim shores loomed through the driving snow, and the ragged pines tossed wildly in the wind; through marsh and musky and tangled wood, and all the long monotony of dreary savagery which lies on that dim ridge, from whose sides the waters roll east to the Bay of Hudson, north to the Frozen Ocean.

We reached the Methy Portage, and turned north-west through a long region of worthless forest. Now and again a wood Cariboo crossed the track; a marten showed upon a frozen lake; but no other sign of life was visible. The whole earth seemed to sleep in savage desolation; the snow lay deep upon the ground, and slowly we plodded on.

To rise at half-past two o'clock a.m., start at four, and plod on until sunset, halting twice for an hour during the day, this was the history of each day's toil. Yet, with this long day of work, we could only travel about twenty-five miles. In front, along the track, went a young Chipewyan Indian; then came a train of dogs floundering deep in the soft snow; then the other trains wound along upon firmer footing. Camp-making in the evening in this deep snow was tedious work. It was hard, too, to hunt up the various dogs in the small hours of the morning, from their lairs in snow-drift or beneath root of tree; but some dogs kept uncomfortably close to camp, and I well remember waking one night out of a deep sleep, to find two huge beasts tearing each other to pieces on the top of the buffalo bag in which I lay.

After three days of wearisome labour on this summit ridge of the northern continent we reached the edge of a deep glen, 700 feet below the plateau. At the bottom of this valley a small river ran in many curves between high-wooded shores. The sleds bounded rapidly down the steep descent, dogs and loads rolling frequently in a confused heap together. Night had fallen when we gained the lower valley, and made a camp in the darkness near the winding river; the height of land was passed, and the river in the glen was the Clearwater of the Athabasca.

I have before spoken of the life of hardship to which the wintering agents of the Hudson's Bay Company are habituated, nor was I without some practical knowledge of the subject to which I have alluded. I had now, however, full opportunity of judging the measure of toil contained in the simple encomium one often utters in the north, "He is a good traveller."

Few men have led, even in the hard regions of the north, a life of greater toil than Mr. Roderick Macfarlane. He had left his island home when almost a boy, and in earliest manhood had entered the remote wilds of the Mackenzie River. For seventeen years he had remained cut off from the outer world; yet his mind had never permitted itself to sink amidst the oppressive solitudes by which he was surrounded: it rose rather to the level of the vastness and grandeur which Nature wears even in her extreme of desolation.

He entered with vigour into the life of *toil* before him. By no means of a strong constitution or frame of body, he nevertheless fought his way to hardiness; midst cold and darkness and scant living, the natural accompaniments of remote travel, he traversed the country between the Peel, Mackenzie, and Liard rivers, and pushed his explorations to the hitherto unknown River Anderson. Here, on the borders of the Barren Ground, and far within the Arctic Circle, he founded the most northern and remote of all the trading stations of the Fur Company. In mid-winter he visited the shores of the Frozen Ocean, and dwelt with the Esquimaux along the desolate coasts of that bay which bears the name of England's most hapless explorer.

Nor was it all a land of desolation to him. Directed by a mind as sanguine as his own,[1] he

[1] The late Major McKennicot, U.S.A., who, in charge of United States telegraph exploration, died at Fort Yukon,

entered warmly into the pursuits of natural history, and classed and catalogued the numerous birds which seek in summer these friendless regions, proving in some instances the range of several of the tiniest of the feathered wanderers to reach from Texas to the Arctic shores.

All his travels were performed on snow shoes, driving his train of dogs, or beating the track for them in the snow. In a single winter, as I have before mentioned, he passed from the Mackenzie River to the Mississippi, driving the same train of dogs to Fort Garry, fully 2000 miles from his starting-point; and it was early in the following summer, on his return from England after a hasty visit, the first during twenty years, that I made his acquaintance in the American State of Minnesota. He was not only acquainted with all the vicissitudes of northern travel, but his mind was well stored with the history of previous exploration. Chance and the energy of the old North-West Company had accumulated a large store of valuable books in the principal fort on the Mackenzie. These had been carefully studied during periods of inaction, and arctic exploration in reality or in narrative was equally familiar to him.

"I would have given my right arm to have been allowed to go on one of these search expeditions," he often said to me; and perhaps, if those wise and sapient men, who, acting in a corporate or individual capacity, have the power of selection for the work of relief or exploration, would only accustom themselves to make choice of such materials, the bones that now dot the sands of King William's Land or the estuary of the Great Fish River, might in the flesh yet move amongst us.

One night we were camped on a solitary island in the Swan Lake. The camp had been made after sunset, and as the morning's path lay across the lake, over hard snow where no track was necessary, it was our intention to start on our way long before daybreak. In this matter of early starting it is almost always impossible to rely on the Indian or the half-breed *voyageur*. They will lie close hid beneath their blankets, unless, indeed, the cold should become so intense as to force them to arise and light a fire; but, generally speaking, they will lie huddled so closely together that they can defy the elements, and it becomes no easy matter to arouse them from their pretended slumbers at two or three o'clock of a dead-cold morning. My companion, however, seemed to be able to live without sleep. At two o'clock he would arise from his deer-skin robe and set the camp astir. I generally got an hour's law until the fire was fairly agoing and the tea-kettle had been boiled.

No matter what the morning was, he never complained. This morning on Swan Lake was bitterly cold—30° below zero at my head.

"Beautiful morning!" he exclaimed, as I emerged from my buffalo robe at three o'clock; and he really meant it. I was not to be done.

"Oh, delightful!" I managed to chatter forth, with a tolerable degree of acquiescence in my voice, a few mental reservations and many bodily ones all over me.

But 30° below zero, unaccompanied by wind, is not so bad after all when one is fairly under weigh and has rubbed one's nose for a time, and struck the huge "mittained" hands violently together, and run a mile or so; but let the faintest possible breath of wind arise—a "zephyr" the poets would call it, a thing just strong enough to turn smoke or twist the feather which a wild duck might detach from beneath his wing as he cleft the air above—then look out, or rather look down, cast the eye so much askant that it can catch a glimpse of the top of the nose, and you will see a ghostly sight.

We have all heard of hard hearts, and stony eyes, and marble foreheads, alabaster shoulders, snowy necks, and firm-set lips, and all the long array of silicious similitudes used to express the various qualities of the human form divine; but firmer, and colder, and whiter, and harder than all stands forth prominently a frozen nose.

A study of frozen noses would be interesting; one could work out from it an essay on the admirable fitness of things, and even history read by the light of frozen noses might teach us new theories. The Roman nose could not have stood an arctic winter, hence the limits of the Roman empire. The Esquimaux nose is admirably fitted for the climate in which it breathes, hence the limited nature it assumes.

CHAPTER XII.

The Clearwater.—A bygone Ocean.—A Land of Lakes.—The Athabasca River.—Who is he?—Chipewyan Indians.—Echo.—Major succumbs at last.—Mal de Raquette.

THE Clearwater, a river small in a land where rivers are often a mile in width, meanders between its lofty wooded hills; or rather one should say, meanders in the deep valley which it has worn for itself through countless ages.

Ever since the beginning of the fur trade it has been the sole route followed into the North. More practicable routes undoubtedly exist, but hitherto the Long Portage (a ridge dividing the waters of the chain of lakes and rivers we have lately passed from those streams which seek the Arctic Ocean) and the Clearwater River have formed as it were the gateway of the North.

This Long Portage, under its various names of La Loche and Methy, is not a bad position from whence to take a bird's-eye view of the Great North.

Once upon a time, how long ago one is afraid to say (some Right Reverend gentlemen being as particular about the age of Mother Earth as an elderly female is anxious on the score of years about the Census times), a great sea rolled over what is now the central continent. From the Gulf of Mexico to the Arctic Ocean, from the Gulf of St. Lawrence to the base of the Rocky Mountains, this ocean has left its trace. It had its shores, and to-day these shores still show the trace of where the restless waves threw their surge upon the earlier earth. To the eye of the geologist the sea-shell, high cast upon some mountain ridge, tells its story of the sea as plainly as the tropic sea-shell, held to the dreamer's ear, whispers its low melody of sounding billow.

To the east of this ocean the old earth reared its iron head in those grim masses which we name Laurentian, and which, as though conscious of their hoary age, seem to laugh at the labour of the new comer, man.

The waters went down, or the earth went up, it little matters which; and the river systems of the continent worked their ways into Mother Ocean: the Mississippi south, the St. Lawrence east, the Mackenzie north. But the old Laurentian still remained, and to-day, grim, filled with wild lakes, pine-clad, rugged, almost impassable it lies, spread in savage sleep from Labrador to the Arctic Ocean.

At the Methy Portage we are on the western boundary of this Laurentian rock; from here it runs south-east to Canada, north to the Frozen Ocean.

It is of the region lying between this primary formation and the Rocky Mountains, the region once an ocean, of which we would speak.

I have said in an earlier chapter that the continent of British America, from the United States' boundary, slopes to the north-east, the eastern slope terminates at this Portage la Loche, and henceforth the only slope is to the north; from here to the Frozen Sea, one thousand miles, as wild swan flies, is one long and gradual descent. Three rivers carry the waters of this slope into the Arctic Ocean; the great Fish River of Sir George Back, at the estuary of which the last of Franklin's gallant crew lay down to die; the Coppermine of Samuel Hearne; and the Mackenzie which tells its discoverer's name. The first two flow through the Barren Grounds, the last drains by numerous tributaries, seventeen hundred miles of the Rocky Mountains upon both sides of that snow-capped range. All its principal feeders rise beyond the mountains, cutting through the range at right angles, through tremendous valleys, the sides of which overhang the gloomy waters.

The Liard, the Peel, the Peace rivers, all have their sources to the west of the Rocky Mountains. Even the parent rill of the Great Athabasca is on the Pacific side also. Nor is this mountain, thus curiously rent in twain by large rivers, a mere ridge, or lofty table-land; but huge and vast, capped by eternal snow, it lifts its peaks full fifteen thousand feet above the sea level.

Many large lakes lie spread over this ancient sea bottom; Lake Athabasca, Great Slave, and Great Bear Lake continue across the continent, that great Lacustrine line, which, with Winnipeg, Superior, Huron, and Ontario, forms an aggregate of water surface larger than Europe.

Of other lakes, the country is simply a vast network, beyond all attempt at name or number; of every size, from a hundred yards to a hundred miles in length, they lie midst prairie, or midst forest, lonely and silent, scarce known even to the wild man's ken.

And now, having thus imperfectly tried to bring to the reader's mind a vision of this vast North, let us descend from the height of land into the deep valley of the Clearwater, and like it, hurry onward to the Athabasca.

Descending the many-curving Clearwater for

one day, we reached, on the last day of February, its junction with the Athabasca, a spot known as the Forks of the Athabasca. The aspect of the country had undergone a complete change; the dwarf and ragged forest had given place to lofty trees, and the white spruce from a trunk of eight feet in circumference lifted its head fully one hundred and fifty feet above the ground. Nor was it only the aspect of the trees that might have induced one to imagine himself in a land of plenty. In the small fort at the Forks, luxuries unseen during many a day met the eye; choice vegetables, the produce of the garden; moose venison, and better than all, the tender steak of the wood buffalo, an animal now growing rare in the North.

There was salmon too, and pears and peaches; but these latter luxuries I need hardly say were not home produce; they came from the opposite extremes of Quebec and California. Here, then, in the midst of the wilderness was a veritable Eden. Here was a place to cry Halt, to build a hut, and pass the remainder of one's life. No more dog-driving, no more snow shoes, no smoky camp, no aching feet, no call in midnight; nothing but endless wood buffalo steaks, fried onions, moose moofle, parsnips, fresh butter, rest and sleep: alas! it might not be; nine hundred miles yet lay between me and the Rocky Mountains; nine hundred miles had still to be travelled, ere the snow had left bare the brown banks of the Peace River.

And now our course led straight to the north, down the broad bed of the Athabasca. A river high shored, and many islanded, with long reaches, leagues in length, and lower banks thick wooded with large forest trees.

From bank to bank fully six hundred yards of snow lay spread over the rough frozen surface; and at times, where the prairie plateau approached the river's edge, black bitumen oozed out of the clayey bank, and the scent of tar was strong upon the frosty air.

On Sunday, the 2nd of March, we remained for the day in a wood of large pines and poplars. Dogs and men enjoyed that day's rest. Many were footsore, some were sick, all were tired.

"The Bheel is a black man, and much more hairy; he carries archers in his hand, with these he shoots you when he meets you; he throws your body into a ditch: by this you will know the Bheel." Such, word for word, was the written reply of a young Hindoo at an examination of candidates for a Government Office in Bombay a few years ago. The examiners had asked for a description of the hill-tribe known as Bheels, and this was the answer. It is not on record what number of marks the youthful Brahmin received for the information thus lucidly conveyed, or whether the examiners were desirous of making further acquaintance with the Bheel, upon the terms indicated in the concluding sentence; but, for some reason or other, the first sight of a veritable Chipewyan Indian brought to my mind the foregoing outline of the Bheel, and I found myself insensibly repeating, "The Chipewyan is a red man, and much more hairy." There I stopped, for he did not carry archers in his hand, nor proceed in the somewhat abrupt and discourteous manner which characterized the conduct of the Bheel. And here, perhaps, it will be necessary to say a few words about the wild man who dwells in this Northern Land.

A great deal has been said and written about the wild man of America. The white man during many years has lectured upon him, written learned essays upon him, phrenologically proved him this, chronologically demonstrated him that, ethnologically asserted him to be the tother! I am not sure that the conchologists even have not thrown a shell at him, and most clearly shown that he was a conglomerate of this, that, and tother all combined. They began to dissect him very early. One Hugh Grotius had much to say about him a long time ago. Another Jean de Leut also descanted upon him, and so far back as the year of grace 1650, one Thorogood (what a glimpse the date gives of the name and the name of the date!) composed a godly treatise entitled " Jews in America, or a probability that Americans are of that race." Perhaps, if good Master Thorogood was in the flesh to-day he might, arguing from certain little dealings in boundary cases, consequential claims and so forth, prove incontestably that modern American statesmen were of that race too. But to proceed. This question of the red man's origin has not yet been solved; the doctors are still disputing about him. One professor has gotten hold of a skull delved from the presumed site of ancient Atazlan, and by the most careful measurements of the said skull has proceeded to show that because one skull measures in circumference the hundredth and seventy-seventh decimal of an inch more than it ought, it must of necessity be of the blackamoor type of headpiece.

Another equally learned professor, possessed of another equally curious skull (of course on shelf not on shoulders), has unfortunately come to conclusions directly opposite, and incontestably proven from careful occipital measurements that the type is Mongolian.

While thus the doctors differ as to what he is, or who he is, or whence he came, the force of theory changes to the stern tragedy of fact; and over the broad prairie, and upon the cloud-capped mountain, and northwards in the gloomy pine-forest, the red man withers and dies out before our gaze: soon they will have nothing but the skulls to lecture upon.

From the Long Portage which we have but lately crossed, to the barren shores where dwell the Esquimaux of the coasts, a family of cognate tribes inhabit the continent; from east to west the limits of this race are even more extensive. They are found at Churchill, on Hudson's Bay, and at Fort Simpson, on the rugged coast of New Caledonia. But stranger still, far down in Arizona and Mexico, even as far south as Nicaragua, the guttural language of the Chipewyan race is still heard, and the wild Navago and fierce Apache horseman of the Mexican plains are kindred races with the distant fur-hunters of the North. Of all the many ramifications of Indian race, this is perhaps the most extraordinary. Through what vicissitudes of war and time, an offshoot from the shores of Athabasca wandered down into Mexico, while a hundred fierce, foreign, warlike tribes occupied the immense intervening distance, is more than human conjecture can determine.

To the east of the Rocky Mountains these races

call themselves "Tumeh," a name which signifies "People," with that sublimity of ignorance which makes most savage people imagine themselves the sole proprietors of the earth. Many subdivisions exist among them; these are the Copper Indians, and the Dog Ribs of the Barren Grounds; the Loucheux or Kutchins, a fierce tribe on the Upper Yukon; the Yellow Knives, Hares, Nehanies, Sickanies, and Dahas of the Mountains and the Mackenzie River; the Slaves of the Great Slave Lake; the Chipewyans of Lake Athabasca, and Portage la Loche, the Beavers of the Peace River.

West of the Rocky Mountains, the Carriers, still a branch of the Chipewyan stock, intermingle with the numerous Atnah races of the coast. On the North Saskatchewan, a small wild tribe called the Surcees also springs from this great family, and as we have already said, nearly three thousand miles far down in the tropic plains of Old Mexico, the harsh, stuttering "tch" accent grates upon the ear. Spread over such a vast extent of country it may be supposed they vary much in physiognomy. Bravery in men and beauty in women are said to go hand in hand. Of the courage of the Chipewyan men I shall say nothing; of the beauty of the women I shall say something. To assert that they are very plain would not be true; they are undeniably ugly. Some of the young ones are very fat; all of the old ones are very thin. Many of the faces are pear-shaped; narrow foreheads, wide cheeks, small deep-set *fat* eyes. The type is said to be Mongolian, and if so, the Mongolians should change their type as soon as possible.

Several of the men wear sickly-looking moustaches, and short, pointed chin tufts; the hair, coarse and matted, is worn long. The children look like rolls of fat, half melted on the outside. Their general employment seems to be eating moose meat, when they are not engaged in deriving nourishment from the maternal bosom.

This last occupation is protracted to an advanced age of childhood, a circumstance which probably arises from the fact that the new-born infant receives no nourishment from its mother for four days after its birth, in order that it shall in after life be able to stand the pangs of hunger; but the infant mind is no doubt conscious itself that it is being robbed of its just rights, and endeavours to make up for lost time by this postponement of the age of weaning.

This description does not hold good of the Beaver Indians of Peace River; many of them, men and women, are good-looking enough, but of them more anon.

All these tribes are excellent hunters. The moose in the south and wooded country, the reindeer in the barren lands, ducks and geese in vast numbers during the summer, and, generally speaking, inexhaustible fish in the lakes yield them their means of living. At times, one prodigious feast; again, a period of starvation.

For a time living on moose nose, or buffalo tongue, or daintiest tit-bit of lake and forest; and then glad to get a scrap of dry meat, or a putrid fish to satisfy the cravings of their hunger. While the meat lasts, life is a long dinner. The child just able to crawl is seen with one hand holding the end of a piece of meat, the other end of which is held between the teeth; while the right hand wields a knife a foot in length, with which it saws steadily, between lips and fingers, until the mouthful is detached. How the nose escapes amputation is a mystery I have never heard explained.

A few tents of Chipewyans were pitched along the shores of the Athabasca River, when we descended that stream. They had long been expecting the return of my companion, to whose arrival they looked as the means of supplying them with percussion gun-caps, that article having been almost exhausted among them.

Knowing the hours at which he was wont to

travel they had marked their camping-places on the wooded shores, by planting a line of branches in the snow across the river from one side to the other. Thus even at night it would have been impossible to pass their tents without noticing the line of marks. The tents inside or out always presented the same spectacle. Battered-looking dogs of all ages surrounded the dwelling-place. In the trees or on a stage, meat, snow-shoes, and dog sleds, lay safe from canine ravage. Inside, some ten or twelve people congregated around a bright fire burning in the centre. The lodge was usually large, requiring a dozen moose skins in its construction. Quantities of moose or buffalo meat, cut into slices, hung to dry in the upper smoke. The inevitable puppy dog playing with a stick; the fat, greasy child pinching the puppy dog, drinking on all fours out of a tin pan, or sawing away at a bit of meat; and the women, old or young, cooking or nursing with a naïveté which Rubens would have delighted in. All these made up a Chipewyan "Interior," such as it appeared wherever we halted in our march, and leaving our dogs upon the river, went up into the tree-covered shore to where the tents stood pitched.

Anxious to learn the amount of game destroyed by a good hunter in a season, I caused one of the men to ask Chripo what he had killed. Chripo counted for a time on his fingers, and then informed us that since the snow fell he had killed ten wood buffalo and twenty-five moose; in other words, about seventeen thousand pounds of meat, during four months. But of this a large quantity went to the Hudson's Bay Fort, at the Forks of the Athabasca.

The night of the 4th of March found us camped in a high wood, at a point where a "cache" of provisions had been made for ourselves and our dogs. More than a fortnight earlier these provisions had been sent from Fort Chipewyan, on Lake Athabasca, and had been deposited in the " cache " to await my companion's arrival. A bag of fish for the dogs, a small packet of letters, and a bag of good things for the master swung from a large tripod close to the shore. Some of these things were very necessary, all were welcome, and after a choice supper we turned in for the night.

At four o'clock next morning we were off. My friend led the march, and the day was to be a long one. For four hours we held on, and by an hour after sunrise we had reached a hut, where dwelt a Chipewyan named Echo. The house was deserted, and if anybody had felt inclined to ask, Where had Echo gone to? Echo was not there to answer where. Nobody, however, felt disposed to ask the question, but in lieu thereof dinner was being hastily got ready in Echo's abandoned fireplace. Dinner? Yes, our *first* dinner took place usually between seven and eight o'clock a.m. Nor were appetites ever wanting at that hour either.

Various mishaps, of broken snow-shoe and broken-down dog, had retarded my progress on this morning, and by the time the leading train had reached Echo's I was far behind. One of my dogs had totally given out, not Cerf-vola, but the Ile à la Crosse dog "Major." Poor brute! he had suddenly lain down, and refused to move. He was a willing, good hauler, generally barking vociferously whenever any impediment in front detained the trains. I saw at once it was useless to coerce him after his first break-down, so there was nothing for it but to take him from the harness and hurry on with the other three dogs as best I could. Of the old train which had shared my fortunes ever since that now distant day in the storm, on the Red River steam-boat, two yet remained to me.

Pony had succumbed at the Rivière la Loche, and had been left behind at that station, to revel in an abundance of white fish. The last sight I got of him was suggestive of his character. He was careering wildly across the river with a huge stolen white fish in his mouth, pursued by two men and half-a-dozen dogs, vainly attempting to recapture the purloined property. Another dog, named "Sans Pareil," had taken his place, and thus far we had "marched on into the bowels of the land without impediment."

From the day after my departure from Ile à la Crosse I had regularly used snow-shoes, and now I seldom sought the respite of the sled, but trudged along behind the dogs. I well knew that it was only by sparing my dogs thus that I could hope to carry them the immense distance I purposed to travel; and I was also aware that a time might come when, in the many vicissitudes of snow travel, I would be unable to walk, and have to depend altgoether on my train for means of movement. So, as day by day the snow-shoe became easier, I had tramped along, until now, on this 5th of March, I could look back at nigh three hundred miles of steady walking.

Our meal at Echo's over we set out again. Another four hours passed without a halt, and another sixteen or seventeen miles lay behind us. Then came the second dinner—cakes, tea, and sweet pemmican; and away we went once more upon the river. The day was cold, but fine; the dogs trotted well, and the pace was faster than before. Two Indians had started ahead to hurry on to a spot, indicated by my companion, where they were to make ready the camp, and await our arrival.

Night fell, and found us still upon the river. A bright moon silvered the snow; we pushed along, but the dogs were now tired, all, save my train, which having only blankets, guns, and a few articles to carry, went still as gamely as ever. At sundown our baggage sleds were far to the rear. My companion driving a well-loaded sled led the way, while I kept close behind him.

For four hours after dark we held steadily on; the night was still, but very cold; the moon showed us the track; dogs and men seemed to go forward from the mere impulse of progression. I had been tired hours before, and had got over it; not half-tired, but regularly weary; and yet somehow or other the feeling of weariness had passed away, and one stepped forward upon the snow-shoe by a mechanical effort that seemed destitute of sense or feeling.

At last we left the river, and ascended a steep bank to the left, passing into the shadow of gigantic pines. Between their giant trunks the moonlight slanted; and the snow, piled high on forest wreck, glowed lustrous in the fretted light. A couple of miles more brought us suddenly to the welcome glare of firelight, and at ten o'clock at night we reached the blazing camp. Eighteen hours earlier we had started for the day's march, and only during two hours had we halted on the road. We had, in fact, marched steadily during sixteen hours, twelve of which had been at rapid pace. The distance run that day is unmeasured, and is likely to remain so for many a day; but at the most moderate estimate it would not have been less than fifty-six miles. It was the longest day's march I ever made, and I had cause long to remember it, for on arising at daybreak next morning I was stiff with Mal de Raquette.

In the North, Mal de Raquette or no Mal de Raquette, one must march; sick or sore, or blistered, the traveller must frequently still push on. Where all is a wilderness, progression frequently means preservation; and delay is tantamount to death.

In our case, however, no such necessity existed; but as we were only some twenty-five miles distant from the great central distributing point of the Northern Fur Trade, it was advisable to reach it without delay. Once again we set out: debouching from the forest we entered a large marsh. Soon a lake, with low-lying shores, spread before us. Another marsh, another frozen river, and at last, a vast lake opened out upon our gaze. Islands, rocky, and clothed with pine-trees, rose from the snowy surface. To the east, nothing but a vast expanse of ice-covered sea, with a blue, cold sky-line; to the north, a shore of rocks and hills, wind-swept, and part covered with dwarf firs, and on the rising shore, the clustered buildings of a large fort, with a red flag flying above them in the cold north blast.

The "lake" was Athabasca, the "clustered buildings" Fort Chipewyan, and the Flag—well; we all know it; but it is only when the wanderer's eye meets it in some lone spot like this that he turns to it, as the emblem of a Home which distance has shrined deeper in his heart.

CHAPTER XIII.

Lake Athabasca.—Northern Lights.—Chipewyan.—The real Workers of the World.

ATHABASCA, or more correctly "Arabascon," "The Meeting-place of many Waters," is a large lake. At this fort of Chipewyan we stand near its western end. Two hundred miles away to the east, its lonely waters still lave against the granite rocks.

Whatever may be the work to which he turns hand or brain, an Indian seldom errs. If he names a lake or fashions a piece of bark to sail its waters, both will fit the work for which they were intended.

"The meeting-place of many waters" tells the story of Athabasca. In its bosom many rivers unite their currents; and from its north-western rim pours the Slave River, the true Mackenzie. Its first English discoverer called it the "Lake of the Hills;" a more appropriate title would have been "The Lake of the Winds," for fierce and wild the storms sweep over its waves.

Over the Lake Athabasca the Northern Lights hold their highest revels. They flash, and dance, and stream, and intermingle, and wave together their many colours like the shapes and hues of a kaleidoscope. Sometimes the long columns of light seem to rest upon the silent, frozen shores, stretching out their rose-tipped tops to touch the zenith; again the lines of light traverse the sky from east to west as a hand might sweep the chords of some vast harp, and from its touch would flow light instead of music. So quickly run the colours along these shafts, that the ear listens instinctively for sound in the deep stillness of the frozen solitude; but sound I have never heard. Many a time I have listened breathless to catch the faintest whisper of these wondrous lightnings; they were mute as the waste that lay around me.

Figures convey but a poor idea of cold, yet they are the only means we have, and by a comparison of figures some persons, at least, will understand the cold of an Athabascan winter. The citadel of Quebec has the reputation of being a cold winter residence; its mean temperature for the month of January is 11° 7′ Fahr. The mean temperature of the month of January, 1844, at Fort Chipewyan, was 22° 74′, or nearly 30° colder, and during the preceding month of December the wind blew with a total pressure of one thousand one hundred and sixty pounds to the square foot.

It is perhaps needless to say more about the rigour of an Athabascan winter.

As it is the "meeting-place of many waters" so also is it the meeting-place of many systems. Silurian and Devonian approach it from the west. Laurentian still holds five-sixths of its waters in the same grasp as when what is now Athabasca lay a deep fiord along the ancient ocean shore. The old rock caught it to his rough heart then, and when in later ages the fickle waves which so long had kissed his lips left him stern and lonely, he still held the clear, cold lake to his iron bosom.

Athabasca may be said to mark also the limits of some great divisions of the animal kingdom. The reindeer and that most curious relic of an older time, the musk ox, come down near its north-eastern shores, for there that bleak region known as the " Barren Grounds " is but a few miles distant. These animals never pass to the southern end of the lake; the Cariboo, or reindeer of the woods, being a distinct species from that which inhabits the treeless waste. The wood buffalo and the moose are yet numerous on the north-west and south-west shores: but of these things we shall have more to say anon.

All through the summer, from early May to mid-October, the shores of the lake swarm with wild geese, and the twilight midsummer midnight is filled with the harsh sounds of the cries of the snow goose, or the " wavy " flying low over their favourite waters.

In early days Chipewyan was an important centre of the fur trade, and in later times it has been made the starting-point of many of the exploratory parties to the northern coast. From Old Fort Chipewyan Mackenzie set forth to explore the great northern river, and to the same place he returned when first of all men north of the 40th parallel he had crossed in the summers of 1792-93 the continent to the Pacific Ocean.

It was from New Fort Chipewyan that Simpson set out to trace the coast-line of the Arctic Ocean; and earlier than either, it was from Fond du Lac, at the eastern end of Fort Athabasca, that Samuel Hearne wandered forth to reach the Arctic Sea.

To-day it is useful to recall these stray items of adventure from the past in which they lie buried. It has been said by some one that a "nation cannot be saved by a calculation;" neither can she be made by one.

If to-day we are what we are, it is because a thousand men in bygone times did not stop to count the cost. The decline of a nation differs from that of an individual in the first symptoms of its decay. The heart of the nation goes first, the extremities still remain vigorous. France, with many a gallant soul striking hard for her in the Carnatic or in Canada, sickens in the pomp and luxury of Versailles, and has nothing to offer to her heroes but forgetfulness, debt, or the rack. Her colonial history was one long tissue of ingratitude.

Bimcourt, De Chastes, Varrene de la Verendrie, or Lally might fight and toil and die, what cared the selfish heart of old France ? The order of St. Louis long denied, and 40,000 livres of debt rewarded the discovery of the Rocky Mountains. Frenchmen gave to France a continent. France thought little of the gift, and fate took it back again. History sometimes repeats itself. There is a younger if not a greater Britain waiting quietly to reap the harvest of her mother's mistakes.

But to Chipewyan. It is emphatically a lonely spot; in summer the cry of the wild bird keeps time to the lapping of the wave on the rocky shore, or the pine islands rustle in the western breeze; nothing else moves over these 8000 square miles of crystal water. Now and again at long intervals the beautiful canoe of a Chipewyan glides along the bay-indented shores, or crosses some traverse in the open lake.

When Samuel Hearne first looked upon the "Arabascon," buffalo were very numerous along its southern shore, to-day they are scarce; all else rests as then in untamed desolation. At times this west end of the lake has been the scene of strange excitements. Men came from afar and pitched their tents awhile on these granite shores, ere they struck deeper into the heart of the great north. Mackenzie, Franklin, Back, Richardson, Simpson, Rae, rested here; on piercing further into unknown wilds, they flew the red-cross flag o'er seas and isles upon whose shores no human foot had pressed a sand-print.

Eight hundred thousand pounds sunk in the Arctic Sea! will exclaim my calculating friend behind the national counter; nearly a million gone for ever! No, head cash-keeper, you are wrong. That million of money will bear interest higher than all your little speculations in times not far remote, and in times lying deep in the misty future. In hours when life and honour lie at different sides of the "to do" or "not to do," men will go back to times when other men battling with nature or with man, cast their veto on the side of honour, and by the white light thrown into the future from the great dead Past, they will read their roads where many paths commingle.

CHAPTER XIV.

A Hudson's Bay Fort.—It comes at last.—News from the outside world.—Tame and wild Savages.—Lac Clair.—A treacherous deed.—Harper.

THE term "Fort" which so frequently occurs in these pages may perhaps convey an erroneous impression to the reader's mind. An imposing array of rampart and bastion, a loop-holed wall or formidable fortalice may arise before his mind's eye as he reads the oft-recurring word. Built generally upon the lower bank of a large river or lake, but sometimes perched upon the loftier outer bank, stands the Hudson's Bay Fort. A square palisade, ten to twenty feet high, surrounds the buildings; in the prairie region this defence is stout and lofty, but in the wooded country it is frequently dispensed with altogether.

Inside the stockade some half-dozen houses are grouped together in square or oblong form. The house of the Bourgeois and Clerks, the store wherein are kept the blankets, coloured cloths, guns, ammunition, bright handkerchiefs, ribbons, beads, &c., the staple commodities of the Indian trade; another store for furs and peltries, a building from the beams of which hang myriads of skins worth many a gold piece in the marts of far-away London city;—martens and minks, and dark otters, fishers and black foxes, to say nothing of bears and beavers, and a host of less valuable furs. Then came the houses of the men.

Lounging at the gate, or on the shore in front, one sees a half-breed in tasselated cap, or a group of Indians in blanket robes or dirty-white capôtes; everybody is smoking; the pointed poles of a wigwam or two rise on either side of the outer palisades, and over all there is the tapering flag-staff. A horse is in the distant river meadow. Around the great silent hills stand bare, or fringed with jagged pine tops, and some few hundred yards away on either side, a rude cross or wooden railing blown over by the tempest, discoloured by rain or snow-drift, marks the lonely resting-place of the dead.

Wild, desolate and remote are these isolated trading spots, yet it is difficult to describe the feelings with which one beholds them across some ice-bound lake, or silent river as the dog trains wind slowly amidst the snow. Coming in from the wilderness, from the wrack of tempest, and the bitter cold, wearied with long marches, footsore or frozen, one looks upon the wooden house as some palace of rest and contentment.

I doubt if it be possible to know more acute comfort, for its measure is exactly the measure of that other extremity of discomfort which excessive cold and hardship have carried with them. Nor does that feeling of home and contentment lose aught for want of a welcome at the threshold of the lonely resting-place. Nothing is held too good for the wayfarer; the best bed and the best supper are his. He has, perhaps, brought letters or messages from long absent friends, or he comes with news of the outside world; but be he the bearer of such things, or only the chance carrier of his own fortunes, he is still a welcome visitor to the Hudson's Bay Fort.

Three days passed away in rest, peace, and plenty. It was nearing the time when another start would be necessary, for after all, this Athabascan Fort was scarce a half-way house in my winter journey. The question of departure was not of itself of consequence, but the prospect of leaving for a long sojourn in deeper solitudes, without one word of news from the outside world, without that winter packet to which we had all

L

looked so long, was something more than a mere disappointment.

All this time we had been travelling in advance of the winter packet, and as our track left a smooth road for whatever might succeed us, we reckoned upon being overtaken at some point of the journey by the faster travelling express. Such had not been the case, and now three days had passed since our arrival without a sign of an in-coming dog-train darkening the expanse of the frozen lake.

The morning of the 4th of March, however, brought a change. Far away in the hazy drift and "poudre" which hung low upon the surface of the lake, the figures of two men and one sled of dogs became faintly visible. Was it only Antoine Larungeau, a solitary "Freeman" from the Quatre Fourche, going like a good Christian to his prayers at the French Mission? Or was it the much-wished-for packet?

It soon declared itself; the dogs were steering for the fort, and not for the mission. Larungeau might be an indifferent church member, but had the whole college of cardinals been lodged at Chipewyan they must have rejoiced that it was not Larungeau going to mass, and that it was the winter packet coming to the fort.

What reading we had on that Sunday afternoon!

News from the far-off busy world; letters from the far-off quiet home; tidings of great men passed away from the earth; glad news and sorry news, borne through months of toil 1500 miles over the winter waste.

And now came a short busy time at the fort. A redistribution of the packet had to be made. On to the north went a train of dogs for the distant Yukon; on to the west went a train of dogs for the head of the Peace River. In three days more I made ready to resume my journey up the Peace River. Once more the sleds were packed, once more the untiring Cerf-vola took his place in the leading harness, and the word "march" was given.

This time I was to be alone. My good friend, whose unvarying kindness had made an acquaintanceship of a few weeks ripen into a friendship destined I trust to endure for many years, was no longer to be my companion.

He came, in company with another officer, some miles of the way, to see me off; and then at the Quatre Fourche we parted, he to return to his lonely fort, I to follow across the wide-spreading Lake Marnoway the long trail to the setting sun.

If the life of the wanderer possesses many moments of keen enjoyment, so also has it its times of intense loneliness; times when no excitement is near to raise the spirits, no toil to render thought impossible; nothing but a dreary, hopeless prospect of labour, which takes day after day some little portion from that realm of space lying before him, only to cast it to augment that other dim land of separation which lies behind him.

Honest Joe Gargery never with his blacksmith hand nailed a sadder truth upon the wheel of time, than when he defined life to be made up of "partings welded together." But in civilization generally when we part we either look forward to meeting again at some not remote period, or we have so many varied occupations, or so many friends around us, that if the partings are welded together, so also are the meetings.

In the lone spaces it is different. The endless landscape, the monotony of slow travel, the dim vision of what lies before, seen only in the light of that other dim prospect lying behind; lakes, rivers, plains, forests, all hushed in the savage sleep of winter;—these things bring to the wanderer's mind a sense of loneliness almost as vast as the waste which lies around him.

On the evening of the 12th of March I camped alone in the wilderness. Far as eye could reach, on every side, there lay nothing but hard, drifted snow, and from its surface a few scant willows raised their dry leafless saplings. The three or four men were busy scraping the deep snow from the lee side of some low willow bushes, but they were alien in every thought and feeling; and we were separated by a gulf impossible to bridge: so that I was quite alone. I will not say on whose side the fault lay, and possibly the admission may only prove a congeniality of feeling between myself and my train; but, for all that, I felt a far stronger tie of companionship with the dogs that drew my load, than for the men with whom I now found myself in company.

They were by no means wild; far from it, they were eminently tame. One of them was a scoundrel of a very low type, as some of his actions will hereafter show. In him the wild animal had been long since destroyed, the tame brute had taken its place.

The man who had been my servant from the Saskatchewan was a French half-breed; strong, active, and handsome, he was still a sulky, good-for-nothing fellow. One might as well have tried to make friends with a fish to which one cast a worm, as with this good-looking, good-for-nothing man. He had depth sufficient to tell a lie which might wear the semblance of truth for a day; and cunning enough to cheat without being caught in the actual fact. I think he was the most impudent liar I have ever met. The motive which had induced him to accept service in this long journey was, I believe, a domestic one. He had run away with a young English half-breed girl, and then ran away from her. If she had only known the object of her affections as well as I did, she would have regarded the last feat of activity as a far less serious evil than the first.

The third man was a Swampy Indian of the class one frequently meets in the English-speaking settlement on Red River. Taken by himself, he was negatively good; but placed with others worse than himself, he was positively bad. He was, however, a fair traveller, and used his dogs with a degree of care and attention seldom seen amongst the half-breeds.

Small wonder, then, that with these three worthies who, though strangers, now met upon a base of common rascality, that I should feel myself more completely alone than if nothing but the waste had spread around me. Full thirty days of travel must elapse ere the mountains, that great break to which I looked so long, should raise their snowy peaks across my pathway.

The lameness of the last day's travel already gave ominous symptoms of its presence. The snow was deeper than I had yet seen it; heretofore, at the longest, the forts lay within five days' journey of each other; now there was one gap in which, from one post to the next, must, at the shortest, be a twelve days' journey.

At dawn, on the 13th of March, we quitted our burrow in the deep drift of the willow bushes, and held our way across what was seemingly a shoreless sea.

The last sand ridge or island top of Lake Athabasca had sunk beneath the horizon, and as the sun came up, flashing coldly upon the level desert of snow, there lay around us nought but the dazzling surface of the frozen lake.

Lac Clair, the scene of our present day's journey, is in reality an arm of the Athabasca. Nothing but a formation of mud and drift, submerged at high summer water, separated it from the larger lake; but its shores vary much from those of its neighbour, being everywhere low and marshy, lined with scant willows and destitute of larger timber. Of its south-western termination but little is known, but it is said to extend in that direction from the Athabasca for fully seventy miles into the Birch Hills. Its breadth from north to south would be about half that distance. It is subject to violent winter storms, accompanied by dense drift; and from the scarcity of wood along its shores, and the absence of distinguishing landmarks, it is much dreaded by the winter *voyageur*.

The prevailing north-west wind of the Lake Athabasca has in fact the full sweep of 250 miles across Lac Clair. To lose one's way upon it would appear to be the first rule of travel amongst the trip-men of Fort Chipewyan. The last adventure of this kind which had taken place on its dim expanse had nearly a tragic end.

On the southern shore of the lake three moose had been killed. When the tidings reached the fort, two men and two sleds of dogs set off for the "cache;" it was safely found, the meat packed upon the sleds, and all made ready for the return. Then came the usual storm: dense and dark the fine snow (dry as dust under the biting cold) swept the surface of the lake. The sun, which on one of these "poudre" days in the North seems to exert as much influence upon the war of cold and storm as some good bishop in the Middle Ages was wont to exercise over the belligerents at Cressy or Poictiers, when, as it is stated, "He withdrew to a neighbouring eminence, and there remained during the combat;"—the sun, I say, for a time, seemed to protest, by his presence, against the whole thing, but then finding all protests equally disregarded by the wind and cold, he muffled himself up in the nearest cloud and went fast asleep until the fight was over.

For a time the men held their way across the

lake ; then the dogs became bewildered ; the leading driver turned to his companion, and telling him to drive both trains, he strode on in front of his dogs to give a "lead" in the storm.

Driving two trains of loaded dogs is hard work; the second driver could not keep up, and the man in front deliberately increasing his pace walked steadily away, leaving his comrade to the mercies of cold and drift. He did this coward act with the knowledge that his companion had only three matches in his possession, he having induced him to give up the rest to Indians whom they had fallen in with.

The man thus abandoned on the dreaded lake was a young Hudson's Bay clerk, by no means habituated to the hardships of such a situation. But it requires little previous experience to know when one is lost. The dogs soon began to wander, and finally headed for where their instinct told them lay the shore. When they reached the shore night had fallen, the wind had gone down, but still the cold was intense; it was the close of January, the coldest time of the year, when 80° of frost is no unusual occurrence. At such a time it was no easy matter to light a fire; the numbed, senseless hands cannot find strength to strike a match; and many a time had I seen a hardy *voyageur* fail in his first attempts with the driest wood, and with full daylight to assist him.

But what chance had the inexperienced hand, with scant willow sticks for fuel and darkness to deceive him? His wood was partly green, and one by one his three matches flashed, flickered, and died out.

No fire, no food—alone somewhere on Lac Clair in 40° to 50° below zero! It was an ugly prospect. Wrapping himself in a blanket, he got a dog at his feet and lay down. With daylight he was up, and putting the dogs into harness set out; but he knew not the landmarks, and he steered heedless of direction. He came at last to a spring of open water; it was highly charged with sulphur, and hence its resistance to the cold of winter. Though it was nauseous to the taste he drank deeply of it; no other spring of water existed in all the wide circle of the lake.

For four days the wretched man remained at this place; his sole hope lay in the chance that men would come to look for him from the fort, but ere that would come about a single night might suffice to terminate his existence.

These bad nights are bad enough when we have all that food and fuel can do. Men lose their fingers or their toes sometimes in the hours of wintry daylight, but here fire there was none, and food without fire was not to be had. The meat upon the sled had frozen almost as solid as the stone of a quarry.

He still hoped for relief, but had he known of the conduct of the ruffian whose desertion had thus brought him to this misery his hope would have been a faint one.

On the day following his desertion, the deserter appeared at the Quatre Fourche; he pretended to be astounded that his comrade had not turned up. On the same evening he reached Fort Chipewyan: he told a plausible story of having left his companion smoking near a certain spot on the north side of the lake; on his return to the spot the sleds were gone, and he at once concluded they had headed for home. Such was his tale.

A search expedition was at once despatched, but acting under the direction of the scoundrel Harper no trace of the lost man could be found.

No wonder! for the scene of his desertion lay many miles away to the south, but the villain wished to give time for cold and hunger to do their work; not for any gratification of hatred or revenge towards his late comrade, but simply because "dead men tell no tales." Upon the return of this unsuccessful expedition suspicions were aroused; the man was besought to tell the truth, all would be forgiven him if he now confessed where it was he had left his companion. He still however asserted that he had left him on the shore of the lake at a spot marked by a single willow. Again a search party goes out, but this time under experienced leadership, and totally disregarding the story of the deserter.

Far down, near the south shore of the lake, the quick eye of a French half-breed caught the faint print of a snow-shoe edge on the hard drifted surface; he followed the clue—another print—and then another;—soon the shore was reached, and the impress of a human form found among the willows.

Never doubting for an instant that the next sight would be the frozen body of the man they sought for (since the fireless camping-place showed that he was without the means of making a fire), the searchers went along. They reached the Sulphur Spring, and there, cold, hungry, but safe, sat the object of their search. Five days had passed, yet he had not frozen!

If I wished to learn more of the deserter Harper, I had ample opportunity of doing so. His villainous face formed a prominent object at my camp fire. He was now the packet bearer to Fort Vermilion on the Peace River; he was one of the worthies I have already spoken of.

We crossed Lac Clair at a rapid pace, and

reached at dusk the north-western shore; of course we had lost ourselves; but the evening was calm and clear, and the error was set right by a two-hours' additional march.

It was piercingly cold when, some time after dark, the shore was gained; but wood was found by the yellow light of a full moon, and a good camp made on a swampy island. From here our path lay through the woods and ridges nearly due west again.

On the fourth day after leaving Fort Chipewyan we gained a sandy ridge covered with cypress, and saw beneath us a far-stretching valley; beyond, in the distance to the north and west, the blue ridges of the Cariboo Mountains closed the prospect. In the valley a broad river lay in long sweeping curves from west to east.

We were on the banks of the Peace River.

CHAPTER XV.

The Peace River.—Volcanos.—M. Jean Batiste St. Cyr.—
Half a loaf is better than no bread.—An oasis in the desert.
—Tecumseh and Black Hawk.

IT is possible that the majority of my readers have never heard of the Peace River. The British empire is a large one, and Britons can get on very well without knowing much of any river, excepting perhaps the Thames, a knowledge of which, until lately, Londoners easily obtained by the simple process of smelling. Britannia it is well known rules the waves, and it would be ridiculous to expect rulers to bother themselves much about the things which they rule; perchance, in a score of years or so, when our lively cousins bring forth their little Alaska Boundary question, as they have already brought forth their Oregon, Maine, and San Juan boundary questions, we may pay the Emperor of Morocco, or some equally enlightened potentate, the compliment of asking him to tell us whether the Peace River has always been a portion

THE VALLEY OF THE PEACE RIVER.

[*Page* 158.

of the British empire? or whether we knew the meaning of our own language when we framed the treaty of 1825 ? Until then, the Peace River may rest in the limbo of obscurity; and in any case, no matter who should claim it, its very name must indicate that it was never considered worth fighting about.

Nevertheless the Peace River is a large stream of water, and some time or other may be worth fighting for too. Meantime we will have something to say about it.

Like most of the streams which form the headwaters of the great Mackenzie River system, the Peace River has its sources west of the Chipewyan or Rocky Mountains. Its principal branch springs from a wild region called the Stickeen, an alpine land almost wholly unknown. There at a presumed elevation of 6000 feet above the sea level, amidst a vast variety of mountain peaks, the infant river issues from a lake to begin its long voyage of 2500 miles to the Arctic Sea.

This region is the birthplace of many rivers, the Yukon, the Liard, the Peace River, and countless streams issue from this impenetrable fastness. Situated close to the Pacific shore, at their source, these rivers nevertheless seek far distant oceans. A huge barrier rises between them and the nearest coast. The loftiest range of mountains in North America here finds its culminating point; the coast or cascade range shoots up its volcanic peaks to nigh 18,000 feet above the neighbouring waves. Mounts Cri-Hon and St. Elias cast their crimson greeting far over the gloomy sea, and Ilyamna and Island Corovin catch up the flames to fling them further to Kamchatka's fire-bound coast.

The Old World and the New clasp hands of fire across the gloomy Northern Sea; and amidst ice and flame Asia and America look upon each other.

Through 300 miles of mountain the Peace River takes its course, countless creeks and rivers seek its waters; 200 miles from its source it cleaves the main Rocky Mountain chain through a chasm whose straight, steep cliffs frown down on the black water through 6000 feet of dizzy verge. Then it curves into the old ocean bed, of which we have already spoken, and for 500 miles it flows in a deep, narrow valley, from 700 to 800 feet below the level of the surrounding plateau. Then it reaches a lower level, the banks become of moderate elevation, the country is densely wooded, the large river winds in serpentine bends through an alluvial valley; the current once so strong becomes sluggish, until at last it pours itself through a delta of low-lying drift into the

Slave River, and its long course of 1100 miles is ended.

For 900 miles only two interruptions break the even flow of its waters. A ridge of limestone underlies the whole bed of the river at a point some 250 miles from its mouth, causing a fall of eight feet with a short rapid above it. The other obstacle is the mountain cañon on the outer and lower range of the Rocky Mountains, where a portage of twelve miles is necessary.

In its course through the main chain of the Rocky Mountains no break occurs, the current runs silently under the immense precipice as though it fears to awaken even by a ripple the sleeping giant at whose feet it creeps.

Still keeping west, we began to ascend the Peace River; we had struck its banks more than 100 miles above its delta, by making this direct line across Lac Clair and the intervening ridges.

Peace River does not debouch into Lake Athabasca, but as we have said into the Slave River some twenty miles below the lake; at high water, however, it communicates with Athabasca through the canal-like channel of the Quatre Fourche, and when water is low in Peace River, Athabasca repays the gift by sending back through the same channel a portion of her surplus tide.

M

Since leaving Lac Clair I had endured no little misery; the effects of that long day's travel from the river Athabasca had from the outset been apparent, and each day now further increased them. The muscles of ancles and instep had become painfully inflamed, to raise the snow-shoe from the ground was frequently no easy matter, and at last every step was taken in pain. I could not lie upon my sled because the ground was rough and broken, and the sled upset at every hill side into the soft snow; besides there was the fact that the hills were short and steep, and dogs could not easily have dragged me to the summit. There was nothing for me but to tramp on in spite of aching ancles.

At the camp I tried my remedies, but all were useless. From pain-killer, moose fat, laudanum and porpoise oil I concocted a mixture, which I feel convinced contains a vast fortune for any enterprising professor in the next century, and which even in these infant ages of "puffing" might still be made to realize some few millions of dollars; but nevertheless, my poor puffed foot resisted every attempt to reduce it to symmetry, or what was more important, to induce it to resume work.

That sixteen-hour day had inflamed its worst passions, and it had struck for an "eight-hour movement." One can afford to laugh over it all now, but then it was gloomy work enough; to make one step off the old hidden dog-track of the early winter was to sink instantly into the soft snow to the depth of three or four feet, and when we camped at night on the wooded shore, our blankets were laid in a deep furrow between lofty snow walls, which it had taken us a full hour to scoop out. At last, after six days of weary travel through ridge and along river reach, we drew near a house.

Where the little stream called the Red River enters from the south the wide channel of the Peace River, there stands a small Hudson's Bay post. Here, on the evening of the 17th of March, we put in for the night. At this solitary post dwelt M. Jean Batiste St. Cyr; an old and faithful follower of the Hudson's Bay Company. When the powerful North-West Fur Company became merged into the wealthier but less enterprising corporation of the Hudson's Bay, they left behind them in the North a race of faithful servitors—men drawn in early life from the best rural *habitans* of Lower Canada—men worthy of that old France from which they sprung, a race now almost extinct in the north, as indeed it is almost all the world over. What we call "the spirit of the age" is against it; faithful service to powers of earth, or even to those of Heaven, not being included in the catalogue of virtues taught in the big school of modern democracy.

From one of this old class of French Canadians, M. Jean Batiste St. Cyr was descended.

Weary limbs and aching ancles pleaded for delay at this little post, but advancing spring, and still more the repeated assaults of my servant and his comrades upon my stock of luxuries, urged movement as the only means of saving some little portion of those good things put away for me by my kind host at Chipewyan. It seems positively ridiculous now, how one could regard the possession of flour and sugar, of sweet cake and sweet pemmican, as some of the most essential requisites of life. And yet so it was. With the grocer in the neighbouring street, and the baker round the corner, we can afford to look upon flour and sugar as very common-place articles indeed; but if any person wishes to arrive at a correct notion of their true value in the philosophy of life let him eliminate them from his daily bill of fare, and restrict himself solely to moose meat, grease, and milkless tea. For a day or two he will get on well enough, then he will begin to ponder long upon bread, cakes, and other kindred subjects; until day by day he learns to long for bread, then the Bath buns of his earlier years will float in enchanting visions before him; and like Clive at the recollection of that treasure-chamber in the Moorshedabad Palace, he will marvel at the moderation which left untouched a single cake upon that wondrous counter.

It is not difficult to understand the feelings which influenced a distant northern Missionary, when upon his return to semi-civilization, his friends having prepared a feast to bid him welcome, he asked them to give him bread and nothing else. He had been without it for years, and his mind had learned to hunger for it more than the body.

My servitor, not content with living as his master lived, was helping the other rascals to the precious fare. English half-breed, French ditto, and full Christian Swampy had apparently formed an offensive and defensive alliance upon the basis of a common rascality, Article I. of the treaty having reference to the furtive partition of my best white sugar, flour, and Souchong tea; things which, when they have to be "portaged" far on men's shoulders in a savage land, are not usually deemed fitted for savage stomachs too.

One night's delay, and again we were on the endless trail; on along the great silent river, between the rigid bordering pines, amidst the diamond-shaped islands where the snow lay deep and soft in "shnay" and "batture," on out into the long reaches where the wild March winds swept the river bed, and wrapt isle and shore in clouds of drift.

On the evening of the 19th of March our party drew near a lonely post, which, from the colour of the waters in the neighbouring stream, bears the name of Fort Vermilion. The stormy weather had sunk to calm; the blue sky lay over mingled forest and prairie; far off to the north and south rose the dark outlines of the Reindeer and Buffalo Mountains; while coming from the sunset and vanishing into the east, the great silent river lay prone amidst the wilderness of snow.

A gladsome sight was the little fort, with smoke curling from its snow-laden roof, its cattle standing deep in comfortable straw-yard, and its master at the open gateway, waiting to welcome me to his home: pleasant to any traveller in the wilderness, but doubly so to me, whose every step was now taken in the dull toil of unremitting pain.

Physicians have termed that fellow-feeling which the hand sometimes evinces for the hand, and the eye for the eye, by the name of "sympathy." It is unfortunate that these ebullitions of affection which the dual members of our bodies manifest towards each other, should always result in doubling the amount of pain and inconvenience suffered by the remainder of the human frame. For a day or two past my right foot had shown symptoms of sharing the sorrows of its fellow-labourer; and however gratifying this proof of good feeling should have been, it was nevertheless accompanied by such an increase of torture that one could not help wishing for more callous conduct in the presence of Mal de Raquette.

A day's journey north of the Peace River at Fort Vermilion, a long line of hills approaching the altitude of a mountain range stretches from east to west. At the same distance south lies another range of similar elevation. The northern range bears the name of the Reindeer; the southern one that of the Buffalo Mountains. These names nearly mark the two great divisions of the animal kingdom of Northern America.

It is singular how closely the habits of those two widely differing animals, the reindeer and the buffalo, approximate to each other. Each have their treeless prairie, but seek the woods in winter; each have their woodland species; each separate when the time comes to bring forth their young; each mass together in their annual migrations. Upon both the wild man preys in unending hostility. When the long days of the Arctic summer begin to shine over the wild region of the Barren Grounds, the reindeer set forth for the low shores of the Northern Ocean; in the lonely wilds whose shores look out on the Archipelago where once the ships of England's explorers struggled midst floe and pack, and hopeless iceberg, the herds spend the fleeting summer season, subsisting on the short grass, which for a few weeks changes these cold, grey shores to softer green.

With the approach of autumn the bands turn south again, and uniting upon the borders of the barren grounds, spend the winter in the forests which fringe the shores of the Bear, Great Slave, and Athabascan Lakes. Thousands are killed by the Indians on this homeward journey; waylaid in the passes which they usually follow, they fall easy prey to Dog-rib and Yellow-knife and Chipewyan hunter; and in years of plenty the forts of the extreme north count by thousands the fat sides of Cariboo, piled high in their provision stores.

But although the hills to the north and south of Vermilion bore the names of Reindeer and Buffalo, upon neither of these animals did the fort depend for its subsistence. The Peace River is the land of the moose; here this ungainly and most wary animal has made his home, and winter and summer, hunter and trader, along the whole length of 900 miles, between the Peace and Athabasca, live upon his delicious venison.

Two days passed away at Fort Vermilion; outside the March wind blew in bitter storm, and drift piled high around wall and palisade. But within there was rest and quiet, and many an anecdote of time long passed in the Wild North Land.

Here, at this post of Vermilion, an old veteran spent the winter of his life; and from his memory the scenes of earlier days came forth to interest the chance wanderer, whose footsteps had led him to this lonely post. Few could tell the story of these solitudes better than this veteran pensioner. He had come to these wilds while the century was yet in its teens. He had seen Tecumseh in his glory, and Black Hawk marshal his Sauk warriors, where now the river shores of Illinois wave in long lines of yellow corn. He had spoken with men who had seen the gallant La Perouse in Hudson's Bay, when, for the last time in History, France flew the *fleur-de-lis* above the ramparts of an English fort in this northern land.

The veteran explorers of the Great North had been familiar to his earlier days, and he could speak of Mackenzie and Frazer and Thompson, Harmon and Henry, as men whom he had looked on in his boyhood.

For me these glimpses of the bygone time had a strange charm. This mighty solitude, whose vastness had worn its way into my mind; these leagues and leagues of straight, tall pines, whose gloomy moan seemed the voice of 3000 miles of wilderness; these rivers so hushed and silent, save when the night owl hooted through the twilight; all this sense of immensity was so impressed on the imagination by recent travel, that it heightened the rough colouring of the tale which linked this shadowy land of the present with the still more shadowy region of the past.

Perhaps at another time, when I too shall rest from travel, it will be my task to tell the story of these dauntless men; but now, when many a weary mile lies before me, it is time to hold westward still along the great Unchagah.

The untiring train was once again put into the moose-skin harness, after another night of wild storm and blinding drift; and with crack of whip and call to dog, Vermilion soon lay in the waste behind me.

CHAPTER XVI.

The Buffalo Hills.—A fatal Quarrel.—The exiled Beavers.—
"At-tal-loo" deplores his wives.—A Cree Iuterior.—An
attractive Camp.—I camp alone.—Cerf-vola without a
Supper.—The Recreants return.—Dunvegan.—A Wolf-hunt.

A LONG distance, destitute of fort or post, had now to be passed. For fully 300 miles above Vermilion, no sign of life but the wild man and his prey (the former scant enough) are to be found along the shores of the Peace River.

The old fort known as Dunvegan lies twelve long winter days' travel to the south-west, and to reach it even in that time requires sustained and arduous exertion.

For 200 miles above Vermilion the course of the Peace River is north-west; it winds in long, serpentine curves between banks which gradually become more lofty as the traveller ascends the stream. To cut the long curve to the south by an overland portage now became our work; and for three days we followed a trail through mingled prairie and forest-land, all lying deep in snow. Four trains of dogs now formed our line. An Ojibbeway, named "White Bear," led the advance, and the trains took in turn the work of breaking the road after him.

Mal de Raquette had at last proved more than a match for me, and walking had become impossible; but the trains returning to Dunvegan were lightly loaded, and as the officer at Vermilion had arranged that the various dogs should take their turn in hauling my cariole, I had a fresh train each day, and thus Cerf-vola and his company obtained a two days' respite from their toil.

The old dog was as game as when I had first started, but the temporary change of masters necessitated by our new arrangements seemed to puzzle him not a little; and many a time his head would turn round to steal a furtive look at the new driver, who, "filled with strange oaths," now ran behind his cariole. Our trail led towards the foot of the Buffalo Hills. I was now in the country of the Beaver Indians, a branch of the great Chipewyan race, a tribe once numerous on the river which bears its present name of Peace from the stubborn resistance offered by them to the all-conquering Crees—a resistance which induced that warlike tribe to make peace on the banks of the river, and to leave at rest the beaver-hunters of the Unchagah.

Since that time, though far removed from the white settler, lying remote from the faintest echo of civilization, this tribe of Beaver Indians has steadily decreased; and to-day, in the whole length of 900 miles from beyond the mountains to the Lake Athabasca, scarce 200 families lie scattered over the high prairies and undulating forest belts of the Peace River. Now they live in peace with all men, but once it was a different matter; the Crees were not their only enemies, their Chipewyan cousins warred upon them; and once upon a time a fierce commotion raged amongst their own tribe.

One day a young chief shot his arrow through a dog belonging to another brave. The brave revenged the death of his dog, and instantly a hundred bows were drawn. Ere night had fallen some eighty warriors lay dead around the camp, the pine woods rang with the lamentations of the women, the tribe had lost its bravest men. There was a temporary truce—the friends of the chief whose arrow had killed the dog yet numbered some sixty people—it was agreed that they should separate from the tribe and seek their fortune in the vast wilderness lying to the south.

In the night they commenced their march;

sullenly their brethren saw them depart never to return. They went their way by the shores of the Lesser Slave Lake, towards the great plains which were said to lie far southward by the banks of the swift-rolling Saskatchewan.

The tribe of Beavers never saw again this exiled band, but a hundred years later a Beaver Indian, who followed the fortunes of a white fur-hunter, found himself in one of the forts of the Saskatchewan. Strange Indians were camped around the palisades, they were portions of the great Blackfeet tribe whose hunting-grounds lay south of the Saskatchewan; among them were a few braves who, when they conversed together, spoke a language different from the other Blackfeet; in this language the Beaver Indian recognized his own tongue.

The fortunes of the exiled branch were then traced, they had reached the great plains, the Blackfeet had protected them, and they had joined the tribe as allies in war against Crees or Assineboines. To-day the Surcees still speak the guttural language of the Chipewyan. Notorious among the wild horse-raiders of the prairies, they outdo even the Blackfeet in audacious plundering; and although the parent stock on the Peace River are quiet and harmless, the offshoot race has long been a terror over the prairies of the south. No men in this land of hunters hunt better than the Beavers. It is not uncommon for a single Indian to render from his winter trapping 200 marten skins, and not less than 20,000 beavers are annually killed by the tribe on the waters of the Peace River.

On the morning of the third day after leaving Vermilion we fell in with a band of Beavers. Five wigwams stood pitched upon a pretty rising knoll, backed by pine woods, which skirted the banks of the stream, upon the channel of which the lodges of the animal beaver rose cone-like above the snow.

When we reached the camp, "At-tal-loo," the chief, came forth. A stranger was a rare sight; and "At-tal-loo" was bound to make a speech; three of his warriors, half a dozen children, and a few women filled up the background. Leaning upon a long single-barrelled gun "At-tal-loo" began.

The mayor and corporation of that thriving borough of Porkingham could not have been more solicitous to interrupt a royal progress to the north, than was this Beaver Indian anxious to address the traveller; but there was this difference between them, whereas Mayor Tomkins had chiefly in view the excellent opportunity of hearing his own voice, utterly unmindful of what a horrid bore he was making himself to his sovereign, "At-tal-loo" had in view more practical results : his frequent iteration of the word "tea," in his guttural harangue, told at once the story of his wants :—

"This winter had been a severe one; death had struck heavily into the tribe; in these three wigwams six women had died. It was true each brave still had three or four wives left, but moose were plenty, and a man with six helpmates could be rich in dry meat and moose leather. Tea was the pressing want. Without tea the meat of the moose was insipid; without tea and tobacco the loss of even the fifth or sixth rib became a serious affair."

I endeavoured to find out the cause of this mortality among the poor hunters, and it was not far to seek. Constitutions enfeebled by close intermarriage, and by the hardships attending upon wild life in these northern regions, were fast wearing out. At the present rate of mortality the tribe of the Beavers will soon be extinct, and with them will have disappeared the best and the simplest of the nomad tribes of the north.

"At-tal-loo" was made happy with tea and tobacco, and we went our way. Another doughty chief, named "Twa-poos," probably also regarded tea as the elixir of life, and the true source of happiness; but as my servitor still continued to regard my stock of the luxury as a very excellent medium for the accumulation of stray marten skins for his own benefit, it was perhaps as well that I should only know "Twa-poos" through the channel of hearsay.

On the morning of the 25th of March we emerged from the tortuous little Buffalo River upon the majestic channel of the Peace. Its banks were now deeply furrowed beneath the prairie level, its broad surface rolled away to the south-west, 500 yards from shore to shore. The afternoon came forth bright and warm; from a high ridge on the left shore a far-stretching view lay rolled before us—the Eagle Hills, the glistening river, the wide expanse of dark forest and white prairie; and above, a sky which had caught the hue and touch of spring, while winter still stood intrenched on plain and river.

Late that evening we reached the hut of a Cree Indian. A snow-storm closed the twilight, and all sought shelter in the house: it was eight feet by twelve, in superficial size, yet nineteen persons lay down to rest in it, a Cree and his wife, an Assineboine and his wife, eight or ten children, and any number of Swampy, Ojibbeway, and half-breeds. Whenever the creaky door opened, a dozen dogs found ingress, and dodged under and over the men, women, and children in hopeless confusion.

The Assineboine squaw seemed to devote all her energies to the expulsion of the intruders; the infants rolled over the puppy dogs, the puppy dogs scrambled over the infants, and outside in the snow and on the low roof Cerf-vola and his friends did battle with a host of Indian dogs. So the night passed away. Next morning there was no track. We waded deep in the snow, and made but slow progress. Things had reached a climax with my crew; they had apparently made up their minds to make a long, slow journey. They wanted to camp at any Indian lodge they saw, to start late and to camp early, to eat, smoke, and talk, to do everything in fact but travel.

I was still nearly 150 miles from Dunvegan, and as much more from that mountain range whose defiles I hoped to reach ere the ice road on which I travelled had turned to a rushing stream. Already the sun shone strong in the early afternoon, and the surface snow grew moist under his warm rays, and here were my men ready to seek any excuse for loitering on the way.

About noon one day we reached a camp of Crees on the south shore of the river. Moose-meat was getting scarce, so I asked my yellow rascal to procure some tit-bits from the camp in exchange for tea. The whole party at once vanished into the tents, while I remained with the dogs upon the river. Presently my friend reappeared; he "could only get a rib-piece or a tough leg." "Then don't take them," I said. I saw the rascal was at his old work, so taking some tea and tobacco, I went up myself to the tents; meantime the men, women, and children had all come out to the shore. I held up the tea and pointed to the moose-meat; in an instant the scene changed—briskets, tongues, and moose-noses were brought out, and I could have loaded my dogs with tit-bits had I wished; still I pretended to find another motive for my henchman's conduct. "See," I said to him, "I make a better trader with Indians than you do. They would only give you the tough bits; I can get noses enough to load my dogs with."

But the camp possessed an attraction still more enticing; early that morning I had observed the Indians and half-breeds arraying themselves in their gayest trappings. The half-breed usually in dressing himself devotes the largest share of attention to the decoration of his legs; beads, buckles, and embroidered ribbons flutter from his leggings, and his garters are resplendent with coloured worsted or porcupine-quill work.

These items of finery had all been donned this morning in camp, the long hair had been carefully smeared with bear's fat, and then I had not long to wait for an explanation of all this adornment. In one of the three Cree tents there dwelt two good-looking squaws; we entered this tent, the mats were unrolled, the fire replenished, and the squaws set to work to cook a moose nose and tongue for my dinner. Dinner over, the difficulty began; the quarters were excellent in the estimation of my men. It would be the wildest insanity to think of quitting such a paradise of love and food under at least a twenty-four hours' delay.

So they suddenly announced their intention of "bideing a wee." I endeavoured to expostulate, I spoke of the lateness of the season, the distance I had yet to travel, the necessity of bringing to Dunvegan the train of dogs destined for that post at the earliest period; all was of no avail. Their snow-shoes were broken and they must wait. Very good; put my four dogs into harness, and I will go on alone. So the dogs were put in harness, and taking with me my most lootable effects, I set out alone into the wilderness.

It still wanted some four hours of sunset when I left the Indian lodges on the south shore, and held my way along the far-reaching river.

My poor old dog, after a few glances back to see why he should be alone, settled himself to

ALONE IN THE WILDERNESS.

[*Page* 181.

work, and despite a lameness, the result of long travel, he led the advance so gamely that when night fell some dozen miles lay between us and the Cree lodges.

At the foot of a high ridge whose summit still caught the glow from the low-set sun, while the river valley grew dark in the twilight, I turned the dogs towards the south shore, and looked about for a camping-place. The lower bank sloped down to the ice abruptly, but dogs going to camp will drag a load up, over, or through anything, and the prospect of rest above is even a greater incentive to exertion than the fluent imprecations of the half-breed below. So by dint of hauling we reached the top, and then I made my camp in a pine-clump on the brink. When the dogs had been unharnessed, and the snow dug away, the pine brush laid upon the ground, and the wood cut, when the fire was made, the kettle filled with snow and boiled, the dogs fed with a good hearty meal of dry moose meat, and my own hunger satisfied; then, it was time to think, while the fire lit up the pine stems, and the last glint of daylight gleamed in the western sky. A jagged pine-top laid its black cone against what had been the sunset. An owl from the opposite shore sounded at intervals his lonely call; now and again a passing breeze bent the fir trees until they whispered forth that mournful song which seems to echo from the abyss of the past.

The fir-tree is the oldest of the trees of the earth, and its look and its voice tell the story of its age. If it were possible to have left my worthless half-breeds altogether and to traverse the solitudes alone, how gladly would I have done so!

I felt at last at home. The great silent river, the lofty ridge darkening against the twilight, yon star burning like a beacon above the precipice—all *these* were friends, and midst them one could rest in peace.

And now, as I run back in thought along that winter journey, and see again the many camp-fires glimmering through the waste of wilderness, there comes not to my memory a calmer scene than that which closed around my lonely fire by the distant Unchagah. I was there almost in the centre of the vast wilderness of North America, around, stretched in silence, that mystery we term Nature, that thing which we see in pictures, in landscapes, in memory; which we hear in the voice of wind-swept forests and the long sob of seas against ocean rocks. This mother, ever present, ever mysterious, sometimes terrible, often tender—always beautiful—stood there with nought to come between us save loneliness and twilight. I awoke with the dawn. Soft snow was falling on river and ridge, and the opposite shore lay hid in mist and gloom. A breakfast, which consists of pemmican, tea, and biscuit, takes but a short time to prepare or to discuss, and by sunrise I was on the river.

Until mid-day I held on, but before that time the sun glowed brightly on the dazzling surface of the snow; and the dogs panted as they hauled their loads, biting frequent mouthfuls of the soft snow through which they toiled.

About noon I camped on the south shore. I had still two meals for myself, but none remained for the dogs; the men had, however, assured me that they would not fail to make an early start, and I determined to await their coming in this camp. The day passed and night closed again, but no figure darkened the long stretch of river, and my poor dogs went supperless to sleep. Cerf-vola, it is true, had some scraps of sweet pemmican, but they were mere drops in the ocean of his appetite. The hauling-dog of the North is a queer animal about food; when it is there he likes to have it, but when it isn't there, like his Indian master, he can do without it.

About supper-hour he looks wistfully at his master, and seeing no sign of pemmican-chopping or dry meat-slicing, he rolls himself up into a ball and goes quietly to sleep in his snow bed.

Again the night came softly down, the grey owl hooted his lonely cry, the breeze stirred the forest tops, and the pine-tree murmured softly and low, singing its song of the past to the melody of its million years. At such times the mind of the wanderer sings its own song too. It is the song of home; and as memory rings the cadence, time and distance disappear, and the old land brightens forth amidst the embers of the forest-fire.

These islands which we call "home" are far away; afar off we idealize them, in the forest depths we dream bright visions of their firesides of welcome; in the snow-sheeted lake, and the icy stretch of river, and the motionless musky, how sweetly sound the notes of brook and bird; how brightly rise the glimpses of summer eves when the white mists float over the scented meadows, and the corn-craik sounds from his lair in the meadow-sweet!

It is there, away in the east, far off, where the moon is rising above the forked pines, or the up-coming stars edge the ice piles on the dim eastern shores of yon sheeted lake. Far away, a speck amidst the waves of distance, bright, happy, and peaceful; holding out its welcome, and following with its anxious thoughts the wanderer who sails away over the ocean, and roams the expanses of the earth.

Well, some fine day we come back again; the great steam-ship touches the long idealized shore. Gods, how the scene changes! We feel bursting with joy to see it all again, to say, "Oh! how glad I am to see you all!"

We say it with our eyes to the young lady behind the refreshment buffet at the railroad station. Alas! she mistakes our exuberance for impertinence, and endeavours to annihilate us with a glance, enough to freeze even her high-spirited sherry. We pass the bobby on his beat with a smile of recognition, but that ferocious functionary, not a whit softened, regards us as a "party" likely to afford him transient employment in the matter of "running in." The railway porter alone seems to enter into our feelings of joy, but alas! it is only with a view to that donation with which we are sure to present him. We have enlisted his sympathies as her Majesty enlists her recruits, by the aid of a shilling. Ere an hour has passed, the vision seen so frequently through the mist of weary miles has vanished, and we have taken our place in the vast humming crowd of England's hive, to wish ourselves back into the dreamy solitudes again.

I had been asleep some hours, and midnight

had come, when the sound of voices roused me, and my recreant band approached the dying camp-fire. They had at length torn themselves away from the abode of bliss and moose meat, but either the memory of its vanished pleasures, or a stray feeling of shame, kept them still sullen and morose. They, however, announced their readiness to go on at once, as the crust upon the snow was now hard. I rose from my robe, gave the dogs a late supper, and once more we set out.

Daylight found us still upon the track; the men seemed disposed to make amends for former dilatoriness, the ice-crust was hard, and the dogs went well. When the sun had become warm enough to soften the surface we camped, had supper, and lay down to sleep for the day.

With sunset came the hour of starting, and thus turning night into day, breakfasting at sunset, dining at midnight, supping at sunrise, travelling all night, and sleeping all day, we held our way up the Unchagah. Three nights of travel passed, and the morning of the 1st of April broke upon the silent river. We had travelled well; full one hundred miles of these lonely, lofty shores had vanished behind us in the grey dusky light of twilight, night, and early morning.

As the dawn broke in the east, and gradually grew into a broader band of light, the huge ramparts of

NIGHT INTO DAY. [*Page* 187.

the lofty shores wore strange, unearthly aspects. Six hundred feet above the ice, wind and sun had already swept the snow, and the bare hill-tops rose to view, free, at last, from winter's covering.

Lower down full many a rugged ridge, and steep, scarped precipice, held its clinging growth of pine and poplar, or showed gigantic slides, upon whose gravelly surface the loosened stones rolled with sullen echo, into the river chasm beneath. Between these huge walls lay the river, broadly curving from the west, motionless and soundless, as we swept with rapid stride over its sleeping waters.

Sometimes in the early morning, upon these steep ridges, the moose would emerge from his covert, and look down on the passing dog trains, his huge, ungainly head outstretched to

"Sniff the tainted gale,"

his great ears lying forward to catch the faint jingle of our dog-bells. Nearly all else seemed to sleep in endless slumber, for, alone of summer denizens, the owl, the moose, the wolf, and the raven keep winter watch over the wilderness of the Peace River.

At daybreak, on the 1st of April, we were at the mouth of the Smoking River. This stream enters the Peace River from the south-west. It has its source but a couple of days' journey north of the Athabasca River, at the spot where that river emerges from the Rocky Mountains. And it drains the beautiful region of varied prairie and forest-land, which lies at the base of the mountains between the Peace and Athabasca rivers.

The men made a long march this day. Inspired by the offer of a gratuity, if they could make the fort by night-time, and anxious, perhaps, to atone for past shortcomings, they made up a train of five strong dogs.

Setting out with this train at eight o'clock in the morning, three of them held the pace so gamely that when evening closed we were in sight of the lofty ridge which overhangs at the north shore, the fort of Dunvegan.

As the twilight closed over the broad river we were steering between two huge walls of sandstone rock, which towered up 700 feet above the shore.

The yellow light of the sunset still glowed in the west, lighting up the broad chasm through which the river flowed, and throwing many a weird shadow along the basaltic precipice. Right in our onward track stood a large dusky wolf. He watched us until we approached within 200 yards of him, then turning he held his course up the centre of the river. My five dogs caught sight of

THE WOLF CHASE. [*Page* 189.

him, and in an instant they gave chase. The surface of the snow was now hard frozen, and urged by the strength of so many dogs the cariole flew along over the slippery surface.

The driver was soon far behind. The wolf kept the centre of the river, and the cariole bounded from snow pack to snow pack, or shot along the level ice; while the dusky twilight filled the deep chasm with its spectral light. But this wild chase was not long to last. The wolf sought refuge amidst the rocky shore, and the dogs turned along the trail again.

Two hours later a few lights glimmered through the darkness, beneath the black shadow of an immense hill. The unusual sound of rushing water broke strangely on the ear after such a lapse of silence. But the hill streams had already broken their icy barriers, and their waters were even now hastening to the great river (still chained with the gyves of winter), to aid its hidden current in the work of deliverance.

Here and there deep pools of water lay on the surface of the ice, through which the dogs waded, breast deep, and the cariole floated like a boat. Thus, alternately wading and sliding, we drew near the glimmering lights.

We had reached Dunvegan! If the men and dogs slept well that night it was little wonder.

With the intermission only necessary for food, we had travelled incessantly during four-and-twenty hours. Yet was it the same that night at Dunvegan as it had been elsewhere at various times. Outside the dogs might rest as they pleased, but within, in the huts, Swampy and Half-breed and Ojibbeway danced and fiddled, laughed and capered until the small hours of the morning.

CHAPTER XVII.

Alexander Mackenzie.—The first sign of Spring.—Spanker the suspicious.—Cerf-vola contemplates cutlets.—An Indian hunter.—" Encumbrances."—Furs and finery.—A " dead fall."—The fur trade at both ends.—An old fort.—A night attack.—Wife-lifting.—Cerf-vola in difficulties and boots.—The Rocky Mountains at last.

ABOUT eighty years ago a solitary canoe floated on the waters of the Peace River. Eight sturdy Iroquois or Canadians moved it with dexterous paddle; in the centre sat the figure of a European, busy with field-book and compass.

He was a daring Scotchman from the isles, by name Alexander Mackenzie. He was pushing his way slowly to the West; before him all was vague conjecture. There was a mighty range of mountains the Indians said—a range through which the river flowed in a profound chasm—beyond that all was mystery; but other wild men, who dwelt westward of the chasm in a land of mountains, had told them tales of another big river flowing toward the mid-day sun into the lake that had no shore.

This daring explorer built himself a house not far below the spot where my recreant crew had found a paradise in the wilderness; here he passed the winter. Early in the following spring he continued his ascent of the river. He was the first Englishman that ever passed the Rocky Mountains. He was the first man who crossed the Northern Continent.

His footsteps were quickly followed by men almost as resolute. Findlay, Frazer, and Thompson soon carried the fortunes of the North-West Company through the defiles of the Peace River; and long before Jacob Astor had dreamt his dream of Columbian fur trade, these men had planted on the wild shores of New Caledonia and Oregon the first germs of English domination; little dreaming, doubtless, as they did so, that in after-time, between dulness upon one side and duplicity on the other, the fruits of their labour and their sufferings would pass to hostile hands.

From its earliest days, the fur trade of the North had been carried on from bases which moved northward with the tide of exploration. The first French adventurers had made Tadousac, at the mouth of the rock-shadowed Saguenay, the base of their operations; later on, Montreal had been their point of distribution; then Mackenaw, between Lakes Michigan and Huron. With the fall of French dominion in 1762 the trade passed to English hands, and Fort William on Lake Superior, and Fort Chipewyan on Lake Athabasca, became in time centres of fur trade.

It was from the latter place that Mackenzie and his successors pushed their explorations to the distant shores of Arctic and Pacific Oceans. Among the earlier posts which these men established in the Great Wilderness was this fort, called Dunvegan, on the Peace River. A McLeod, of Skye, founded the post, and named it after the wild, storm-swept fortalice which the chief of his race in bygone times had reared upon the Atlantic verge. As Dunvegan was then, so it is to-day; half a dozen little houses roofed with pine-bark; in front, the broad river in its deep-cut gorge; behind, an abrupt ridge 700 feet in height, at the top of which a rolling table-land spreads out into endless distance.

Unlike the prairies of the Saskatchewan, this plateau is thickly interspersed with woods and thickets of pine and poplar. Its many lakes are free from alkali, and the varied growth of willows which they sustain, yield ample sustenance to the herds of moose which still roam the land. The deep trough through which the river flows increases with singular regularity as the traveller ascends the stream. Thus at Vermilion the banks are scarcely thirty feet above low-water level; 200 miles higher up they rise to 350 feet; at Dunvegan they are 720; and 100 miles still further west they attain an elevation of 900 and 1000 feet. Once upon the summit, however, no indication of ruggedness meets the eye. The country spreads into a succession of prairies, lakes, and copses, through which the traveller can ride with ease, safe from the badger-holes which form such an objectionable feature in more southern prairies. At times the river-bed fills up the entire bottom of the deep valley through which it runs; but more frequently a wooded terrace lies between the foot of the ridge and the brink of the water, or the land rises to the upper level in a series of rounded and less abrupt ascents. The soil is a dark sandy loam, the rocks are chiefly lime and sandstone, and the numerous slides and huge landslips along the lofty shores, render visible strata upon strata of many-coloured earths and layers of rock and shingle, lignite and banded clays in rich succession. A black, bituminous earth in many places forces its way through rock or shingle, and runs in long, dark streaks down the steep descent. Such is the present aspect of the Peace River, as lonely and silent it holds its long course, deep furrowed below the unmeasured wilderness.

April had come; already the sun shone warmly

in the midday hours; already the streams were beginning to furrow the grey overhanging hills, from whose southern sides the snow had vanished, save where in ravine or hollow it lay deep, drifted by the winter winds; but the river was not to be thus easily roused from the sleep into which the Arctic cold had cast it. Solid under its weight of ice, four feet in thickness, it would yet lie for days in motionless torpor. Snow might fly from sky and hill-top, prairie and forest might yield to the soft coming spring; but like a skilful general grim winter only drew off his forces from outlying points to make his last stand in the intrenchments of the frozen river.

From the summit of the steep hill, whose scarped front looks down upon the little huts of Dunvegan, the eye travels over many a mile of wilderness, but no hill top darkens the far horizon; and the traveller, whose steps for months have followed the western sun, feels half inclined to doubt the reality of the mountain barrier he has so long looked in vain for. So it seemed to me, as I scanned one evening the long line of the western sky from this lofty ridge.

Nineteen hundred miles behind me lay that Musk Rat Creek, by whose banks on that now distant day in October, I had bidden civilization a long good-bye.

Prairie and lakelet, broad river, vast forest, dim spreading lake, silent ridge and waste of wilderness—all lay deep sunken again in that slumber from which my lonely passage had for a moment roused them.

Different faces had at times accompanied me; various dogs had toiled and tugged at the oaken sled, or lain at night around the wintry camp-fires; and yet, still remote lay that giant range, for whose defiles my steps had so long been bound. But amid all changes of time and place and persons, two companions still remained with me. Cerf-vola the untiring, Spanker the suspicious, still trotted as briskly as when they had quitted their Dakotan home. If I should feel inclined to doubt their strength and vigour, I had only to look down the hill-side to read a reassurance—a couple of hundred feet beneath where I stood. There Spanker the suspicious might have been observed in company with two other savages, doing his utmost to terminate the career of a yearling calf, which early spring had tempted to the hill-top. It was consolatory to notice that Cerf-vola the untiring took no part in this nefarious transaction. He stood apart, watching it with a countenance expressive of emotions which might be read, either in the light of condemnation of cruelty, or commendation of coming veal cutlets.

About midnight on the 3rd of April I quitted Dunvegan, and turned once more along the frozen river. The moon, verging to its first quarter, shone above the southern shore, lighting half the river, while the remainder lay wrapped in darkness.

A half-breed named Kalder accompanied me— my former servitor having elected to remain at Dunvegan. He had probably heard strange stories of life beyond the mountains. " Miners were fond of shooting ; to keep their hand and eye in practice they would shoot him as soon as they caught sight of him," so it would perhaps be wiser to stay on the eastern slope. He remained behind, and William Kalder, a Scotch half-breed, who spoke French in addition to his Indian tongue, reigned in his stead.

Above Dunvegan, the Peace is a rapid river. We decided to travel by moonlight only, and in the morning, as many places had already become unsound; a great quantity of water lay on the surface of the ice, and wet mocassins and heavy snow-shoes became our constant companions. By daybreak, however, all water would be frozen solid, and except for the effect of the sharp ice on the dogs' feet, the travelling was excellent at that hour.

At daybreak on the fourth we heard ahead a noise of barking, and presently from the wooded shore a moose broke forth upon the river. The crusted snow broke beneath his weight, and he turned at bay near the southern shore. We were yet a long way off, and we hurried on as fast as dogs could run. When we had reached within a couple of hundred yards of where he stood butting the dogs, a shot rang sharply from the woods; the unshapely animal still kept his head lowered to his enemies, but the shot had struck, for as we came panting up, he rolled heavily amidst his baying enemies, who closed around him while the blood bubbled fast over the pure frosted snow. Above, on the wooded banks, under a giant pine, sat a young Indian quietly regarding his quarry. Not a move of limb or countenance betokened excitement; his face was flushed by a long quick chase down the rugged hill-side; but now, though his game lay stretched beneath him, he made no outward sign of satisfaction. He sat unmoved on the rock above, his long gun balanced above his knee—the fitting background to a picture of wild sport in the wilderness. It was now the time when the Indians leave their winter hunting-grounds, and make a journey to the forts with the produce of their season's toil. They come, a motley throng; men, women and children; dogs, sleds and hand-tobogans, bearing the precious freight of fur to the trading-post, bringing in the harvest of marten-skins from the vast field of the desert wilds.

On this morning, ere we reached our camping place, a long cavalcade passed us. A couple of braves in front, too proud and lazy to carry anything but their guns; then old women and young ones, bending under their loads, or driving dogs, or hauling hand-sleds laden with meat, furs, mooseskins, and infants. The puppy-dog and the infant never fail in cabin or *cortége*. Sometimes one may see the two packed together on the back of a woman, who carries besides a load of meat or skins. I believe the term "encumbrance" has sometimes been applied to the human portion of such a load, in circles so elevated that even the humanity of maternity would appear to have been successfully eliminated by civilization. If ever the term carried truth with it, it is here in this wild northern land, where yon wretched woman bears man's burthen of toil as well as her own. Here the child is veritably an encumbrance; yet in some instincts the savage mother might teach her civilized sister a lesson of womanity. Perhaps here, while this motley cavalcade passes along, we may step aside a moment from the track, and tell the story of a marten.

A couple of cotton kerchiefs, which my lady's-maid would disdain to be the owner of, and a couple of ten-pound bank-notes from my lady's purse, mark the two extremes between which lies the history of a marten. We will endeavour to bring together these widely-severed ends.

When the winter is at its coldest, but when the days are beginning to lengthen out a little over the dim pine-woods of the North, the Indian builds a small circular fence of wood, some fourteen inches high. Upon one side this circle is left open, but across the aperture a thick limb or thin trunk of tree is laid with one end resting on the ground. Inside the circle a forked stick holds a small bit of fish or meat as a bait. This forked stick is set so as to support another small piece of wood, upon which in turn rests the half-uplifted log. Pull the baited stick, and you let slip the small supporting one, which in turn lets fall the large horizontal log. Thus runs the sequence. It is a guillotine, with a tree instead of a sharp knife; it is called a "dead fall." Numbers of them are erected in the woods, where martens' tracks are plentiful in the snow. Well, then, the line of "dead falls" being made and set, the Indian departs, and silence reigns in the forest. But once a week he starts forth to visit this line of "dead falls," which may be ten or fifteen miles in length.

Every now and again he finds one of his guillotines down, and underneath it lies a small, thick-furred animal, in size something larger than a ferret, something smaller than a cat. It is needless to describe the colour of the animal; from childhood upwards it is familiar to us. Most persons can recall the figure of maiden aunt or stately visitor, muffed, cuffed, boa'd and pelissed, in all the splendour of her sables. Our little friend under the dead fall is none other than the sable—the marten of North America, the sable of Siberia.

A hundred miles away from the nearest fort this marten has been captured. When the snow and ice begin to show symptoms of softening, the Indian packs his furs together, and sets out, as we have seen, for the fort. There are, perhaps, five or six families together; the squaws and dogs are heavy laden, and the march is slow and toilsome. All the household gods have to be carried along. The leather tent, the battered copper kettle, the axe, the papoose strapped in the moss bag, the two puppy-dogs, yet unable to shift for themselves, the snow-shoes for hunting, the tattered blanket, the dry meat; it makes a big load, all told; and squaw and dog toil along with difficulty under it. The brave of course goes before, deigning only to carry his gun, and not always doing even that. The wife is but as a dog to him—a curious classification, but one for which he might find some authority were he a little more civilized.

Well, day by day the party moves along till

the fort is reached. Then comes the trade. The fifty or a hundred marten-skins are handed over; the debt of the past year is cancelled, partly or wholly; and advances are taken for the coming season.

The wild man's first thought is for the little one,—a child's white capôte, strouds or blanketing for tiny backs, a gaudy handkerchief for some toddling papoose. After that the shot and powder, the flints and ball for his own use; and lastly, the poor wife gets something for her share. She has managed to keep a couple of deer-skins for her own perquisite, and with these she derives a little pin-money.

It would be too long to follow the marten-skin through its many vicissitudes—how it changes from hand to hand, each time more than doubling its price, until at length some stately dowager spends more guineas upon it than its original captor realized pence for it.

Many a time have I met these long processions, sometimes when I have been alone on the march, and at others when my followers were around me; each time there was the inevitable hand-shaking, the good-humoured laughing, the magic word "thé;" a few matches, and a plug or two of tobacco given, and we separated. How easily they were made happy! And now and again among them would be seen a poor crippled Indian, maimed by fall from horse or shot from gun, hobbling along with the women in the rear of the straggling *cortége*, looking for all the world like a wild bird with a broken wing.

The spring was now rapidly approaching, and each day made some change in the state of the ice. The northern bank was quite clear of snow; the water on the river grew daily deeper, and at night the ice cracked and groaned as we walked upon it, as though the sleeping giant had begun to stir and stretch himself previous to his final waking.

On the morning of the 7th of April we passed the site of an old fort on the northern shore. I turned aside to examine it. Rank weeds and grass covered a few mounds, and faint traces of a fireplace could be still discerned. Moose-tracks were numerous around.

Just fifty years earlier, this old spot had been the scene of a murderous attack.

In the grey of the morning, a small band of Beaver Indians approached the fort, and shot its master and four men; a few others escaped in a canoe, leaving Fort St. John's to its fate. It was immediately burned down, and the forest has long since claimed it as its own. In the phraseology of the period, this attack was said to have been made by the Indians in revenge for a series of "wife-lifting" which had been carried on against them by the denizens of the fort. History saith no more, but it is more than probable that this dangerous method of levying "black *female*" was thereafter discontinued by the Highland fur-traders.

We camped not far from the ruined fort, and next night drew near our destination. It was full time. The ice was rapidly going, and already in places dark, treacherous holes showed grimly through to the rushing water beneath.

The dogs were all lame, and Cerf-vola had to be regularly put in boots previous to starting. Still, lame or sound, he always travelled just the same. When his feet were very sore, he would look around now and again for assistance; but if none was forthcoming he bent himself resolutely to the task, and with down-bent head toiled at his collar. Others might tire, others might give out, but he might truly say,—

> "Dogs may come, and dogs may go,
> But I go on for ever,
> Ever, ever, I go on for ever."

Before daybreak on the 8th we stopped for the usual cup of tea and bite of pemmican. The night was dark and overcast. Beside us a huge pile of driftwood lay heaped above the ice. We fired it in many places before starting, and then set out for our last dog-march. The flames rose high through the dry timber, and a long line of light glowed and quivered upon the ice. We were soon far away from it. Day broke; a thick rain began to fall; dogs and men sunk deep in the slushy snow. "Go on, good old Cerf-vola! A little more, and your weary journey will be over; a little more, and the last mile of this 1400 will have been run; a little more, and the collar will be taken from your worn shoulders for the last long time!"

At the bend of the Peace River, where a lofty ridge runs out from the southern side, and the hills along the northern shore rise to nearly 1000 feet above the water, stands the little fort of St. John. It is a remote spot, in a land which is itself remote. From out the plain to the west, forty or fifty miles away, great snowy peaks rise up against the sky. To the north and south and east all is endless wilderness—wilderness of pine and prairie, of lake and stream—of all the vast inanity of that moaning waste which sleeps between the Bay of Hudson and the Rocky Mountains.

So far have we journeyed through that land; here we shall rest awhile. The time of winter travel has drawn to its close; the ice-road has done its work; the dogs may lie down and rest; for those great snowy peaks are the Rocky Mountains.

CHAPTER XVIII.

The wild animals of the Peace River.—Indian method of hunting the moose.—Twa-poos.—The beaver.—The bear.—Bear's butter.—A bear's hug and how it ended.—Fort St. John.—The river awakes.—A rose without a thorn.—Nigger Dan.—A threatening letter.—I issue a Judicial Memorandum.—Its effect is all that could be desired.—Working up the Peace River.

THREE animals have made their homes on the shores of the Peace River and its tributaries. They are the bear, the moose, and the beaver. All are valuable to the Indian for their flesh, fur, or skin; all come to as great perfection here as in any part of the American continent.

The first and last named go to sleep in the long winter months, but the moose still roams the woods and willow banks, feeding with his flesh the forts and the Indians along the entire river. About 100 full-grown moose had been consumed during the winter months at the four posts we have lately passed, in fresh meat alone. He is a huge animal; his carcase will weigh from three to six hundred pounds; yet an ordinary half-breed will devour him in little more than a month.

Between four and five hundred moose are annually eaten at the forts of the Peace River; four of that number are consumed by the Indians, but the range of the animal is vast, the hunters are comparatively few, and to-day there are probably as many moose in Peace River as there were fifty years ago.

Athabasca trades to-day the skins of nearly 2000 moose in a single year. Few animals are more unshapely than this giant deer. His neck slopes down from the shoulder, ending in a head as large as a horse—a head which ends in a nose curled like a camel's—a nose delicious to the taste, but hideous to the eye. The ears are of enormous length. Yet, ugly as are the nose and ears of the moose, they are his chief means of protection against his enemy, and in that great ungainly head there lurks a brain of marvellous cunning. It is through nose and ears that this cunning brain is duly prompted to escape danger.

No man save the Indian, or the half-Indian, can hunt the moose with chance of success.

I am aware that a host of Englishmen and Canadians will exclaim against this, but nevertheless it is perfectly true. Hunting the moose in summer and winter is one thing—killing him in a snow-yard, or running him down in deep snow is another. The two methods are as widely different as killing a salmon which another man has hooked for you is different from rising, hooking, playing, and gaffing one yourself.

To hunt the moose requires years of study. Here is the little game which his instinct teaches him. When the early morning has come, he begins to think of lying down for the day. He has been feeding on the grey and golden willow-tops as he walked leisurely along. His track is marked in the snow or soft clay; he carefully retraces his footsteps, and, breaking off suddenly to the leeward side, lies down a gunshot from his feeding-track. He knows he must get the wind of any one following his trail.

In the morning "Twa-poos," or the Three Thumbs, sets forth to look for a moose; he hits the trail and follows it; every now and again he examines the broken willow-tops or the hoof-marks, when experience tells him that the moose has been feeding here during the early night. Twa-poos quits the trail, bending away in a deep circle to leeward; stealthily he returns to the trail, and as stealthily bends away again from it. He makes as it were the semicircles of the letter B, supposing the perpendicular line to indicate the trail of the moose; at each return to it he examines attentively the willows, and judges his proximity to the game.

At last he is so near that he knows for an absolute certainty that the moose is lying in a thicket a little distance ahead. Now comes the moment of caution. He divests himself of every article of clothing which might cause the slightest noise in the forest; even his moccassins are laid aside; and then, on a pointed toe which a ballet-girl might envy, he goes forward for the last stalk. Every bush is now scrutinized, every thicket examined. See! he stops all at once! You who follow him look, and look in vain; you can see nothing. He laughs to himself, and points to yon willow covert. No, there is nothing there. He noiselessly cocks his gun. You look again and again, but can see nothing; then Twa-poos suddenly stretches out his hand and breaks a little dry twig from an overhanging branch. In an instant, right in front, thirty or forty yards away, an immense dark-haired animal rises up from the willows. He gives one look in your direction, and that look is his *last*. Twa-poos has fired, and the moose is either dead in his thicket or within a few hundred yards of it.

One word now about this sense of hearing possessed by the moose. The most favourable day for hunting is in wild windy weather, when the dry branches of the forest crack in the gale. Nevertheless, Indians have assured me that, on such days, when they have sighted a moose, they have broken a dry stick; and although many branches were waving and cracking in the woods, the animal started at the sound—distinguishing it from the natural noises of the forest.

But although the moose are still as numerous on Peace River as they were in days far removed from the present, there is another animal which has almost wholly disappeared.

The giant form of the wood-buffalo no longer darkens the steep lofty shores. When first Mackenzie beheld the long reaches of the river, the "gentle lawns" which alternated with "abrupt precipices" were "enlivened" by vast herds of buffaloes. This was in 1793. Thirty-three years later, Sir George Simpson also ascended the river with his matchless Iroquois crew. Yet no buffalo darkened the lofty shores.

What destroyed them in that short interval? The answer is not difficult to seek—deep snow. The buffalo grazes on the grass, the moose browses on the tall willows. During one winter of exceptionally deep snow, eighty buffaloes were killed in a single day in the vicinity of Dunvegan. The Indians ran them into the snowdrifts, and then despatched them with knives.

It is still a matter of dispute whether the wood-buffalo is the same species as his namesake of the southern plains; but it is generally believed by the Indians that he is of a kindred race. He is nevertheless larger, darker, and wilder; and although the northern land, in which he is still found, abounds in open prairies and small plains, he nevertheless seeks in preference the thickest woods. Whether he be of the plain race or not, one thing is certain—his habits vary much from his southern cousin. The range of the wood-buffalo is much farther north than is generally believed. There are scattered herds even now on the banks of the Liard River as far as sixty-one degrees of north latitude.

The earth had never elsewhere such an accumulation of animal life as this northern continent must have exhibited some five or six centuries ago, when, from the Great Slave Lake to the Gulf of Florida, millions upon millions of bisons roamed the wilderness.

Have we said enough of animals, or can we spare a few words to the bears and the beavers? Of all the animals which the New World gave to man the beaver was the most extraordinary. His cunning surpassed that of the fox; his skill was greater than that of the honey-bee; his patience was more enduring than the spider's; his labour could turn the waters of a mighty river, and change the face of an entire country. He could cut down forests, and build bridges; he dwelt in a house with rooms, a common hall and a neat doorway in it. He could fell a forest tree in any direction he pleased, or carry it on his back when his sharp teeth had lopped its branches. He worked in companies, with a master beaver at the head of each—companies from whose ranks an idle or a lazy beaver was ignominiously expelled. He dwelt along the shores of quiet lakes, or by the margins of rushing streams, and silent majestic rivers, far in the heart of the solitude.

But there came a time when men deemed his soft, dark skin a fitting covering for their heads; and wild men hunted him out in his lonely home. They trapped him from Texas to the Great Bear Lake; they hunted him in the wildest recesses of the Rocky Mountains; rival companies went in pursuit of him. In endeavouring to cover the heads of others, hundreds of trappers lost their own head-covering; the beaver brought many a white man's scalp to the red man's lodge-pole; and many a red man's life went out with the beaver's. In the West he became well-nigh extinct, in the nearer North he became scarce; yet here in Peace River he held his own against all comers. Nigh 30,000 beavers die annually along its shores, and when spring opens its waters the night is ever broken by the dull plunge of countless beavers in the pools and eddies of the great river.

Along the lofty shores of the Peace River the Saskootum berry grows in vast quantities. In August its fruit is ripe, and the bears come forth to enjoy it; black, brown, and grizzly, stalk along the shores and hill-sides browsing on this luscious berry. On such food Bruin grows fat and unwieldy; he becomes "sleek-headed" and "sleeps of nights," thus falling an easy prey to his hunter.

While he was alive he loved the "poire" berries, and now when he is dead the red man continues the connexion, and his daintiest morsel is the bear's fat and Saskootum berries mixed with powdered moose-meat. It is the dessert of a Peace River feast; the fat, white as cream, is eaten in large quantities, and although at first a little of it suffices, yet after a while one learns to like it, and the dried Saskootum and "bear's butter" becomes a luxury.

But fat or lean, the grizzly bear is a formidable antagonist. Few Indians will follow him alone to his lair; his strength is enormous, he can kill and carry a buffalo-bull; were he as active as he is strong it is probable that he would stand as the most dangerous animal on the earth. But his movements are comparatively slow, and his huge form is upraised upon its hind legs before he grapples his adversary. Woe to that adversary should those great fore-paws ever encircle him. Once only have I known a man live to tell the tale of that embrace: his story was a queer one. He had been attacked from behind, he had only time to fire his gun into the bear's chest when the monster grasped him. The Indian never lost his power of thought; he plunged his left arm into the brute's throat, and caught firm hold of the tongue; with his right hand he drove his hunting-knife into ribs and side; his arm and hand were mangled, his sides were gashed and torn, but the grizzly lay dead before him.

The fort of St. John, on the Upper Peace River, is a very tumble-down old place; it stands on the south shore of the river, some thirty feet above high-water level; close behind its ruined buildings the ridges rise 1000 feet, steep and pine-clad; on the opposite shore bare grassy hills lift their thicket-fringed faces nearly to the same elevation; the river, in fact, runs at the bottom of a very large V-shaped trough 900 feet below the prairie-plateau. Between the base of the hill and the bank of the river lies a tract of wooded and sheltered land, from whose groves of birch, poplar, and pines the loud "drumming" of innumerable partridges now gave token of the coming spring. Yes, we had travelled into the spring—our steps and these never-tiring dogs had carried us farther and quicker than time. It was only the second week in April, and already the earth began to soften; the forest smelt of last year's leaves and of this year's buds; the rills spoke, and the wild duck winged along the river channels. During the whole of the second week of April the days were soft and warm; rain fell in occasional showers; at daybreak my thermometer showed only 3° or 4° of frost, and in the afternoon stood at 50° to 60° in the shade. From the 15th to the 20th the river, which had hitherto held aloof from all advances of the spring, began to show many symptoms of yielding to her soft entreaties. Big tears rose at times upon his iron face and flowed down his frosted cheeks; his great heart seemed to swell within him, and ominous groans broke from his long-silent bosom. At night he recovered himself a little, and looked grim and rigid in the early morning; but, at last, spring, and shower, and sun, and stream were too much for him—all his children were already awake, and prattling, and purling, and pulling at him, and shaking him to open his long-closed eyelids, to look once more at the blue and golden summer.

It was the 20th of April. But the rose of spring had its thorn too (what rose has not?), and with bud, and sun, and shower came the first mosquito on this same 20th of April. He was a feeble insect, and hummed around in a mournful sort of manner, not at all in keeping with the glowing prospect before him. He had a whole long summer of stinging in prospective; "the winter of his discontent" was over, and yet there was nothing hilarious in his hum. I have made a slight error in repeating the old saying, that "no rose is without its thorn," for there is just one—it is the primrose. But there were other thorns than mosquitoes in store for the denizens of this isolated spot, called St. John's, in the wilderness.

On the north shore of the river, directly facing the tumble-down fort, a new log-house was in course of erection by the Hudson's Bay Company. Work moves slowly in the North, and this log-house lay long unfinished. One fine day a canoe came floating down the lonely river; it held a solitary negro—pioneer, cook, trapper, vagrant, idler, or squatter, as chance suited him. This time the black paddler determined to squat by the half-finished log-house of the Company. Four years earlier he had dwelt for a season on this same spot. There were dark rumours afloat about him; he had killed his man it was averred;

nay, he had repeated the pastime, and killed two men. He had robbed several mining shanties, and had to shift his residence more than once beyond the mountains on account of his mode of life. Altogether Nigger Dan, as he was called, bore an indifferent reputation among the solitary white man and his half-breed helpers at the post of St. John's. By the Indians he was regarded as something between a beaver and an American bear, and, had his head been tradeable as a matter of fur, I believe they would have trapped him to a certainty. But despite the hostile feelings of the entire community, Nigger Dan held stout possession of his shanty, and claimed, in addition to his hut, all the land adjoining it, as well as the Hudson's Bay Fort in course of erection. From his lair he issued manifestoes of a very violent nature. He planted stakes in the ground along the river-bank, upon which he painted in red ochre hieroglyphics of a menacing character. At night he could be heard across the silent river indulging in loud and uncalled-for curses, and at times he varied this employment by reciting portions of the Bible in a pitch of voice and accent peculiar to gentlemen of colour. On the 12th of April, four days after my arrival at St. John's, my young host was the recipient of the following ultimatum. I copy it verbatim:—

April 12.

 Kenedy I hear by
Worne you that Com and Gett your
persnol property if eny you
have Got of my prmeeis In 24 hours And then keep away
from me because I shal Not betrubbld Nor trod on
only by her most Noble
    Majesty
    Government
 (Sgd) D. T. Williams.

On the back appeared,—

I have wated longe A-day for an ancer from that Notis you toer Down and now It is my turn to tore down ———

Although the spirit of loyalty which breathed through the latter portion of this document was most admirable, it is nevertheless matter for regret that Dan's views of the subject of "persnol property" were not those of a law-abiding citizen; unfortunately for me, both the Hudson's Bay claimant and the negro occupant appealed to me in support of their rival rights. What was to be done? It is true that by virtue of a commission conferred upon me some years earlier I had been elevated to the lofty title of justice of the peace for Rupert's Land and the North-West Territories, my brother justices consisting, I believe, of two Hudson Bay officials and three half-breed buffalo runners, whose collective wisdom was deemed amply sufficient to dispense justice over something like two million square miles. Nevertheless, it occurred to me that this matter of disputed ownership was one outside even the wide limits of my jurisdiction. To admit such want of jurisdiction would never have answered. "Rupert's Land and the North-West" carried with them a sense of vast indefinite power, that if it were once shaken by an admission of non-competency, two million square miles, containing a population of one twenty-fourth of a wild man to each square mile, might have instantly become a prey to chaotic crime. Feeling the inutility of my lofty office to deal with the matters in question, I decided upon adopting a middle course, one which I have every reason to believe upheld the full majesty of the law in the eyes of the eight representatives of the Canadian, African, and American races of man, now assembled around me. I therefore issued a document which ran thus:—

JUDICIAL MEMORANDUM.

Various circumstances having occurred in the neighbourhood of the Hudson's Bay Fort, known as St. John's, on the Peace River, of a nature to lead to the assumption that a breach of the peace is liable to arise out of the question of disputed ownership, in a plot of land on the north shore of the river, on which the Hudson's Bay Company have erected buildings to serve as their future place of business, and on which it is asserted one Daniel Williams, a person of colour, formerly lived, this is to notify all persons concerned in this question, that no belief of ownership, no former or present possession, will be held in any way to excuse or palliate the slightest infringement of the law, or to sanction any act of violence being committed, or to occasion any threats being made use of by any of the said parties which might lead to a breach of the peace.

Executed by me, as Justice of the Peace for Rupert's Land and the North-West, this 22nd day of April, 1873.

Signed, &c., &c.

I claim for this memorandum or manifesto some slight degree of praise. It bears, I think, a striking analogy to diplomatic documents, for which of late years the British Government has been conspicuous in times of grave foreign complications; but in one important respect my judicial memorandum was very much more successful than any of the political papers upon which it was framed; for whereas they had been received by the respective belligerents to whom they had been addressed in a manner not at all flattering to our national dignity, my very lucid statement that, diplomatically speaking, two and two made four, had a marked impression on the minds of my audience.

On the one hand, I clearly pointed out that murder, arson, and robbery were not singly or collectively in unison with the true interpretation of British law; and on the other, I carefully abstained from giving any indication of what would result from the infringement of that law in the persons of any of the belligerents.

I have reason to believe that the negro Bismarck was deeply impressed by the general tenour of the document; and that a lengthened perusal of the word "executed," in the last sentence, carried with it a sense of profound strangulation under which he long laboured.

And now it was time to think of moving again towards the setting sun.

Many months of travel had carried me across the great plateau of the North to this spot, where from the pine-clad plain arose the white ridges of the Rocky Mountains. Before me lay a land of alps, a realm of mountain peaks and gloomy cañons, where in countless valleys, unseen by the eye of man, this great Peace River had its distant source. In snow that lasts the live-long year these mountain summits rest; but their sides early feel the influence of the summer sun, and from the thousand valleys crystal streams rush forth to swell the majestic current of the great river, and to send it foaming in mighty volume to the distant Athabasca.

At such a time it is glorious work for the *voyageur* to launch his cotton-wood canoe on the rushing water and glance down the broad bosom of the river. His paddle lies idle in the water, or is used only to steer the swift-flying craft; and when evening darkens over the lofty shores, he lights his camp-fire full half a hundred miles from his starting-point of the morning.

But if it be idle, easy work to run down the river at its summer level, what arduous toil it is to ascend it during the same season! Bit by bit, little by little, the upward way must be won; with paddle, with pole, with line dragged along shore and pulled round tree-stump or projecting boulder; until evening finds the toiler often not three river reaches from his starting-point.

When the river finally breaks up, and the ice has all passed away, there is a short period when the waters stand at a low level; the sun is not yet strong enough to melt the snow quickly, and the frosts at night are still sharp in the mountain valleys. The river then stands ten feet below its level of mid-June; this period is a short one, and not an hour must be lost by the *voyageur* who would gain the benefit of the low water in the earlier days of May.

Seventy miles higher up the Peace River stands a solitary house called Hudson's Hope. It marks the spot where the river first emerges from the cañon of the Rocky Mountains, and enters the plain country. A trail, passable for horses, leads along the north shore of the river to this last trading-post of the Hudson's Bay Company on the verge of the mountains. Along this trail I now determined to continue my journey, so as to gain the west side of the Great Cañon before the ice had left the river, and thus reap the advantage of the low water in ascending still farther into the mountains.

It is no easy matter to place an exact picture of the topography of a country before a reader: we must, however, endeavour to do so.

Some fifty miles west of St. John, the Peace River issues from the cañon through which it passes the outer range of the Rocky Mountains. No boat, canoe, or craft of any kind has ever run the gauntlet of this huge chasm; for five-and-thirty miles it lies deep sunken through the mountains; while from its depths there ever rises the hoarse roar of the angry waters as they dash furiously against their rocky prison. A trail of ten miles leads across this portage, and at the western end of this trail the river is reached close to where it makes its first plunge into the rock-hewn chasm. At this point the traveller stands within the outer range of the mountains, and he has before him a broad river, stretching far into a region of lofty peaks, a river with strong but even current, flowing between banks 200 to 300 yards apart. Around great mountains lift up their heads dazzling with the glare of snow, 10,000 feet above the water which carries his frail canoe.

It was through this pass that I now proposed

to journey westward towards the country which lies between the Pacific Ocean, Alaska, and the multitudinous mountains of Central British Columbia, a land but little known; a vast alpine region, where, amidst lakes and mountains nature reigns in loneliness and cloud.

CHAPTER XIX.

Start from St. John's.—Crossing the ice.—Batiste La Fleur.
—Chimeroo.—The last wood-buffalo.—A dangerous weapon.
—Our raft collapses.—Across the Half-way River.

THE 22nd of April had come. For some days we were engaged at St. John's in preparing supplies for the ascent of the river, and in catching and bringing in from the prairie the horses which were to carry me to the point of embarcation at the west end of the cañon; the snow had nearly all disappeared from the level prairie. The river opposite the fort was partly open, but some distance below a bridge of ice yet remained, and on the 20th we moved our horses across this connecting link to the north shore. The night of the 20th made a serious change in the river, and when the 22nd came, it was doubtful whether we should be able to cross without mishap.

From the fort of St. John's to the gold mines on the Ominica River was some twenty or thirty days' travel, and as no supplies were obtainable

Q

en route, save such as my gun might afford, it became necessary to carry a considerable quantity of moose pemmican and dry meat, the sole luxuries which St. John's could boast of.

By the 22nd all preparations were declared complete, and we began to cross the river over the doubtful ice-bridge. First went two men dragging a dog-sled, on which was piled the stores and provisions for the journey; next came old Batiste La Fleur, who was to accompany me as far as the Half-way River, a torrent which we would have to raft across on the second day of our journey.

Batiste carried a long pole, with which he sounded the ice previous to stepping upon it. I brought up the rear, also carrying a pole, and leading by a long line the faithful Cerf-vola. Spanker and his six companions here passed from my hands, and remained at St. John's to idle through the approaching summer, and then to take their places as Hudson Bay hauling-dogs; but for Cerf-vola there was to be no more hauling, his long and faithful service had at length met its reward, and the untiring Esquimaux was henceforth to lounge through life collarless and comfortable.

Coasting down along the shore-ice we reached the crossing-point, and put out into the mid-river;

once on the dangerous part, there was no time to think whether it was safe or not. A Salteaux Indian, dragging the sled, went in, but light and quick as thought he dragged himself from the ice and sped along its yielding surface. Below rumbled the river, and in the open places its dark waters gurgled up and over the crumbling ice. Only a narrow tongue of ice spanned the central current; we crossed it with nothing worse than wet feet and legs, and to me a dislocated thumb, and then we breathed freer on the farther side.

Loading the horses with luggage and provisions, I bade good-bye to my host, and we turned our faces towards the steep north shore. The day was gloriously bright. The hill up which the horses scrambled for a thousand feet was blue with wild anemones; spring was in the earth and in the air. Cerf-vola raced in front, with tail so twisted over his back that it threatened to dislocate his spine in a frantic attempt to get in front of his nose. The earth, bare of snow, gave forth a delicious fragrance, which one drank with infinite delight after the long, long scentless winter; and over the white river below, and the pine forest beyond, summer, dressed in blue sky and golden sunbeam, came moving gently up on the wing of the soft south wind.

We reached the summit. Below lay a long line of frosted river; the little fort, dwarfed by distance, the opposing ridges, the vast solitude, and beyond all, snow-white against the western sky, the peaks and pinnacles of nameless mountains. Through varied prairie and wooded country, and across many a rushing brook, deep hidden in tangled brake and thicket, we held our way on that bright spring afternoon; and evening found us on a bare and lofty ridge, overlooking the valley of the Peace River. Batiste had lived his life in these solitudes, and knew the name of creek and prairie, and the history (for even the wilderness has a history) of each hill or widespread meadow.

The beautiful prairie which lay beneath our camping-place was Chimeroo's prairie, and the great ridge of rock which frowned above it was also Chimeroo's; and away there where the cleft appeared in the hills to the north, that was where Chimeroo's river came out to join the Peace. In fact, Chimeroo played such a conspicuous part in the scenery that one naturally asked, Who was Chimeroo?

"Chimeroo! Oh, he is a Beaver Indian; he lived here for a long time, and he killed the last wood-buffalo in yonder valley, just three years ago."

The last of his race had wandered down from

the banks of the Liard, and Chimeroo had struck his trail, and followed him to the death.

When twilight fell, that peculiar orange light of the American wilderness lay long in the west. Against this vivid colour, Chimeroo's hill stood out in inky profile the perfect image of a colossal face. Forehead, nose, lips, and chin seemed cut in the huge rock, and, like a monstrous sphinx, looked blankly over the solitude.

"It is the head of Chimeroo," I said to Batiste; "see, he looks over his dominions." We were perched upon a bare hill-top, many hundred feet above the river. The face rose between us and the west, some three miles distant; the head, thrown slightly back, seemed to look vacantly out on the waste of night and wilderness, while a long beard (the lower part of the ridge) descended into the darkness. Gradually day drew off his orange curtain from the horizon, and the darkness had blotted out the huge features of Chimeroo. We slept upon our lonely hill-top.

Pursuing our journey on the morrow, we descended to the river, and held our way over Chimeroo's prairie, passing beneath the lofty ridge, whose outline had assumed the image of a human face.

About mid-day we reached the banks of Chimeroo's river, which, being flooded, we forded, and, climbing its steep north shore, halted for dinner. It would not be easy to exaggerate the beauty of the country through which the trail had carried us, or the sensation of rest which came to one as, looking out over the landscape, the fair spring scene stole insensibly on the mind. Everywhere the blue anemone, like a huge primrose, looked up to the bluer sky; butterflies fluttered in the clear, pure air; partridges drummed in the budding thickets. The birch-trees and willows were putting forth their flowers, precursors of the leaves so soon to follow. The long-hushed rippling of the streams fell on the ear like music heard after lapse of time; and from the blue depths of sky at times fell the cry of the wild goose, as with scarce-moving wing he held his way in long waving w's to his summer home. Chimeroo's prairie was golden with the long grass of the old year. Chimeroo's hill glistened in the bright sun of the new spring; and winter, driven from the lower earth, had taken refuge in the mountains, where his snow-white flag of surrender floated out from crag and cliff, high above the realm of pines. Such a scene as this, might the first man have beheld when he looked over the virgin earth. It was far too fine a day to work: we would rest. Batiste La Fleur knew of a lake not far off, and we would go to it and spend the evening in hunting beaver and wild ducks; so we put the saddles on and journeyed slowly to Batiste's paradise.

Through many a devious path and tortuous way did Batiste guide us, until his hunting-ground was gained. On a knoll we made our camp; and while Kalder remained to look after it, Batiste and I sallied forth to hunt.

Batiste's gun was an excellent weapon, were it not for a tendency to burst about the left barrel. This was made observable by two or more ominous bulges towards the centre of the piece; but Batiste appeared to have unlimited confidence in the integrity of his weapon, and explained that these blemishes were only the result of his having on two or three occasions placed a bullet over a charge of shot, and then directed the united volley against the person of a beaver. When loading this gun, Batiste had a risky method of leaning it against his chest while drawing a charge of shot from his shot-bag. I pointed out to him that this was not a safe method of loading, as it was quite possible the other barrel might explode while the gun thus rested against his side. It was true, he said, for only last year the gun under similar treatment had exploded, carrying away the brim of his hat, and causing no slight alarm to the rest of his person.

Our success that afternoon was not great; ducks and geese but lately arrived from the peopled south were yet wild and wary, and had not learned to look on man in any light save that of an enemy; and altogether Batiste's hunter's paradise did not justify his glowing accounts of it. To do him justice, however, it must be stated that the wet ground was literally ploughed up with moose-tracks; and the golden willows lay broken down and bruised by the many animals which had browsed upon them during the winter.

It was mid-day on the 24th of April when we reached the banks of the Half-way River, whose current, swollen by the melting snow, rolled swiftly from the north, between banks piled high with ice-floe. This was the first serious obstacle to the journey, and as soon as dinner was over we set to work to overcome it. From a neighbouring grove of pines Kalder and Baptiste got dry trees; half a dozen of these lashed together formed the groundwork of a raft. Three other pine-trees tied on top completed the craft, and with a long pole and a rough paddle, all fashioned by the axe, the preparations were declared finished. This craft was put together in a sheltered part of the river; and when all was completed, the goods and chattels were placed upon it. But one more piece of work remained to be accomplished ere we set sail upon our raft—the horses had to be crossed. By dint of driving and shouting we forced them across the boulders of ice into the water. It was cold as ice, and they stood knee-deep, afraid to venture farther. But Kalder was a very demon when work had to be done. In an instant he was across the ice-floe, and upon the back of one of the horses; then with knees and hands and voice and heels he urged the brute into the flood. The horse reared and snorted and plunged, but Kalder sat him like the half-breed that he was, and in another second, horse and rider plunged wildly into the torrent. Down they went out of sight, and when they reappeared the horse was striking out for the far shore, and Kalder was grappling with the projecting ice. The other horses soon followed their leader, and all four went swimming down the current. Gradually the back eddy near the farther shore caught them, and, touching ground, they disappeared in the forest. Now came our turn to cross. We towed the crazy raft up the bordering ice, and, mooring her for a moment in an eddy, took our places on the upper logs. Scarcely had we put out from the shore than the fastening gave way, and the whole fabric threatened instant collapse. We got her back to the eddy, repaired the damage, and once more put out. Our weight and baggage sunk us down, so that the body of the raft was quite submerged, and only the three trees on top showed above the water; upon these we crowded. Old Batiste waved a good-bye. Kalder was at the bow with a pole. I worked a paddle on the stern. Once out of the sheltering eddy, the current smote our unwieldy platform, and away we went. Another instant and the pole failed to reach the bottom. With might and main I worked the paddle; down we shot, and across; but ten yards down to every one across. Would we save the eddy? that was the question; for if we missed it, there was nought to stay our wild career. Far as eye could reach, the current ran wild and red. For an anxious minute we rushed down the stream, and then the eddy caught us, and we spun round like a teetotum. "The other side!" roared Kalder; and to the other side went the paddle to keep us in the eddy. Then we headed for the shore; and, ere the current could catch us again, Kalder was breast-deep in the water, holding on with might and main to the raft.

We were across the Half-way River. To unload the raft, build a fire, to dry our wet garments, and shout good-bye to old Batiste, who stood on an ice boulder, anxiously watching our fortunes from the shore we had quitted, took us but a short time.

The horses were captured and saddled, and, ascending through tangled forest into a terraced land of rich-rolling prairies, we pushed on briskly towards the west.

Thus, trotting through a park-like land of wood and glade and meadow, where the jumping deer glanced through the dry grass and trees, we gradually drew near the Rocky Mountains. At times the trail led up the steep face of the outer hill to the plateau above, and then a rich view would lie beneath—a view so vast with the glories of the snowy range, and so filled with nearer river and diamond-shaped island, that many a time I drew rein upon some lofty standpoint to look, as one looks upon things which we would fain carry away into the memory of an after-time.

About the middle of the afternoon of the 25th of April we emerged from a wood of cypress upon an open space, beneath which ran the Peace River. At the opposite side a solitary wooden house gave token of life in the wilderness. The greater part of the river was still fast frozen, but along the nearer shore ran a current of open water. The solitary house was the Hope of Hudson!

CHAPTER XX.

Hudson's Hope.—A lover of literature.—Crossing the Peace.—An unskilful pilot.—We are upset.—Our rescue.—A strange variety of arms.—The Buffalo's Head.—A glorious view.

DISMOUNTING from our tired horses, we loosened saddles and bridles, hobbled the two fore-legs together, and turned them adrift in the forest. Then we *cached* our baggage in the trees, for wolves were plentiful around, and a grey wolf has about as extensive a bill of fare in the matter of man's clothing and appointments as any animal in creation, except perhaps a monkey.

In my early days, in Burmah and India I once possessed a rare specimen of the last-named genus, who, when he found the opportunity, beautifully illustrated his descent from the lower orders of man by devouring a three-volume novel in less time than any young lady of the period could possibly accomplish it. He never knew a moment's starvation as long as he had a photograph album to appease his insatiable love of literature. But to proceed :—

By the time we had *cached* our baggage, two men had come forth from the house on the other side of the river, and started out upon the ice, dragging a very small canoe; when they reached the open water at our side, they launched their craft and paddled across to the shore; then, ascending the hill, they joined us at the cache.

Their news was soon told; the river was open at the west end of the portage (ten miles away). Jaques Pardonet, a French miner, who had been trapping during the winter, was about to start for the mines on the Ominica River; he was now patching up an old canoe which he had found stranded on the shore, and when it was ready he would be off: for the rest, no Indians had come in for a very long time, and moose meat was at a very low ebb in Hudson's Hope.

We descended to the river, and Kalder and Charette (a half-breed in charge of the fort) crossed first in the beaver canoe; it was much too small to carry us all. When they had disembarked safely on the ice, they fastened a long line to the bow of the canoe and shoved her off to our side; as she neared our shore she was caught by an English miner who had been living with Charette for some days, and whom I had engaged to accompany me to the mines. He had declared himself a proficient in the art of canoeing, and I was now about to experience my first example of his prowess.

We took our places and shoved from the shore. I lay low in the canoe, with legs stretched under the narrow thwarts to steady her as much as possible. I took in no baggage, but placed gun and revolver in the bottom alongside of me. Cerf-vola was to swim for himself.

A——, the miner, took a paddle at the stern. We had scarcely left the shore when the canoe lurched quickly to one side, shipping water as she did so. Then came another lurch on the other side, and I knew all was over. I heard the men on shore shouting to the miner to sit low—to keep down in the canoe—but all was too late. There came another lurch, a surge of water, and we were over into the icy quick-running river. I could not free myself from the thwarts which held me like a vice; the water gurgled and rushed around, about, and above me; and the horrid sensation of powerlessness, which the sleeper often experiences in a nightmare, came full upon my waking senses.

Of struggling I have but a faint recollection; at such times one struggles with a wild instinct that knows no rule or thought; but I vividly

CLINGING TO THE CANOE. [Page 239.

recollect the prevalent idea of being held head downwards in the icy current, in a grasp which seemed as strong as that of death.

I remembered, too, without trouble, all the surroundings of the scene; the bordering ice which was close below us—for the channel of water took a central course a little bit lower down the river, and the ice lay on both sides of it—while the current ran underneath as water can only run when four feet of solid ice is pressing upon it. Once under that ice and all was over with us. How it came about I cannot tell, but all at once I found myself free; I suppose one struggle something wilder than the rest had set me free, for long afterwards one of my legs bore tokens of the fight. In another second I was on the surface. I grasped the canoe, but it was round as a log, and turned like a wheel in the water, rolling me down each time, half-drowned as I already was.

My companion, the miner, had gone at once clear of the canoe, and, catching her by the stern, had held himself well above the water. One look at Kalder and Charette on the ice told me they were both utterly demoralized: Kalder had got behind Charette, while the latter held the line without well knowing what to do with it. Perhaps it was better that he did so, as the line was a miserably frail one, little better than a piece of twine, and the weight upon it now in this strong current was very great. Very slowly Charette hauled in the line that held us to Mother Earth; then Kalder recovered his presence of mind, and flung a leathern line across the upturned canoe. I grasped it, and in another instant the bark grated against the edge of the ice. Numbed and frozen I drew myself on to the canoe, then on to the crumbling ice along the edge, and finally to the solid pack itself. Wet, water-logged, numbed, and frozen, we made our way across the ice to the shore. My gun and revolver had vanished; they lay somewhere under twenty feet of water.

Thus, without arms, with watch feebly ticking—as though endeavouring to paddle itself with its hands through billows of water, with Aneroid so elevated, I presume, at its escape from beneath the water, that in a sudden revulsion of feeling it indicated an amount of elevation above the sea level totally inconsistent with anything short of a Himalayan altitude, at which excited state it continued to exist during the remainder of my wandering — we reached the Hope of Hudson. There never was truer saying than that when things go to the worst they mend. When I had changed my dripping clothes for a suit of Charette's Sunday finery, when Mrs. Charette had got ready a cup of tea and a bit of moose steak, and when the note-book, letters, and likenesses, which one carries as relics of civilization into the realms of savagery, had all been duly dried and renovated, matters began to look a good deal better.

Early on the following morning Charette and Kalder moored a couple of canoes in the open water, and began to drag for the gun with a fish-hook fastened to the end of a long pole; the gun was in a leathern case, and an hour's work resulted in its recovery, none the worse for its submersion. My ammunition was still safe, but as the supply of it available for a breech-loader was limited, we were on the whole badly off for arms. I armed Kalder with a flint trading-gun—a weapon which, when he had tried it at a mark, and then hammered the barrel, first on one side then on the other, he declared to be a good "beaver gun." The miner also possessed a gun, but as the hammer of one barrel hung dangling gracefully down the side, and as he possessed no percussion-caps for the other barrel (a want he supplied by an ingenious use of wax vestas), the striking of his match conveyed a similar idea to the mind of any bird or beast at whose person he presented the muzzle; and while the gun was thinking about going off, the bird or beast had already made up its mind to take a similar course.

Now this matter of weapons was a serious item in our affairs, for numerous are the delays and mishaps of an up-river journey in the wild land we were about to penetrate. Down stream all is well; a raft can always be made that will run from four to six miles an hour; but the best craft that men can build will not go a mile an hour upstream on many parts of these rivers, and of this up-river we had some 200 miles before us.

On the 27th of April I set out from Hudson's Hope to cross the portage of ten miles, which avoids the Great Cañon, at the farther end of which the Peace River becomes navigable for a canoe.

We crossed the river once more at the scene of our accident two days previously; but this time, warned by experience, a large canoe was taken, and we passed safely over to the north shore. It took some time to hunt up the horses, and mid-day had come before we finally got clear of the Hope of Hudson.

The portage trail curved up a steep hill of 800 or 900 feet; then on through sandy flats and by small swamps, until, at some eight or nine miles from the Hope of Hudson, the outer spurs of the mountains begin to flank us on either side. To the north a conspicuous ridge, called the Buffalo's Head, rises abruptly from the plain, some 3000 feet above the pass; its rock summit promised a wide view of mountain ranges on one side, and of the great valley of the Peace River on the other. It stood alone, the easternmost of all the ranges, and the Cañon of the Peace River flowed round it upon two sides, south and west.

Months before, at the forks of the Athabasca River, a man who had once wandered into these wilds told me, in reply to a question of mine, that there was one spot near the mouth of the Peace River pass which commanded a wide range of mountain and prairie. It was the Buffalo's Head.

Nine hundred miles had carried me now to that spot. The afternoon was clear and fine; the great range had not a cloud to darken the glare of the sun upon its sheen of snow; and the pure cool air came over the forest trees fresh from the thousand billows of this sea of mountains. The two men went on to the portage end; I gave them my horse, and, turning at right angles into a wood, made my way towards the foot of the Buffalo's Head.

Thick with brulé and tangled forest lay the base of the mountain; but this once passed, the steep sides became clear of forest, and there rose abruptly before me a mass of yellow grass and soft-blue anemones. Less than an hour's hard climbing brought me to the summit, and I was a thousand times repaid for the labour of the ascent.

I stood on the bare rocks which formed the frontlet of the Buffalo's Head. Below, the pines of a vast forest looked like the toy-trees which children set up when Noah is put forth to watch the animals emerging from his ark, and where everything is in perfect order, save and except that perverse pig, who will insist on lying upon his side in consequence of a fractured leg, and who must either be eliminated from the procession altogether, or put in such close contact to Mrs. Noah, for the sake of her support, as to detract very much from the solemnity of the whole procession.

Alas, how futile is it to endeavour to describe such a view! Not more wooden are the ark animals of our childhood, than the words in which man would clothe the images of that higher nature which the Almighty has graven into the shapes of lovely mountains! Put down your wooden woods bit by bit; throw in colour here, a little shade there, touch it up with sky and cloud, cast about it that perfume of blossom or breeze, and in Heaven's name what does it come to after all? Can the eye wander away, away, away until it is lost in blue distance as a lark is lost in blue heaven, but the sight still drinks the beauty of the landscape, though the source of the beauty be unseen, as the source of the music which falls from the azure depths of sky.

That river coming out broad and glittering from the dark mountains, and vanishing into yon profound chasm with a roar which reaches up even here—billowy seas of peaks and mountains beyond number away there to south and west—that huge half dome which lifts itself above all others sharp and clear cut against the older dome of heaven! Turn east, look out into that plain—that endless plain where the pine-trees are dwarfed to spear-grass and the prairie to a meadow-patch—what do you see? Nothing, poor blind reader, nothing, for the blind is leading the blind; and all this boundless range of river and plain, ridge and prairie, rocky precipice and snow-capped sierra, is as much above my poor power of words, as He who built this mighty nature is higher still than all.

Ah, my friend, my reader! Let us come down from this mountain-top to our own small level again. We will upset you in an ice-rapid; Kalder will fire at you; we will be wrecked; we will have no food; we will hunt the moose, and do anything and everything you like,—but we cannot put in words the things that we see from these lonely mountain-tops when we climb them in the sheen of evening. When you go into your church, and the organ rolls and the solemn chant floats through the lofty aisles, you do not ask your neighbour to talk to you and tell you what it is like. If he should do anything of the kind, the beadle takes him and puts him out of doors, and then the policeman takes him and puts him in-doors, and he is punished for his atrocious conduct; and yet you expect me to tell you about this church, whose pillars are the mountains, whose roof is the heaven itself, whose music comes from the harp-strings which the earth has laid over her bosom, which we call pine-trees; and from which the hand of the Unseen draws forth a ceaseless symphony rolling ever around the world.

CHAPTER XXI.

Jacques, the French miner.—A fearful abyss.—The Great Cañon of the Peace River.—We are off on our western way.—Unfortunate Indians.—A burnt baby.—The moose that walks.

It was dusk when I reached the ruined hut which stood at the western end of the portage. My men had long preceded me, and Kalder had supper ready before the great fireplace. The fire shed its light upon a fourth figure; it was that of Jacques, the French miner, five feet two inches in height; miner, trapper, trader, and wanderer since he left his home in Lorraine, near the war-famous citadel of Belfort, some twenty years ago.

I brought one piece of news to the hut: it was that although the river was free from ice opposite our resting-place, and to the end of the reach in view, yet it was fast closed in for the twenty or thirty miles which my mountain climb had enabled me to scan. So here in the midst of the mountains we awaited the disruption of the ice and the opening of our watery way.

The delay thus occasioned was unexpected, and fell heavily on my supply of food; but rabbits and partridges were numerous, and Kalder's gun proved itself to be a worthy weapon at these denizens of the forest, as well as at the beaver. On the evening of my arrival at the hut I had seen two moose drinking on a sand-bar near the mouth of the Cañon, but the river lay between me and them, and we could find no further trace of them on the following day.

In one respect the delay was not irksome to me; it gave me an opportunity of exploring a portion of the Great Cañon, and forming some idea of the nature of the difficulties and dangers which made it an impassable chasm for the hardiest *voyageurs*.

On the 29th of April the ice in the upper part of the river broke up, and came pouring down with great violence for some hours; blocks of ice many feet in thickness, and weighing several tons, came down the broad river, crushing against each other, and lining the shore with huge crystal masses.

The river rose rapidly, and long after dark the grating of the ice-blocks in the broad channel below told us that the break-up must be a general one; the current before our hut was running six miles an hour, and the ice had begun to run early in the afternoon.

All next day the ice continued to run at intervals, but towards evening it grew less, and at nightfall it had nearly ceased.

During the day I set out to explore the Cañon. Making my way along the edge of what was, in ages past, the shore of a vast lake, I gained the summit of a ridge which hung directly over the Cañon. Through a mass of wrack and tangled forest I held on, guided by the dull roar of waters until I reached an open space, where a ledge of rock dipped suddenly into the abyss: on the outer edge of this rock a few spruce-trees sprung from cleft and fissure, and from beneath, deep down in the dark chasm, a roar of water floated up into the day above. Advancing cautiously to the smooth edge of the chasm, I took hold of a spruce-tree and looked over. Below lay one of those grim glimpses which the earth holds hidden, save from the eagle and the mid-day sun. Caught in a dark prison of stupendous cliffs (cliffs which hollowed out beneath, so that the topmost ledge literally hung over the boiling abyss of waters), the river foamed and lashed against rock and precipice, nine hundred feet below me. Like some caged beast that finds escape impossible on one side, it flew as madly and as vainly against the other; and then fell back in foam and roar and raging whirlpool. The rocks at the base held the record of its wrath in great trunks of trees, and blocks of ice lying piled and smashed in shapeless ruin.

Looking down the Cañon towards the south, a great glen opened from the west; and the sun, now getting low in the heavens, poured through this valley a flood of light on red and grey walls of rugged rock; while half the pine-clad hills lay dark in shade, and half glowed golden in this level light; and far away, beyond the shadowy chasm and the sun-lit glen, one great mountain-peak lifted his dazzling crest of snow high into the blue air of the evening.

There are many indications above the mouth of the Cañon, that the valley in which our hut stood was once a large lake. The beaches and terrace levels are distinctly marked, but the barrier fall was worn down into a rapid, and the Cañon became a slant of water for some thirty miles. At the entrance the rock is worn smooth and flat in many places, and huge cisterns have been hollowed in its surface—"kettles," as the *voyageur* calls them—perfectly round, and holding still the granite boulder which had chiselled them, worn to the size and roundness of a cannon-ball from ages of revolution. Some of these kettles are tiny as a tea-cup; others are huge as the tun of Heidelberg.

When I got back to the hut, night had fallen. At the end of the long river-reach a new moon hung in the orange-tinted west; the river was almost clear of ice, and it was resolved to start on the morrow.

There was a certain amount of vagueness in the programme before me. For seventy miles the course was perfectly clear—there was, in fact, only one road to follow—but at the end of that distance two paths lay open, and circumstances could only determine the future route at that point.

If the reader will imagine an immense letter Y laid longitudinally from west to east, he will have a fair idea of the Peace River above the Cañon. The tail of the Y will be the seventy miles of river running directly through the main range of the Rocky Mountains; the right arm will be the Findlay, having its source 300 miles higher up in that wilderness of mountains known as the Stickeen; the left arm will be the Parsnip River, sometimes called by mistake the Peace River, having its source 260 miles to the south near the waters of the upper Frazer. Countless lesser streams (some of them, nevertheless, having their 200 miles of life) roll down into these main systems; and it would seem as though the main channel had, like a skilful general, united all its widely-scattered forces at the forks, seventy miles above us, before entering on the gigantic task of piercing the vast barrier of the central mountains.

Standing on the high ground at the back of the hut in which we awaited the opening of the great river, and looking westward at the mountains piled together in endless masses, it was difficult to imagine by what process a mighty river had cloven asunder this wilderness of rock,—giving us the singular spectacle of a wide, deep, tranquil stream flowing through the principal mountain range of the American continent.

May-day broke in soft showers of rain; the mountains were shrouded in mist; the breeze was not strong enough to lift the gauze-like vapour from the tree-tops on the south shore. By nine o'clock the mists began to drift along the hill-sides; stray peaks came forth through rifts, then shut themselves up again; until finally the sun drew off the vapours, and clad mountain and valley in blue and gold.

We loaded the canoe, closed the door of the old shanty, and shoved off upon our western way. There were four of us and one dog—two miners, my half-breed Kalder, myself, and Cerf-vola. I had arranged with Jacques to travel together, and I made him captain of the boat. None knew better the secrets of the Upper Peace River; for ten years he had delved its waters with his paddle, and its sand-bars with his miner's shovel.

Little Jacques—he was a curious specimen of humanity, and well worth some study too. I have already said that he was small, but that does not convey any idea of his real size. I think he was the smallest man I ever saw—of course I mean a man, and not a dwarf; Jacques had nothing of the dwarf about him—nay, he was a very giant in skill and craft of paddle, and pluck and daring. He had lived long upon his own resources, and had found them equal to most emergencies.

He could set his sails to every shift of fortune, and make some headway in every wind. In summer he hunted gold; in winter he hunted furs. He had the largest head of thick bushy hair I ever saw. He had drawn 3000 dollars' worth of pure gold out of a sand-pit on the Ominica River during the preceding summer; he had now a hundred fine marten-skins, the produce of his winter's trapping. Jacques was rich, but all the same, Jacques must work. As I have said, Jacques was a native of Belfort. Belfort had proved a tough nut for Kaiser William's legions; and many a time as I watched this little giant in times of peril, I thought that with 200,000 little Jacqueses one could fight big Bismarck's beery battalions as often as they pleased. Of course Jacques had a pair of miner's boots. A miner without a pair of miner's boots would be like Hamlet with Hamlet left out. When Jacques donned these boots, and swung himself out on a huge forest trunk prostrate in a rapid, and hewed away at the giant to give our canoe a passage, he looked for all the world like his prototype the giant-killer, and the boots became the seven-leagued friends of our early days.

How the big axe flew about his little head, until crash went the monster, and Jacques sprang back to rock or boat as lively as a squirrel.

He had many queer stories of early days, and could recount with pride the history of the stirring times he had seen. What miner's heart does not soften at the recollection, in these degenerate days, of how the Vigilants hanged six roughs one morning in the market-place of Frisco, just two-and-twenty years ago?

We poled and paddled along the shore of the river; now on one side, now on the other, dodging the heavy floes of ice which still came at intervals along the current.

In the evening we had gained a spot some twelve miles from the hut, and we made our camp on a wooded flat set in a wide amphitheatre of hills. The next morning broke wet and stormy, and we lay in camp during the early part of the day. Towards mid-day the silence was broken by the discharge of a gun at the opposite side of the river. We at once answered it, and soon another report replied to ours. There were Indians in the vicinity, so we might expect a visit. About an hour later a most wretched group appeared at our camp. It consisted of two half-clad women, one of whom carried a baby on her back; a wild-looking boy, apparently about twelve or fourteen years of age, led the way, carrying an old gun; two dogs brought up the rear. A glance at the dogs showed that food, at least, was plentiful in the Indian camp—they were fat and sleek. If an Indian has a fat dog, you may know that game is abundant; if the dog is thin, food is scarce; if there be no dog at all, the Indian is starving, and the dog has been killed and eaten by his master. But to proceed :—

In a network of tattered blankets and dripping rags, these three wretched creatures stalked into our camp; they were as wet as if they had come underneath the river instead of across it; but that seemed to give them little thought. Jacques understood a few words of what they said, and the rest was made out by signs;—all the men were sick, and had been sick for months. This boy and another were alone able to hunt; but moose were plenty, and starvation had not come to supplement sickness; the women were "packing" the men.

Reader, what do you imagine that means? I will soon tell you. It means that when the camp moves—which it does every few days, as the game gets hunted away from one locality—the women carried the men on their backs in addition to the household gods. Literally these poor women carried on their bent backs the house, the clothes, the food, the baby, and the baby's father.

What was the disease? They could not tell.

My slender stock of drugs was long since exhausted; I had nothing left but the pain-killer. I gave them half of my last bottle, and had it been the golden wealth of the sand-bars of this Peace River itself, it could not have been more thought of. To add to their misfortunes, the baby had come to grief about a week previously—it had tumbled head foremost into the fire. It was now unslung from its mother's back for my inspection. Poor little Beaver! its face and head had got a dreadful burning; but, thanks to mountain air and Indian hardiness, it was getting all right.

Had I anything to rub on it? A little of the Mal de Racquette porpoise-oil and pain-killer yet remained, and with such an antidote the youthful Beaver might henceforth live in the camp-fire.

I know some excellent Christians at home who occasionally bestow a shilling or a half-crown upon a poor man at a church-door or a street-crossing, not for the humanity of the act, but just to purchase that amount of heaven in the next world. I believe they could tell you to a farthing how much of Paradise they had purchased last week or the week before. I am not sure that they are quite clear as to whether the quantity of heaven thus purchased, is regulated by the value set on the gift by the beggar or by the rich man; but if it be by the value placed on it by him who gets it, think, my Christian friends, think what a field for investment does not this wilderness present to you. Your shilling spent here amongst these Indians will be rated by them at more than its weight in gold; and a pennyworth of pain-killer might purchase you a perpetuity of Paradise.

Jacques, an adept in Indian trade, got a large measure of dried moose meat in exchange for a few plugs of tobacco; and the Indians went away wet, but happy.

One word more about Indians—and I mean to make it a long word and a strong word, and perhaps my reader will add, a wrong word; but never mind, it is meant the other way.

This portion of the Beaver tribe trade to Hudson's Hope, the fort we have but lately quitted.

Here is the story of a trade made last summer by " the moose that walks."

" The moose that walks" arrived at Hudson's Hope early in the spring. He was sorely in want of gunpowder and shot, for it was the season when the beaver leave their winter houses, and when it is easy to shoot them. So he carried his thirty marten-skins to the fort, to barter them for shot, powder, and tobacco.

There was no person at the Hope. The dwelling-house was closed, the store shut up, the man in charge had not yet come up from St. John's; now what was to be done? Inside that wooden house lay piles and piles of all that the walking moose most needed; there was a whole keg of powder; there were bags of shot and tobacco—there was as much as the moose could smoke in his whole life.

Through a rent in the parchment window the moose looked at all these wonderful things, and at the red flannel shirts, and at the four flint guns, and the spotted cotton handkerchiefs, each worth a sable skin at one end of the fur trade, half a sixpence at the other. There was tea, too—tea, that magic medicine before which life's cares vanished like snow in spring sunshine.

The moose sat down to think about all these things, but thinking only made matters worse.

He was short of ammunition, therefore he had no food, and to think of food when one is very hungry is an unsatisfactory business. It is true that "the moose that walks" had only to walk in through that parchment window, and help himself till he was tired. But no, that would not do.

"Ah!" my Christian friend will exclaim, "Ah! yes, the poor Indian had known the good missionary, and had learnt the lesson of honesty and respect for his neighbour's property."

Yes; he had learnt the lesson of honesty, but his teacher, my friend, had been other than human. The good missionary had never reached the Hope of Hudson, nor improved the morals of "the moose that walks."

But let us go on.

After waiting two days he determined to set off for St. John, two full days' travel. He set out, but his heart failed him, and he turned back again.

At last, on the fourth day he entered the parchment window, leaving outside his comrade, to whom he jealously denied admittance. Then he took from the cask of powder three skins' worth, from the tobacco four skins' worth, from the shot the same; and sticking the requisite number of martens in the powder-barrel and the shot-bag and the tobacco-case, he hung up his remaining skins on a nail to the credit of his account, and departed from this El Dorado, this Bank of England of the Red man in the wilderness, this Hunt and Roskell of Peace River.

And when it was all over he went his way, thinking he had done a very reprehensible act, and one by no means to be proud of. Poor moose that walks! in this trade for skins you are but a small item!

Society muffles itself in your toil-won sables in distant cities, while you starve and die out in the wilderness.

The credit of your twenty skins, hung to the rafter of Hudson's Hope, is not a large one; but surely there is a Hope somewhere else, where your account is kept in golden letters, even though nothing but the clouds had baptized you, no missionary had cast water on your head, and God only knows who taught you to be honest.

Let me not be misunderstood in this matter. I believe, gentlemen missionaries, you mean well by this Indian. I will go further; you form, I think, almost the only class who would deal fairly by him, but you go to work in a wrong direction; your mode of proceeding is a mistake. If you would only be a little more human, and a little less divine—if you would study the necessities of the savage races amidst whom you have cast your lot—what good might ye not effect?

This Cree, this Blackfoot, this Chipewyan, this Beaver—what odds is it, in the name of all goodness, whether he fully understands the numbered or unnumbered things you tell him. Teach him the simple creed which you would teach a child. He is starving, and the feast you give him is of delicate and subtle food, long since compounded from the brain of schoolman and classicist. He is naked, and you would clothe him in mysterious raiment and fine tissue, which time has woven out of the webs of doubt and inquiry. All this will not warm him from the terrible blast of winter, or shelter him from the drenching rains of early summer. He has many faults, some virtues, innumerable wants. Begin with these. Preach against the first; cultivate the second; relieve as much as possible the third. Make him a good man before you attempt to make him an indifferent Christian. In a word, do more for his body; and after a bit, when you have taught him to help his wife in toil and trouble—to build a house and to live in it—to plant a few potatoes when the ground thaws, and to hoe them out ere it hardens again—when you have loosed the bands of starvation, nakedness, and hardship from the grasp in which they now hold him, then will come the moment for your books and your higher teaching. And in his hut, with a well-filled stomach, he will have time to sift truth from falsehood, amidst all the isms and arians under the guise of which you come to teach him. But just now he is only a proletarian and an open-arian, and not much even of these. Meantime I know that you wish well by him. You are ready to teach him—to tell him about a host of good, and some very indifferent, persons; but lo ! in the middle of your homilies he falls asleep, and his sleep is the sleep of death. He starves and dies out before you. Of course I know the old old answer: "He is hopeless; we have tried everything; we can do nothing." How often have I not been told, "He is hopeless; we can do nothing for this Red man!" But will any person dare to say that men such as this Indian at Hudson's Hope are beyond the cure of man? If they be, then your creed must be a poor weak thing.

CHAPTER XXII.

Still westward.—The dangers of the ice.—We enter the main range.—In the mountains.—A grizzly.—The death of the moose.—Peace River Pass.—Pete Joy.—The Ominica.— "Travellers" at home.

WE held our way up the river, fighting many a battle with the current. Round the points the stream ran strong, and our canoe was a big, lumbering affair, hollowed out of a single cottonwood tree by Jacques, years before on the Fraser River, and ill-adapted to the ice, which was our most dangerous enemy. Many a near shave we had of being crushed under its heavy floes as we coasted along beneath their impending masses. When the river breaks up, portions of it stronger than the rest remain still frozen. At the back of these the floating ice jams, and the river rises rapidly behind the barrier thus flung across it. Then the pack gives way, and the pent-up waters rapidly lower. But along the shore, on either side, the huge blocks of ice lie stranded, heaped one upon another, and the water, still falling, brushes off from beneath the projecting pieces, leaving a steep wall of ice, sometimes twenty and thirty feet, brightly rising above the water. Along these impending masses we had to steer our canoe, and hazardous work it was, for every now and again some huge fragment, many tons in weight, would slide from its high resting-place, and crash into the river with a roar of thunder, driving the billows before it half-way across the wide river, and making our hearts jump half as much again.

At one point where the river ran with unusual velocity we battled long beneath a very high ice-wall. Once or twice the current carried us against its sides. We dared not touch it with our poles, for it hung by a thread, so far did its summit project over our heads.

Gently we stole our way up from beneath it, and were still within thirty yards of it when the great boulder, looming high, crashed into the river.

On the fourth day we got clear of this shore ice, and drew near the main range of the mountains. But there was one important question which experience soon told me there was no cause for anxiety about—it was the question of food.

Game was abundant; the lower hills were thickly stocked with blue grouse—a noble bird, weighing between three and four pounds.

The bays of the river held beaver, swimming through the driftwood, and ere we had reached the mountain gate a moose had fallen to my trusty smooth-bore, in one of the grassy glens between the river and the snowy range. It was literally a hunter's paradise. This was the worst time of the year, except for beaver, but necessity knows no game law, and the wilderness at all times must find its wanderers.

We usually camped a couple of hours before sundown, for in this northern land the daylight was more than long enough to stiffen our shoulders, and make our arms ache from pole or paddle. Then came the time to stretch one's legs over these great grassy uplands, so steep, yet so free of rock; so full of projecting point and lofty promontory, beneath which the river lay in long silvery reaches, while around on every side the mountains in masses of rock and snow, lay like giant sentinels, guarding the great road which Nature had hewn through their midst.

At the entrance to the main range, the valley of the river is about two miles wide. The river itself preserves its general width of 250 to 300 yards with singular uniformity. The reaches are from one to three miles in length, the banks are dry, the lower beaches are level and well wooded, and the current becomes deeper and less rapid.

On the 8th of May we reached, early in the morning, the entrance to the main range. A short rapid marks it, a rapid easy to run at all stages of water, and up which we towed our canoe, carrying the more perishable articles to save them from the spray—a precaution which was, however, not necessary, as no water was shipped.

We were now in the mountains. From the low terrace along the shore they rose in stupendous masses; their lower ridges clothed in forests of huge spruce, poplar, and birch; their middle heights covered in dense thickets of spruce alone; their summits cut into a thousand varied peaks, bare of all vegetation, but bearing aloft into the sunshine 8000 feet above us the glittering crowns of snow which, when evening stilled the breezes, shone reflected in the quiet waters, vast and motionless.

Wonderful things to look at are these white peaks, perched up so high above our world. They belong to us, yet they are not of us. The eagle links them to the earth; the cloud carries to them the message of the sky; the ocean sends them her tempest; the air rolls her thunders beneath their brows, and launches her lightnings from their sides; the sun sends them his first greeting, and leaves them his latest kiss. Yet motionless they keep their crowns of snow, their glacier crests of

MOUNT GARNET WOLSELEY AND THE PEACE RIVER.

[*Page* 266.

jewels, and dwell among the stars heedless of time or tempest.

For two days we journeyed through this vast valley, along a wide, beautiful river, tranquil as a lake, and bearing on its bosom, at intervals, small isles of green forest. Now and again a beaver rippled the placid surface, or a bear appeared upon a rocky point for a moment, looked at the strange lonely craft, stretched out his long snout to sniff the gale, and then vanished in the forest shore. For the rest all was stillness; forest, isle, river and mountain—all seemed to sleep in unending loneliness; and our poles grating against the rocky shore, or a shot at some quick-diving beaver, alone broke the silence; while the echo, dying away in the vast mountain cañons, made the relapsing silence seem more intense.

Thus we journeyed on. On the evening of the 8th of May we emerged from the pass, and saw beyond the extremity of a long reach of river a mountain range running north and south, distant about thirty miles from us. To the right and left the Rocky Mountains opened out, leaving the river to follow its course through a long forest valley of considerable width.

We had passed the Rocky Mountains, and the range before us was the central mountain system of North British Columbia.

It was a very beautiful evening; the tops of the birch-trees were already showing their light green leaves amidst the dark foliage of the spruce and firs.

Along the shore, where we landed, the tracks of a very large grizzly bear were imprinted freshly in the sand. I put a couple of bullets into my gun and started up the river, with Cerf-vola for a companion. I had got about a mile from the camp when, a few hundred yards ahead, a large dark animal emerged from the forest, and made his way through some lower brushwood towards the river. Could it be the grizzly? I lay down on the sand-bank, and pulled the dog down beside me. The large black animal walked out upon the sand-bar two or three hundred yards above me. He proved to be a moose on his way to swim the river to the south shore. I lay still until he had got so far on his way that return to the forest would have been impracticable; then I sprang to my feet and ran towards him. What a spring he gave across the sand and down into the water! Making an allowance for the force of the current, I ran towards the shore. It was a couple of hundred yards from me, and when I gained it the moose was already three-parts across the river, almost abreast where I stood, swimming for his very life, with his huge unshapen head thrust out along the surface, the ears thrown forward, while the large ripples rolled from before his chest as he clove his way through the water.

It was a long shot for a rifle, doubly so for a smooth-bore; but old experience in many lands, where the smooth-bore holds its own despite all other weapons, had told me that when you do get a gun to throw a bullet well, you may rely upon it for distances supposed to be far beyond the possibilities of such a weapon; so, in a tenth of the time it has taken me to say all this, I gave the moose the right barrel, aiming just about his long ears. There was a single plunge in the water; the giant head went down, and all was quiet. And now to secure the quarry. Away down stream he floated, showing only one small black speck above the surface; he was near the far side, too. Running down shore I came within calling-distance of the camp, from which the smoke of Kalder's fire was already curling above the tree-tops. Out came Kalder, Jacques, and A——. Of course it was a grizzly, and all the broken flint-guns of the party were suddenly called into requisition. If it had been a grizzly, and that I had been retiring before him in skirmishing order, gods! what a support I was falling back upon! A——'s gun is already familiar to the reader; Kalder's beaver-gun went off about one shot in three; and Jacques possessed a weapon (it had been discarded by an Indian, and Jacques had resuscitated it out of the store of all trades which he possessed an inkling of) the most extraordinary I had ever seen. Jacques always spoke of it in the feminine gender. "She was a good gun, except that a trifle too much of the powder came out the wrong way. He would back her to shoot 'plum' if she would only go off after a reasonable lapse of time, but it was tiring to him to keep her to the shoulder for a couple of minutes after he had pulled her trigger, and then to have her go off when he was thinking of pulling the gun-coat over her again." When she was put away in the canoe, it was always a matter of some moment to place her so that in the event of any sudden explosion of her pent-up wrath, she might discharge herself harmlessly along the river, and on this account she generally lay like a stern-chaser projecting from behind Jacques, and endangering only his paddle.

All these maimed and mutilated weapons were now brought forth, and such a loading and priming and hammering began, that, had it really been a grizzly, he must have been utterly scared out of all semblance of attack.

Kalder now mastered the position of affairs, and like an arrow he and Jacques were into the canoe, and out after the dead moose. They soon over-

CUTTING UP THE MOOSE. [*Page* 271.

hauled him, and, slipping a line over the young antlers, towed him to the shore. We were unable to lift him altogether out of the water, so we cut him up as he lay, stranded like a whale.

Directly opposite a huge cone mountain rose up some eight or nine thousand feet above us, and just ere evening fell over the scene, his topmost peak, glowing white in the sunlight, became mirror'd in most faithful semblance in the clear quiet river, while the life-stream of the moose flowed out over the tranquil surface, dyeing the nearer waters into brilliant crimson.

If some painter in the exuberance of his genius had put upon canvas such a strange contrast of colours, people would have said it is not true to nature; but nature has many truths, and it takes many a long day, and not a few years' toil, to catch a tenth of them. And, my dear friend with the eye-glass—you who know all about nature in a gallery and with a catalogue—you may take my word for it.

And now, ere quitting, probably for ever, this grand Peace River Pass—this immense valley which receives in its bosom so many other valleys, into whose depths I only caught a moment's glimpse as we floated by their outlets—let me say one other word about it.

Since I left the Wild North Land, it has been

my lot to visit the chief points of interest in Oregon, California, the Vale of Shasta, and the Yosemite. Shasta is a loftier mountain than any that frown above the Peace River Pass. Yosemite can boast its half-dozen waterfalls, trickling down their thousand feet of rock; but for wild beauty, for the singular spectacle of a great river flowing tranquilly through a stupendous mountain range,—these mountains presenting at every reach a hundred varied aspects,—not the dizzy glory of Shasta nor the rampart precipices of Yosemite can vie with that lonely gorge far away on the great Unchagah.

On the 9th of May we reached the Forks of the river, where the two main streams of the Parsnip and the Findlay came together. A couple of miles from their junction a second small rapid occurs; but, like the first one, it can be run without difficulty.

Around the point of junction the country is low and marshy, and when we turned into the Findlay, it was easy to perceive from the colour of the water that the river was rising rapidly.

Some miles above the Forks there is a solitary hut on the south bank of the river. In this hut dwelt Pete Joy, a miner of vast repute in the northern mining country.

Some ten years ago Pete had paddled his canoe

into these lonely waters. As he went, he prospected the various bars. Suddenly he struck one of surpassing richness. It yielded one dollar to the bucket, or one hundred dollars a day to a man's work. Pete was astonished; he laid up his canoe, built this hut, and claimed the bar as his property. For a long time it yielded a steady return; but even gold has a limit—the bar became exhausted. Where had all his gold come from?

Ah, that is the question! Even to-day, though the bank has been washed year after year, "it is still rich in colour;" but the "pay-dirt" lies too far from the water's edge, hence the labour is too great.

Well, Pete, the Cornish miner, built his hut and took out his gold; but that did not satisfy him. What miner ever yet was satisfied? Pete went in for fifty things; he traded with the Indians, he trapped, he took an Indian wife; yet, through all, he maintained a character for being as honest and as straightforward a miner as ever found "a colour" from Mexico to Cariboo.

My little friend Jacques expected to meet his old brother miner Pete at his hut; but, as we came within five miles of it, a beaver swam across the river. We all fired at him, and when the smoke had vanished, I heard Jacques mutter, "Pete's not hereabouts, or that fellow wouldn't

T

be there." He was right, for, when we reached the hut an hour later, we found a notice on the door, saying that Pete and two friends had departed for the Ominica just six days earlier, being totally out of all food, and having only their guns to rely upon. Now this fact of Pete's absence rendered necessary new arrangements, for here the two courses I have already alluded to lay open—either to turn south, along the Parsnip; or north and west, along the Findlay and Ominica.

The current of the Parsnip is regular; that of the Ominica is wild and rapid. But the Parsnip was already rising, and at its spring level it is almost an impossibility to ascend it, owing to its great depth; while the Ominica, though difficult and dangerous in its cañons, is nevertheless possible of ascent, even in its worst stage of water.

I talked the matter over with Jacques, as we sat camped on the gold-bar opposite Pete Joy's house. Fortunately we had ample supplies of meat; but some luxuries, such as tea and sugar, were getting dangerously low, and flour was almost exhausted. I decided upon trying the Ominica.

About noon, on the 10th of May, we set out for the Ominica, with high hopes of finding the river still low enough to allow us to ascend it.

Ten miles above Joy's hut the Ominica enters the Peace River from the south-west. We reached its mouth on the morning of the 11th, and found it high and rapid. There was hard work in store for us, and the difficulties of passing the Great Cañon loomed ominously big. We pushed on, however, and that night reached a spot where the river issued from a large gap in a high wall of dark rock. Above, on the summit of this rock, pine-trees projected over the river. We were at the door of the Ominica cañon. The warm weather of last week had done its work, and the water rushed from the gate of the cañon in a wild and impetuous torrent. We looked a moment at the grim gate which we had to storm on the morrow, and then put in to the north shore, where, under broad and lofty pines, we made our beds for the night.

The Findlay River, as it is called, after the fur-trader, who first ascended it, has many large tributaries. It is something like a huge right hand spread out over the country, of which the middle finger would be the main river, and the thumb the Ominica. There is the North Fork, which closely hugs the main Rocky Mountain range. There is the Findlay itself, a magnificent river, flowing from a vast labyrinth of mountains, and being unchanged in size or apparent volume, 120 miles above the Forks we had lately left. At that distance it issues from a cañon similar to that at whose mouth we are now camped; and there is the second South Fork, a river something smaller than the Ominica, from whose mouth it is distant about a hundred miles.

Of these rivers nothing is known. These few items are the result of chance information picked up from the solitary miner who penetrated to this cañon's mouth, and from the reports which a wandering band of Sickanies give of the vast unknown interior of the region of the Stickeen. And yet it is all British territory. It abounds with game; its scenery is as wild as mountain peak and gloomy cañon can make it; it is free from fever or malaria. In it Nature has locked up some of her richest treasures—treasures which are open to any strong, stout heart who will venture to grasp them.

I know not how it is, but sometimes it seems to me that this England of ours is living on a by-gone reputation; the sinew is there without the soul!

It is so easy to be a traveller in an easy chair—to lay out a map and run one's finger over it and say, "This river is the true source of the Hunky-dorum, and that lake finds its outlet in the Rumtifoozle;" and it is equally easy, particularly after our comfortable dinner at the club, to stroll over to the meeting of the Society for the Preservation of Sticklebacks in Tahitian Seas, and to prove to the fashionable audience there assembled, that a stickleback was the original progenitor of the human race.

Our modern Briton can be a traveller without any trouble. He is a member of "the Club," and on the strength of his membership he can criticize "that fellow Burton," or "that queer fish Palgrave," and prove to you how, if that "poor devil" Hayward had tried the Chittral Pass instead of the Pamirsteppa, "he would never have come to grief, you know."

I know one or two excellent idiots, who fancy they are wits because they belong to the Garrick. It is quite as easy to be a traveller by simply belonging to a Travellers' Club.

Now all this would be a very harmless pastime, if something more serious did not lie behind it; just as the mania to dress ourselves in uniform and carry a rifle through the streets, would also be a very harmless, if a very useless, pastime, if a graver question did not again lie hidden beneath "our noble Volunteers;" but the club traveller and the club soldier are not content with the *rôle* of lounging mediocrity for which nature destined them. They must needs stand between the spirit of England's better genius, and England's real toilers of the wilds. They must supervise and criticize and catechize, and generally play the part of Fuzbuz to the detriment of everything which redounds to the true spirit of England's honour in the fair field of travel and discovery.

Let there be no mistake in this matter. To those veterans who still stand above the waves of time, living monuments of England's heroism, in Arctic ice or Africa's sun, we owe all honour and love and veneration. They are the old soldiers of an army passed from the world, and when Time sums up the record of their service here below, it will be but to hand up the roll to the Tribunal of the Future.

But it is of the younger race of whom we would speak—that race who buy with gold the right to determine what England shall do, and shall not do, in the wide field of geographical research; who are responsible for the wretched exploratory failures of the past few years; who have allowed the palm of discovery and enterprise to pass away to other nations, or to alien sons. But if we were to say all we think about this matter, we might only tire the reader, and stop until doomsday at the mouth of this Black Cañon of the Ominica.

CHAPTER XXIII.

The Black Cañon.—An ugly prospect.—The vanished boat.—We struggle on.—A forlorn hope.—We fail again.—An unhoped for meeting and a feast of joy.—The Black Cañon conquered.

CASTING off from camp, on the morning of the 12th, we pushed right into the mouth of the cañon. At once our troubles began. The steep walls of smooth rock rose directly out of the water—sometimes washed by a torrent, at others beaten by a back-whirl and foaming eddy. In the centre ran a rush of water that nothing could stem. Poling, paddling, clinging with hands and nails to the rock; often beaten back and always edging up again, we crept slowly along under the overhanging cliff, which leaned out two hundred feet above us to hold upon its dizzy verge some clinging pine-tree. In the centre of the chasm, about half a mile from its mouth, a wild cataract of foam forbade our passage; but after a whole morning's labour we succeeded in bringing the canoe safely to the foot of this rapid, and moored her in a quiet eddy behind a sheltering rock. Here we unloaded, and, clambering up a cleft in the cañon wall two hundred feet above us, passed along the top of the cliff, and bore our loads to the upper or western end of the cañon, fully a mile from the boat. The day was hot and sweltering, and it was hard work.

In one of these many migrations between camp and canoe, it chanced one evening that, missing the trail, my footsteps led me to the base of a small knoll, the sides and summit of which were destitute of trees. Climbing to the top of this hill I beheld a view of extraordinary beauty. Over the sea of forest, from the dark green and light green ocean of tree-tops, the solid mountain mass lay piled against the east. Below my stand-point the first long reach of the cañon opened out; a grim fissure in the forest, in the depths of which the waters caught the reflection of the sun-lit skies above, glowing brightly between the walls of gloomy rock deep hidden beneath the level rays of the setting sun, high above the cañon, high above the vast forest which stretched between me and the mountains. And the eye, as it wandered over the tranquil ocean upon whose waves the isles of light green shade lay gold-crested in the sunset, seemed to rest upon fresh intervals of beauty, until the solid ramparts rent and pinnacled, silent and impassive, caught and rivetted its glance;

as their snow-white, motionless fingers, carved in characters that ever last, the story of earth's loveliness upon the great blue dome of heaven.

We pushed through the dense underwood, loaded down with all the paraphernalia of our travel, and even Cerf-vola carried his load of boots and moose-meat. When we had finished carrying our loads, it was time for dinner; and that over, we set to work at once for the stiffer labour of hauling the canoe up the rapid of the cañon; for, remember, there was no hope of lifting her, she was too heavy, and the rocky walls were far too steep to allow of it. Up along shore, through rapid and eddy we dragged our craft, for here the north side had along its base ledges of rock and bits of shore, and taking advantage of these, sometimes in the canoe and sometimes out of it in the water, we reached at length the last edge or cliff round which it was possible to proceed at the north shore.

For a long time we examined the spot, and the surrounding cañon. Jacques and I climbed up to the top above, and then down on hands and knees to a ledge from which we could look over into the chasm, and scan its ugly features. Beyond a doubt it was ugly—the rock on which we lay hollowed down beneath us until it roofed the shore of the cañon with a half cavern, against which a wild whirlpool boiled up now and again, sinking suddenly into stillness. Even if we could stretch a line from above the rock to where our canoe lay below it, she might have been knocked to atoms in the whirlpool in her passage beneath the cavern; but the distance was too great to stretch a line across. The next and only course was to make a bold crossing from below the rock, and gain the other shore, up which it was possible to drag our canoe. Once over, the thing would be easy enough for at least a couple of hundred yards more.

We climbed back to the canoe and imparted the result of our investigation to the other two men. From the level of the boat the proposed crossing looked very nasty. It was across a wild rush of water, in the centre of the cañon, and if we failed to make a small eddy at the farther shore we must drive full upon the precipice of rock where, below us boiled and seethed the worst rapid in the cañon—a mass of wave, and foam, and maddened surge. Once out of the sheltering eddy in which we lay watching this wild scene, we would be in the midst of a rock close above the rapid. There was no time to get headway on the canoe. It would shoot from shelter into furious current, and then, if it missed yon little eddy, look out; and if you have any good angels away at home, pray that they may be pray-

RUNNING STERN FOREMOST THE BLACK CAÑON.

ing for you—for down that white fall of water you must go broadside or stern on.

The more we looked at it, the less we liked it; but it was the sole means of passing the cañon, and retreat came not yet into our heads. We took our places—Kalder at the bow, Jacques at the stern, A—— and I in the middle; then we hugged the rock for the last time, and shoved out into the swirl of waters. There was no time to think; we rose and fell; we dipped our paddles in the rushing waves with those wild quick strokes which men use when life is in the blow; and then the cañon swung and rocked for a second, and with a wild yell of Indian war-whoop from Kalder, which rose above the rush of the water, we were in the eddy at the farther shore.

It was well done. On again up the cañon with line from rock to rock, bit by bit, until, as the sun began to slope low upon the forest, we reach the foot of the last fall—the stiffest we had yet breasted. Above it lies our camp upon the north shore; above it will be easy work— we will have passed the worst of the Ominica River.

Made bold by former victory we passed our line round the rock, and bent our shoulders to haul the canoe up the slant of water. Kalder with a long pole held the frail craft out from the rock.

A—— and I were on the line, and Jacques was running up to assist us, when suddenly there came upon the rope a fierce strain; all at once the canoe seemed to have the strength of half a dozen runaway horses. It spun us round, we threw all our strength against it, and snap went the rope midway over the water; the boat had suddenly sheered, and all was over. We had a second line fastened to the bow; this line was held by Kalder at the moment of the accident, but it was in loose coils about him, and of no service to stay the doomed rush. Worse than all, the canoe, now going like an arrow down the rapid, tightened the tangled coils around Kalder's legs, and I saw with horror that he ran every chance of being dragged feet foremost from the smooth rock on which he stood, into the boiling torrent beneath.

Quicker than thought he realized his peril; he sprang from the treacherous folds, and dragged with all his strength the quick-running rope clear of his body; and then, like the Indian he was, threw all his weight to stay the canoe.

It was useless; his line snapped like ours had done, and away went the canoe down the surge of water—down the lip of the fall—away, away—bearing with her our sole means of travel through the trackless wilderness! We crouched together on the high rock, which commanded a long view down the Black Cañon, and gazed wistfully after our vanishing boat.

In one instant we were reduced to a most wretched state. Our canoe was gone; but that was not half our loss – our meat and tent had also gone with her; and we were left on the south shore of the river, while a deep, wide and rapid stream rolled between us and our camp, and we had no axe wherewith to cut trees for a raft—no line to lash them together. Night was coming on; we were without food, shipwrecked in the wilderness.

When the canoe had vanished, we took stock of all these things, and then determined on a course. It was to go back along the upper edge of the cañon to the entrance opposite our camping-place of the last night, there to make a raft from some logs which had been collected for a *cache* in the previous year, then to put together whatever line or piece of string we possessed, and, making a raft, endeavour to cross to the north shore, and thus gain our camp above the cañon.

It was a long piece of work, and we were already tired with the day's toil, but it was the sole means by which we could hope to get back to our camp and to food again. After that we would deliberate upon further movements.

When men come heavily to grief in any enterprise, the full gravity of the disaster does not break all at once upon their minds; nay, I have generally found that the first view of the situation is the ludicrous one. One is often inclined to laugh over some plight, which means anything but a laughing matter in reality.

We made our way to the mouth of the cañon, and again held a council. Jacques did not like the idea of the raft; he would go down through the Beaver swamps along the south shore, and, it might be, find the canoe stranded on some beach lower down. Anyhow he would search, and next morning he would come up again along the river and hail us across the water in our camp with tidings of his success : so we parted.

We at once set to work to make our raft. We upset the logs of the old *cache*, floated them in the water, and lashed them together as best we could, with all the bits of line we could fasten together; then we got three rough poles, took our places on the rickety raft, and put out into the turbid river. Our raft sank deep into the water; down, down we went; no bottom for the poles, which we used as paddles in the current. At last we reached the shore of a large island, and our raft was thrown violently amidst a pile of driftwood. We scrambled on shore, broke our way through drift and thicket to the upper end of the island, and found a wide channel of water separating us still from the north shore. Wading up to our middles across a shallow part of this channel, we finally reached the north shore and our camp of the previous night; from thence we worked through the forest, and just at dusk we struck our camp of the morning. Thus, after many vicissitudes and much toil, we had got safely back to our camp; and though the outlook was dreary enough—for three large rivers and seventy miles of trackless forest lay between us and the mining camp to which we were tending, while all hope of assistance seemed cut off from us—still, after a hearty supper, we lay down to sleep, ready to meet on the morrow whatever it might bring forth.

Early next morning the voice of little Jacques sounded from the other side. He had had a rough time of it; he had gone through slough and swamp and thicket, and finally he had found the canoe stranded on an island four miles below the cañon, half full of water, but otherwise not much the worse for her trip. "Let us make a raft and go down, and we would all pull her up again, and everything would yet be right." So, taking axes and line with us, we set off once more for the mouth of the cañon, and built a big raft of dry logs, and pushed it out into the current.

Jacques was on the opposite shore, so we took him on our raft, and away we went down current at the rate of seven miles an hour. We reached the island where our castaway canoe lay, and once more found ourselves the owners of a boat. Then we poled up to the cañon again, and, working hard, succeeded in landing the canoe safely behind the rock from which we had made our celebrated crossing on the previous day. The day was hot and fine, the leaves of the cotton-wood were green, the strawberries were in blossom, and in the morning a humming-bird had fluttered into the camp, carrying the glittering colours which he had gathered in the tropics. But these proofs of summer boded ill for us, for all around the glittering hills were sending down their foaming torrents to flood the Ominica.

On the night of the 13th the river, already high, rose nearly two feet. The morning of the 14th came, and, as soon as breakfast was over, we set out to make a last attempt to force the cañon. The programme was to be the same as that of two days ago; to cross above the rapid, and then with double-twisted line to drag the canoe up the fatal fall! We reached the canoe and took our places the same as before. This time, however, there was a vague feeling of uneasiness in every one's mind; it may have been because we went at the work coldly, unwarmed by previous exercise; but despite the former successful attempt, we felt the presage of disaster ere we left the sheltering rock. Once more the word was given, and we shot into the boiling flood. There was a moment's wild struggle, during which we worked with all the strength of despair. A second of suspense, and then we are borne backwards—slowly, faster, yet faster—until with a rush as of wings, and amid a roar of maddened water, we go downwards towards the cañon's wall.

"The rock! the rock!—keep her from the rock!" roared Jacques. We might as well have tried to stop an express train. We struck, but it was the high bow, and the blow split us to the centre; another foot and we must have been shivered to atoms. And now, ere there was time for thought, we were rushing, stern foremost, to the edge of the great rapid. There was no escape; we were as helpless as if we had been chained in that black cañon. "Put steerway on her!" shouted Jacques, and his paddle dipped a moment in the surge and spray. Another instant and we were in it; there was a plunge—a dash of water on every side of us; the waves hissed around and above us, seeming to say, "Now we have got you; for two days you have been edging along us, flanking us, and fooling us; but now it is our turn!"

The shock with which we struck into the mass of breakers was but the prelude to total wreck, and the first sensation I experienced was one of surprise that the canoe was still under us. But after the first plunge she rose well, and amidst the surge and spray we could see the black walls of the cañon flitting by us as we glanced through the boiling flood. All this was but the work of a moment, and lo! breathless and dripping, with canoe half filled, we lay safe in quiet eddies where, below the fall, the water rested after its strife.

Behind the rock we lay for a few minutes silent, while the flooded canoe rose and fell upon the swell of the eddy.

If, after this escape, we felt loth to try the old road again, to venture a third time upon that crossing above the rapid, let no man hold our courage light.

We deliberated long upon what was best to be done. Retreat seemed inevitable; Kalder was strongly opposed to another attempt; the canoe was already broken, and with another such blow she must go to pieces. At last, and reluctantly, we determined to carry all our baggage back from the camp, to load up the boat, and, abandoning the Black Cañon and the Ominica altogether, seek through the Parsnip River an outlet towards the South. It was our only resource, and it was a poor one. Wearily we dragged our baggage back to the canoe, and loaded her again. Then, casting out into the current, we ran swiftly down the remainder of the cañon, and shot from beneath the shadows of its sombre walls. As we emerged from the mouth into the broader river, the sheen of coloured blankets struck our sight on the south shore.

In the solitudes of the North one is surprised at the rapidity with which the eye perceives the first indication of human or animal existence, but the general absence of life in the wilderness makes its chance presence easily detected.

We put to shore. There was a camp close to the spot where we had built our first raft on the night of the disaster; blankets, three fresh beavers, a bundle of traps, a bag of flour, and a pair of miner's boots. The last item engaged Jacques's attention. He looked at the soles, and at once declared them to belong to no less an individual than Pete Joy, the Cornish miner; but where, meantime, was Pete? A further inspection solved that question too. Pete was "portaging" his load from the upper to the lower end of the cañon —he evidently dreaded the flooded chasm too much to attempt its descent with a loaded canoe. In a little while appeared the missing Pete, carrying on his back a huge load. It was as we had anticipated—his canoe lay above the rapids, ours was here below. Happy coincidence! We would exchange crafts; Pete would load his goods in our boat, we would once again carry our baggage to the upper end of the cañon, and there, taking his canoe, pursue our western way. It was indeed a most remarkable meeting to us. Here were we, after long days of useless struggle, after many dangers and hair-breadth escapes amid the whirlpools and rapids of the Black Chasm, about to abandon the Ominica River altogether, and to seek by another route, well known to be almost impassable at high water, a last chance of escape from the difficulties that beset us; and now, as moody and discouraged, we turned our faces to begin the hopeless task, our first glance was greeted, on emerging from the dismal prison, by a most unlooked-for means of solving all our difficulties. Little wonder if we were in high spirits, and if Pete, the Cornish miner, seemed a friend in need.

But before anything could be done to carry into effect this new arrangement, Pete insisted upon our having a royal feast. He had brought with him from the mining camp many luxuries; he had bacon, and beans, and dried apples, and sugar, and flour, and we poor toilers had only moose-meat and frozen potatoes and sugarless tea in our lessening larders. So Pete set vigorously to work; he baked and fried, and cut and sliced, and talked all the time, and in less than half an hour laid out his feast upon the ground. I have often meditated over that repast in after-time, and wondered if Pete really possessed the magic power of transmuting the baser victuals known to us as pork, beans, and molasses into golden comestibles, or had scarcity and the wilderness anything to say to it? It was getting late when we broke up from the feast of Joy, and, loading once more all our movables upon our backs, set out to stagger for the last time to the west end of the portage. There the canoe of the Cornish miner stood ready for our service; but the sun was by this time below the ridges of the Ominica Mountains, and we pitched our camp for the night beneath the spruce-trees of the southern shore.

At break of day next morning we held our way to the west. It was a fresh, fair dawn, soft with the odours of earth and air; behind us lay the Black Cañon, conquered at last; and as its sullen roar died away in distance, and before our canoe rose the snow-covered peaks of the Central Columbian range, now looming but a few miles distant, I drew a deep breath of satisfaction—the revulsion of long, anxious hours.

CHAPTER XXIV.

The Untiring over-estimates his powers.—He is not particular as to the nature of his dinner.—Toil and temper.—Farewell to the Ominica.—Germansen.—The mining camp.—Celebrities.

In the struggle which it was our daily work to wage with Nature, whose dead weight seemed to be bent on holding us back, the wear and tear of the things of life had been considerable. Clothes we will say nothing of—it is their function to go— but our rough life had told heavily against less perishable articles. My aneroid was useless; my watch and revolver slept somewhere beneath the Peace River; ammunition was reduced to a few rounds, to be used only upon state occasions; but to make up for every loss, and to counterbalance each misfortune, Cerf-vola had passed in safety through rapid, wreck, and cañon. On several occasions he had had narrow escapes. A fixed idea pervaded his mind that he was a good hunting-dog; it was an utterly erroneous impression upon his part, but he still clung to it with the tenacity I have not unfrequently seen evinced by certain sporting individuals who fancy themselves sportsmen; and as the impression sometimes leads its human holders into strange situations, so also was Cerf-vola betrayed into dangers by this unfortunate belief in his sporting propensities. A very keen sense of smell enabled him to detect the presence of bird or beast on shore or forest, but absence from the canoe usually obliged him to swim the swollen river—a feat which resulted in his being carried down sometimes out of sight on the impetuous torrent. He swam slowly, but strongly, and his bushy tail seemed incapable of submersion, remaining always upon the surface of the water. But about this time an event occurred which by every rule of science should have proved fatal to him.

One evening, it was the 16th of May, our larder being low, we camped early at the mouth of a river called the Ozalinca. Beaver were plentiful, fish were numerous; and while I went in quest of the former with my gun, Jacques got ready a few large cod-hooks, with bait and line. I pushed my way up the Ozalinca, and soon reached a beaver-dam. Stealing cautiously to the edge, I saw one old veteran busily engaged in the performance of his evening swim; every now and again he disappeared beneath the crystal water, rising again to the surface to look around him with evident satisfaction; presently a younger beaver appeared, and began to nibble some green willows beneath the water. They were a little too far to afford a certain shot, so I waited, watching the antics of this strangest denizen of American rivers. All at once the old veteran caught sight of me; his tail flogged loudly on the water, and down he went out of sight. I waited a long time, but he never reappeared, and I was obliged to content myself with a couple of ducks ere night closed over the pond.

When I reached the camp on the Ominica River my three companions wore long faces: the cause was soon told. Jacques had baited his hooks with moose-meat; in an evil moment he had laid one of these upon the shore ere casting it into the water; Cerf-vola had swallowed bait, hook, and line in a single mouthful; the hook was no mere salmon-hook, but one fully two inches in length, and of proportionate thickness—a full-sized cod-hook. I turned to the dog; he lay close to my outspread buffalo robe, watching the preparation of supper; he looked as unmoved as though he had recently swallowed a bit of pemmican. One might have fancied from his self-satisfied appearance that large fish-hooks had ever formed a favourite article of food with him. I gave him the greater portion of my supper, and he went to sleep as usual at my head. I have merely to add that from that day to this he has been in most excellent health. I can only attribute this fact to the quantity of fish he had consumed in his career; a moderate computation would allow him many thousand white fish and pike in the course of his life; and as he only made one mouthful of a large white fish, the addition of a fish-hook in the matter was of no consequence.

Passing the mouths of the Mesalinca and the Ozalinca—two wild, swollen torrents flowing through a labyrinth of mountain peaks from the north-west—we entered, on the third day after leaving the cañon, the great central snowy range of North-British Columbia. The Ominica was here only a slant of water, 100 yards in breadth; it poured down a raging flood with a velocity difficult to picture.

We worked slowly on, now holding by the bushes that hung out from the forest shore, now passing ropes around rocks and tree-stumps, and dragging, poling, pushing, as best we could. The unusual toil brought out the worst characteristics of my crew. Kalder worked like a horse with a savage temper, and was in a chronic state of laying violent hands upon the English miner, who, poor fellow, worked his best, but failed to satisfy the expectations of the more athletic Indian. It was no easy matter to keep the peace between them, and once, midway in a rapid, my Indian leaped past me in the canoe, seized the unoffending miner, and hurled him to the bottom of the boat. This was too much. I caught hold of a paddle and quickly informed my red servitor that if he did not instantly loosen his hold, my paddle would descend upon his hot-tempered head; he cooled a little, and we resumed our upward way.

But for all this Kalder was a splendid fellow. In toil, in difficulty, in danger, alone he was worth two ordinary men; and in camp no better wild man lived to cut, to carry, or to cook; to pitch a tent, or portage a load—no, not from Yukon to wild Hudson's Bay.

On the night of the 19th of May we reached the mouth of the Wolverine Creek, and camped at last by quiet water. We were worn and tired from continuous toil. The ice-cold water in which we so frequently waded, and which made the pole-handles like lumps of ice to the touch, had begun to tell on hands and joints. Nevertheless, when at night the fire dried our dripping clothes and warmed us again, the plate of pemmican and cup of tea were relished, and we slept that sleep which is only known when the pine-trees rock the tired wanderer into forgetfulness.

The last rapid was passed, and now before us lay a broad and gentle current, lying in long serpentine bends amid lofty mountains. So, on the morning of the 20th, we paddled up towards the mining camp with easy strokes. Around us lay misty mountains, showing coldly through cloud-rift and billowy vapour. The high altitude, to which by such incessant labour we had worked our way, was plainly visible in the backward vegetation. We were nearing the snow-line once more, but still the sheltered valleys were bursting forth into green, and spring was piercing the inmost fastness of these far-north hills.

And now I parted with the Ominica. It lay before us, far stretching to the westward, amid cloud-capped cliffs and snowy peaks; known to the gold-seeker for seventy miles yet higher and deeper into the land of mountains, and found there to be still a large, strong river, flowing from an unknown west.

And yet it is but one of that score of rivers which, 2500 miles from these mountains, seek the Arctic Sea, through the mighty gateway of the Mackenzie.

Late on the evening of the 20th of May I reached the mining camp of Germansen, three miles south of the Ominica River. A queer place was this mining camp of Germansen, the most northern and remote of all the mines on the American continent.

Deep in the bottom of a valley, from whose steep sides the forest had been cleared or burned off, stood some dozen or twenty well-built wooden houses; a few figures moved in the dreary valley, ditches and drains ran along the hill-sides, and here and there men were at work with pick and shovel in the varied toil of gold-mining.

The history of Germansen Creek had been the history of a thousand other creeks on the western continent. A roving miner had struck the glittering pebbles; the news had spread. From Montana, from Idaho, from California, Oregon, and Cariboo, men had flocked to this new find in the far north. In 1871, 1200 miners had forced their way through almost incredible hardships to the new field; provisions reached a fabulous price; flour and pork sold at six and seven shillings a pound! The innumerable sharks that prey upon the miner flocked in to reap the harvest; some struck the golden dust, but the majority lost everything, and for about the twentieth time in their lives became "dead broke;" little was known of the severity of the season, and many protracted the time of their departure for more southern winter quarters. Suddenly, on their return march, the winter broke; horses and mules perished miserably along the forest trail. At length the Frazer River was reached, a few canoes were obtained, but the ice was fast filling in the river. The men crowded into the canoes till they were filled to the edge; three wretched miners could find no room; they were left on the shore to their fate; their comrades pushed away. Two or three days later the three castaways were found frozen stiff on the inhospitable shore.

The next summer saw fewer miners at the Congo, and this summer saw fewer still; but if to-morrow another strike were to be made 500 miles to the north of this remote Congo, hundreds would rush to it, caring little whether their bones were left to mark the long forest trail. The miner has ever got his dream of an El Dorado fresh and sanguine. No disaster, no repeated failure will discourage him. His golden paradise is always "away up" in some half-inaccessible spot in a wilderness of mountains. Nothing daunts him in this wild search of his. Mountains, rivers, cañons are the enemies he is constantly wrestling with. Nature has locked her treasures of gold and silver in deep mountain caverns, as though she would keep them from the daring men who strive to rob her. But she cannot save them. When one sees this wonderful labour, this delving into the bowels of rock and shingle, this turning and twisting of river channel, and sluicing and dredging and blasting, going on in these strange out-of-the-way places, the thought occurs, if but the tenth part of this toil were expended by these men in the ordinary avocations of life, they would all be rich or comfortable. The miner cannot settle down—at least for a long time—the life has a strange fascination for him; he will tell you that for one haul he has drawn twenty blanks; he will tell you that he has lost more money in one night at "faro," or "poker," than would suffice to have kept him decently for five years; he will tell you that he has frequently to put two dollars into the ground in order to dig one dollar out of it, and yet he cannot give up the wild, free life. He is emphatically a queer genius; and no matter what his country, his characteristics are the same. It would be impossible to discipline him, yet I think that, were he amenable to even a semblance of restraint and command, 40,000 miners might conquer a continent.

His knowledge of words is peculiar; he has a thousand phrases of his own which it would be needless to follow him into. "Don't prevaricate, sir!" thundered a British Columbian judge to a witness from the mines, "don't prevaricate, sir!" "Can't help it, judge," answered the miner. "Ever since I got a kick in the mouth from a mule that knocked my teeth out, I prevaricate a good deal."

In the bottom of the valley, between the wooden houses and the rushing creek of Germansen, I pitched my tent for a short time, and in the course of a few days had the honour of becoming acquainted, either personally or by reputation, with Doe English, Dancing Bill, Black Jack, Dirty-faced Pete, Ned Walsh, Rufus Sylvester, and several others among the leading "boys" of the northern mining country. I found them men who under the rough garb of mountain miners had a large and varied experience in wild life and adventure—generous, free-hearted fellows too, who in the race for gold had not thrown off as dead weight, half as much of human kindness as many of their brothers, who, on a more civilized course, start for the same race too.

CHAPTER XXV.

Mr. Rufus Sylvester.—The Untiring developes a new sphere of usefulness.—Mansen.—A last landmark.

ON the evening of my arrival at Germansen Mr. Rufus Sylvester appeared from the south, carrying the mail for the camp. Eleven days earlier he had started from Quesnelle on the Frazer River; the trail was, he said, in a very bad state; snow yet lay five feet deep on the Bald, and Nation River Mountains; the rivers and streams were running bank-high; he had swum his horses eleven times, and finally left them on the south side of the Bald Mountains, coming on on foot to his destination. The distance to Quesnelle was about 330 miles. Such was a summary of his report.

The prospect was not encouraging; but where movement is desired, if people wait until prospects become encouraging, they will be likely to rest stationary a long time. My plan of movement to the south was this: I would dispense with everything save those articles absolutely necessary to travel; food and clothing would be brought to the lowest limits, and then, with our goods on our shoulders, and with Cerf-vola carrying on his back a load of dry meat sufficient to fill his stomach during ten days, we would set out on foot to cross the Bald Mountains. Thirty miles from the mining Congo, at the south side of the mountain range, Rufus Sylvester had left a horse and a mule; we would recover them again, and, packing our goods upon them, make our way to Fort St. James on the wild shores of Stuart's Lake—midway on our journey to where, on the bend of the Frazer River, the first vestige of civilization would greet us at the city called Quesnelle.

It was the 25th of May when, having loaded my goods upon the back of a Hydah Indian from the coast, and giving Kalder a lighter load to carry, I set off with Cerf-vola for the south. Idleness during the past three weeks had produced a considerable change in the person of the Untiring. He had grown fat and round, and it was no easy matter to strap his bag of dry meat upon his back so as to prevent it performing the feat known, in the case of a saddle on a horse's back, by the term "turning." It appeared to be a matter of perfect indifference to the Untiring whether the meat destined for his stomach was carried beneath that portion of his body or above his back; he pursued the even tenour of his way in either case, but a disposition on his part to "squat" in every pool of water or patch of mud along the trail, perfectly regardless of the position of his ten days' rations, had the effect of quickly changing its nature, when it was underneath him, from dry meat to very wet meat, and making the bag which held it a kind of water-cart for the drier portions of the trail.

Twelve miles from Germansen Creek stood the other mining camp of Mansen. More ditches, more drains, more miners, more drinking; two or three larger saloons; more sixes and sevens of diamonds and debilitated looking kings and queens of spades littering the dusty street; the wrecks of "faro" and "poker" and "seven up" and "three-card monti;" more Chinamen and Hydah squaws than Germansen could boast of; and Mansen lay the same miserable-looking place that its older rival had already appeared to me. Yet every person was kind and obliging. Mr. Grahame, postmaster, dealer in gold-dust, and general merchant, cooked with his own hands a most excellent repast, the discussion of which was followed by further introductions to mining celebrities. Prominent among many Joes and Davises and Petes and Bills, I recollect one well-known name; it was the name of Smith. We have all known, I presume, some person of that name. We have also known innumerable prefixes to it, such as Sydney, Washington, Buckingham, &c., &c., but here at Mansen dwelt a completely new Smith. No hero of ancient or modern times had been called on to supply a prefix or a second name, but in the person of Mr. Peace River Smith I recognized a new title for the old and familiar family.

Mr. Stirling's saloon at Mansen was a very fair representation of what, in this country, we would call a "public-house," but in some respects the saloon and the public differ widely. The American saloon is eminently patriotic. Western America, and indeed America generally, takes its "cocktails" in the presence of soul-stirring mementoes; from above the lemons, the coloured wine-glass, the bunch of mint, and the many alcoholic mixtures which stand behind the bar—General Washington, Abraham Lincoln, and President Grant look placidly upon the tippling miner; but though Mr. Stirling's saloon could boast its card-tables, its patriotic pictures, and its many "slings" and "juleps," in one important respect it fell far short of the ideal mining paradise. It was not a hurdy-house; music and dancing were both wanting. It was a serious drawback, but it was explained to me that Mansen had become too much " played out " to afford to pay the piper, and hurdies had never penetrated to the fastnesses of the Peace River mines.

When the last mining hero had departed, I lay down in Mr. Grahame's sanctum, to snatch a few hours' sleep ere the first dawn would call us to the march. I lay on the postmaster's bed while that functionary got together his little bags of gold-dust, his few letters and mail matters for my companion, Rufus Sylvester the express man. This work occupied him until shortly before dawn, when he abandoned it to again resume the duties of cook in preparing my breakfast. Day was just breaking over the pine-clad hills as we bade adieu to this kind host, and with rapid strides set out through the sleeping camp. Kalder, the Hydah Indian, and the Untiring, had preceded us on the previous evening, and I was alone with the express man, Mr. Rufus Sylvester. He carried on his back a small, compact, but heavy load, some 600 ounces of gold-dust being the weightiest item; but, nevertheless, he crossed with rapid steps over the frozen ground. We carried in our hands snow-shoes for the mountain range still lying some eight miles away. The trail led o'er hill and through valley, gradually ascending for the first six miles, until through breaks in the pines I could discern the snowy ridges towards which we were tending. Soon the white patches lay around us in the forest, but the frost was severe, and the surface was hard under our mocassins. Finding the snow-crust was sufficient to bear our weight, we *cachéd* the snow-shoes and held our course up the mountain. Deeper grew the snow; thinner and smaller became the pines—dwarf things that hung wisps of blue-grey moss from their shrunken limbs. At last they ceased to be around us, and the summit-ridges of the Bald Mountain spread out under the low-hung clouds. The big white ptarmigan *bleated* like sheep in the thin frosty air. We crossed the topmost ridge, where snow ever dwells, and saw beneath a far-stretching valley. I turned to take a last look to the north; the clouds had lifted, the sun had risen some time; away over an ocean of peaks lay the lofty ridge I had named Galty More a fortnight earlier, when emerging from the Black Cañon. He rose above us then the monarch of the range; now he lay far behind, one of the last landmarks of the Wild North Land.

We began to descend; again the sparse trees were around us; the snow gradually lessened; and after five hours of incessant and rapid walking we reached a patch of dry grass, where Kalder, the English miner, and the Indians with the horses were awaiting us.

CHAPTER XXVI.

British Columbia.—Boundaries again.—Juan de Fuça— Carver.— The Shining Mountains. — Jacob Astor. — The monarch of salmon.—Oregon.—Riding and tying.—Nation Lake.—The Pacific.

WE have been a long time now in that portion of the American continent which is known as British Columbia, and yet we have said but little of its early life, or how it came into the limits of a defined colony.

Sometime about that evening when we lay camped (now a long way back) upon the hill where the grim face of Chimeroo looked blankly out upon the darkening wilderness, we entered for the first time the territory which bears the name of British Columbia.

Nature, who, whether she forms a flower or a nation, never makes a mistake, had drawn on the northen continent of America her own boundaries. She had put the Rocky Mountains to mark the two great divisions of East and West America. But the theory of natural boundaries appears never to have elicited from us much support, and in the instance now under consideration we seem to have gone not a little out of our way to evince our disapprobation of Nature's doings.

It was the business of the Imperial Government a few years ago to define the boundaries of the new province to which they were giving a Constitution.

The old North-West Fur Company had rested satisfied with the Rocky Mountain frontier, but in the new document the Eastern line was defined as follows: " And to the east, from the boundary of the United States northwards to the Rocky Mountains, *and the one hundred and twentieth meridian of West Longitude.*" Unfortunately, although the one hundred and twentieth meridian is situated for a portion of its course in the main range of the mountains, it does not lie altogether within them.

The Rocky Mountains do not run north and south, but trend considerably to the west; and the 120th meridian passes out into the prairie country of the Peace River. In looking at this strangely unmeaning frontier, where nature had already given such an excellent "divide," and one which had always been adopted by the early geographer, it seems only rational to suppose that the framers of the new line lay under the impression that mountain and meridian were in one and the same line. Nor supposing such to be the case, would it be, by any means, the first time that such an error had been made by those whose work it was to frame our Colonial destiny.

Well, let us disregard this rectification of boundary, and look at British Columbia as Nature had made it.

When, some seventy years ago, the Fur Company determined to push their trade into the most remote recesses of the unknown territory lying before them, a few adventurers following this same course which I have lately taken, found themselves suddenly in a labyrinth of mountains. These men named the mountain land "New Caledonia," for they had been nurtured in far Highland homes, and the grim pine-clad steeps of this wild region, and the blue lakes lying lapped amid the mountains, recalled the Loch's and Ben's of boyhood's hours. 'Twas long before they could make much of this new dominion. Mountains rose on every side; white giants bald with age, wrapt in cloud, and cloaked with pines. Cragged and scarped, and towering above valleys filled with boulders, as though in bygone ages, when the old peaks had been youngsters they had pelted each other with Titanic stones; which, falling short, had filled the deep ravines that lay between them.

But if the mountains in their vast irregularity defied the early explorers, the rivers were even still more perplexing. Mountains have a right to behave in an irregular kind of way, but rivers are usually supposed to conduct themselves on more peaceful principles. In New Caledonia they had apparently forgotten this rule; they played all manner of tricks. They turned and twisted behind the backs of hills, and came out just the very way they shouldn't have come out. They rose often close to the sea, and then ran directly away from it. They pierced through mountain ranges in cañons and chasms ; and the mountains threw down stones at them, but that only made them laugh all the louder, as they raced away from cañon to cañon. Sometimes they grew wicked, and, turned viciously the bit, and worried the bases of the hills, and ate trees and rocks and landslips ; and then, over all their feuds and bickerings, came Time at last, as he always does, and threw a veil over the conflict; this was a veil of pine-trees.

But in one respect both mountain and river seemed in perfect accord; they would keep the land to themselves and their child, the wild Indian; but the white man, the child of civilization, must be kept out. Nevertheless the white man came in, and he named the rivers after his own names, though they still laughed him to scorn, and were useless to his commerce. Gradually this white fur-hunter spread himself through the land; he passed the Frazer, reached the Columbia, and gained its mouth; and here a strange rival presented himself. We must go back a little.

Once upon a time a Greek sailor was cast away on the shore, where the northmost Mexican coast merged into unknown lands.

He remained for years a wanderer; but when finally fate threw him again upon Adriatic coasts, he was the narrator of strange stories, and the projector of far distant enterprises.

North of California's shore, there was, he said, a large island. Between this island and the mainland lay a gulf which led to those other gulfs, which, on the Atlantic verge, Cartier and Hudson had made known to Europe.

In these days kings and viceroys gladly listened to a wanderer's story. The Greek was sent back to the coasts he had discovered, commissioned to fortify the Straits he called Annian, against English ships seeking through this outlet the northern passage to Cathay.

Over the rest time has drawn a cloud. It is said that the Greek sailor failed and died. His story became matter of doubt. More than 700 years passed away; Cook sought in vain for the strait, and the gulf beyond it.

Another English sailor was more fortunate; and in 1756 a lonely ship passed between the island and the mainland, and the long, doubtful channel was named "Juan de Fuça," after the nickname of the forgotten Greek.

To fortify the Straits of Annian was deemed the dream of an enthusiast; yet by a strange coincidence, we see to-day its realization, and the Island of San Juan, our latest loss, has now upon its shores a hostile garrison, bent upon closing the Straits of Fuça against the ships of England.

North of California, and south of British Columbia, there lies a vast region. Rich in forest, prairie, snow-clad peak, alluvial meadow, hill pasture, and rolling table-land. It has all that nature can give a nation; its climate is that of England; its peaks are as lofty as Mont Blanc; its meadows as rich as the vales of Somerset.

The Spaniard knew it by repute, and named it Oregon, after the river which we call the Columbia. Oregon was at that time the entire west of the Rocky Mountains, to the north of California. Oregon had long been a mystic land, a realm of fable. Carver, the indefatigable, had striven to reach the great river of the west, whose source lay near that of the Mississipi. The Indians had told him that where the Mississipi had its birth in the shining mountains, another vast river also rose, and flowed west into the shoreless sea. Carver failed to reach the shining mountains; his dream remained to him. "Probably," he writes, "in future ages they (the mountains) may be found to contain more riches in their bowels than those of Indostan or Malabar, or that are produced on the golden Gulf of Guinea, nor will I except even the Peruvian mines." To-day that dream comes true, and from the caverns of the shining mountains men draw forth more gold and silver than all these golden realms enumerated by the baffled Carver ever produced. But the road which Carver had pointed out was soon to be followed.

In the first years of the new century men penetrated the gorges of the shining mountain, and reached the great river of the west; but they hunted for furs, and not for gold; and fur-hunters keep to themselves the knowledge of their discoveries. Before long the great Republic born upon the Atlantic shores began to stretch its infant arms towards the dim Pacific.

In 1792, a Boston ship entered the mouth of the Oregon river.

The charts carried by the vessel showed no

river upon the coast-line, and the captain named the breaker-tossed estuary after his ship "the Columbia." He thought he had discovered a new river; in reality, he had but found again the older known Oregon. It is more than probable, that this new named river would again have found its ancient designation, had not an enterprising German now appeared upon the scene. One Jacob Astor, a vendor of small furs and hats, in New York, turned his eyes to the west.

He wished to plant upon the Pacific the germs of American fur trade. The story of his enterprise has been sketched by a cunning hand; but under the brilliant colouring which a great artist has thrown around his tale of Astoria, the strong bias of the partisan is too plainly apparent. Yet it is easy to detect the imperfect argument by which Washington Irving endeavours to prove the right of the United States to the disputed territory of Oregon. The question is one of " Who was first upon the ground ?"

Irving claims, that Astor, in 1810, was the first trader who erected a station on the banks of the Columbia.

But in order to form his fort, Astor had to induce several of the *employées* of the North-West Fur Company to desert their service. And Irving innocently tells us, that when the overland expedition under Hunt reached the Columbia, they found the Indians well supplied with European articles, which they had obtained from white traders already domiciled west of the Rocky Mountains. He records the fact while he misses its meaning. British fur traders had reached Oregon long before Jacob Astor had planted his people on the estuary of the Columbia. Astor's factory had but a short life. The war of 1813 broke out. A British ship appeared off the bar of the Columbia River, and the North-West Company moving down the river became the owners of Astoria. But with their usual astuteness the Government of the United States claimed, at the conclusion of the war, the possession of Oregon, on the ground that it had been theirs prior to the struggle. That it had not been so, is evident to any person who will carefully inquire into the history of the discovery of the North-West Coast, and the regions lying west of the mountains. But no one cares to ask about such things, and no one cared to do so, even when the question was one of greater moment than it is at present. So, with the usual supineness which has let drift from us so many fair realms won by the toil and daring of forgotten sons, we parted at last with this magnificent region of Oregon, and signed it over to our voracious cousins.

It was the old story so frequently repeated. The country was useless; a pine-forest, a wilderness, a hopeless blank upon the face of nature.

To-day, Oregon is to my mind *the fairest State in the American Union.*

There is a story widely told throughout British Columbia, which aptly illustrates the past policy of Great Britain, in relation to her vast Wild Lands.

Stories widely told are not necessarily true ones; but this story has about it the ring of probability.

It is said that once upon a time a certain British nobleman anchored his ship-of-war in the deep waters of Puget Sound. It was at a time when discussion was ripe upon the question of disputed ownership in Oregon, and this ship was sent out for the protection of British interests on the shores of the North Pacific. She bore an ill-fated name for British diplomacy. She was called the "America."

The commander of the "America" was fond of salmon fishing; the waters of the Oregon were said to be stocked with salmon: the fishing would be excellent. The mighty "Ekewan," monarch of salmon, would fall a victim to flies, long famous on waters of Tweed or Tay. Alas! for the perverseness of Pacific salmon. No cunningly twisted hackle, no deftly turned wing of mallard, summer duck, or jungle cock, would tempt the blue and silver monsters of the Columbia or the Cowlitz Rivers. In despair, his lordship reeled up his line, took to pieces his rod, and wrote in disgust to his brother (a prominent statesman of the day) that the whole country was a huge mistake; that even the salmon in its waters was a fish of no principle, refusing to bite, to nibble, or to rise. In fine, that the territory of Oregon, was not worthy of a second thought. So the story runs. If it be not true, it has its birth in that too true insularity which would be sublime, if it did not cost us something like a kingdom every decade of years.

Such has been the past of Oregon. It still retains a few associations of its former owners. From its mass of forest, from its long-reaching rivers, and above its ever green prairies, immense spire-shaped single peaks rise up 14,000 feet above the Pacific level. Far over the blue waters they greet the sailor's eye, while yet the lower shore lies deep sunken beneath the ocean sky-line. They are literally the "shining mountains" of Carver, and seamen say that at night, far out at sea, the Pacific waves glow brightly 'neath the reflected lustre of their eternal snows.

These solitary peaks bear English titles, and

early fur-hunter, or sailor-discoverer, have written their now forgotten names in snow-white letters upon the blue skies of Oregon.

But perhaps one of these days our cousins will change all that.

Meantime, I have wandered far south from my lofty standpoint on the snowy ridges of the Bald Mountains in Northern New Caledonia.

Descending with rapid strides the mountain trail, we heard a faint signal-call from the valley before us. It was from the party sent on the previous evening, to await our arrival at the spot where Rufus had left his worn-out horses a week before. A few miles more brought us within sight of the blue smoke which promised breakfast—a welcome prospect after six hours forced marching over the steep ridges of the Bald Mountains.

Two Indians, two miners, two thin horses, and one fat dog now formed the camp before the fire, at which we rested with feelings of keen delight. Tom, the " carrier " Indian, and Kalder, my trusty henchman, had breakfast ready; and beans and bacon, to say nothing of jam and white bread, were still sufficient novelties to a winter traveller, long nourished upon the sole luxury of moose pemmican, to make eighteen miles of mountain exercise a needless prelude to a hearty breakfast. The meal over we made preparations for our march to the south. In round numbers I was 300 miles from Quesnelle. Mountain, forest, swamp, river, and lake, lay between me and that valley where the first vestige of civilized travel would greet me on the rapid waters of the Frazer River.

Through all this land of wilderness a narrow trail held its way; now, under the shadow of lofty pine forest; now, skirting the shores of lonely lakes; now, climbing the mountain ranges of the Nation River, where yet the snow lay deep amid those valleys whose waters seek upon one side the Pacific, upon the other the Arctic Ocean. Between me and the frontier "city" of Quesnelle lay the Hudson's Bay Fort of St. James, on the south-east shore of the lake called Stuart's. Here my companion Rufus counted upon obtaining fresh horses; but until we could reach this half-way house, our own good legs must carry us, for the steeds now gathered into the camp were as poor and weak as the fast travel and long fasting of the previous journey could make them. They were literally but skin and bone, and it was still a matter of doubt whether they would be able to carry our small stock of food and blankets, in addition to their own bodies, over the long trail before us.

Packing our goods upon the backs of the skeleton steeds, we set out for the south. Before proceeding far a third horse was captured. He proved to be in better condition than his comrades. A saddle was therefore placed on his back, and he was handed over to me by Rufus in order that we should "ride and tie" during the remainder of the day. In theory this arrangement was admirable; in practice it was painfully defective. The horse seemed to enter fully into the "tying" part of it, but the "riding" was altogether another matter. I think nothing but the direst starvation would have induced that "cayoose" to deviate in any way from his part of the tying. No amount of stick or whip or spur would make him a party to the riding. At last he rolled heavily against a prostrate tree, bruising me not a little by the performance. He appeared to have serious ideas of fancying himself "tied" when in this reclining position, and it was no easy matter to disentangle oneself from his ruins. After this I dissolved partnership with Rufus, and found that walking was a much less fatiguing, and less hazardous performance, if a little less exciting.

We held our way through a wild land of hill and vale and swamp for some fifteen or sixteen miles, and camped on the edge of a little meadow, where the old grass of the previous year promised the tired horses a scanty meal. It was but a poor pasturage, and next morning one horse proved so weak that we left him to his fate, and held on with two horses towards the Nation River. Between us and this Nation River lay a steep mountain, still deep in snow. We began its ascent while the morning was yet young.

Since daylight it had snowed incessantly; and in a dense driving snow-storm we made the passage of the mountain.

The winter's snow lay four feet deep upon the trail, and our horses sunk to their girths at every step. Slowly we plodded on, each horse stepping in the old footprints of the last journey, and pausing often to take breath in the toilsome ascent. At length the summit was reached; but a thick cloud hung over peak and valley. Then the trail wound slowly downwards, and by noon we reached the shore of a dim lake, across whose bosom the snow-storm swept as though the time had been mid-November instead of the end of May.

We passed the outlet of the Nation Lake (a sheet of water some thirty-five miles in length, lying nearly east and west), and held our way for some miles along its southern shore. In the evening we had reached a green meadow, on the banks of a swollen stream.

While Rufus and I were taking the packs off the tired horses, preparatory to making them swim the stream; a huge grizzly bear came out upon

the opposite bank and looked at us for a moment.
The Indians who were behind saw him approach
us, but they were too far from us to make their
voices audible. A tree crossed the stream, and
the opposite bank rose steeply from the water to
the level meadow above. Bruin was not twenty
paces from us, but the bank hid him from our
view; and when I became aware of his proximity
he had already made up his mind to retire.
Grizzlies are seldom met under such favourable
circumstances. A high bank in front, a level
meadow beyond, I long regretted the chance, lost
so unwittingly, and our cheerless bivouac that
night in the driving sleet would have been but
little heeded, had my now rusty double-barrel
spoken its mind to our shaggy visitor. But one
cannot always be in luck.

All night long it rained and sleeted and snowed,
and daylight broke upon a white landscape. We
got away from camp at four o'clock, and held on
with rapid pace until ten. By this hour we had
reached the summit of the table-land "divide"
between the Arctic and Pacific Oceans. It is
almost imperceptible, its only indication being the
flow of water south, instead of north-east. The
day had cleared, but a violent storm swept the
forest, crashing many a tall tree prostrate to the
earth; and when we camped for dinner, it was no

easy matter to select a spot safe from the dangers of falling pine-trees.

As I quitted this Arctic watershed, and stood on the height of land between the two oceans, memory could not help running back, over the many scenes which had passed, since on that evening after leaving the Long Portage, I had first entered the river systems of the North.

Full 1300 miles away lay the camping-place of that evening; and as the many long hours of varied travel rose up again before me, snow-swept, toil-laden, full at times of wreck and peril and disaster; it was not without reason that, turning away from the cold northern landscape, I saluted with joy the blue pine-tops, through which rolled the broad rivers of the Pacific.

"THE LOOK-OUT MOUNTAIN."

CHAPTER XXVII.

The Look-out Mountain.—A gigantic tree.—The Untiring retires before superior numbers.—Fort St. James.—A strange sight in the forest.—Lake Noola.—Quesnelle.—Cerf-vola in civilized life.—Old dog, good-bye.

WE marched that day over thirty miles, and halted in a valley of cotton-wood trees, amid green leaves again. We were yet distant about forty-five miles from the Fort St. James, but my friend Rufus declared that a rapid march on the morrow would take us to the half-way house by sun-down. Rapid marches had long since become familiar, and one more or less did not matter much.

Daybreak found us in motion; it was a fast walk, it was a faster walk, it was a run, and ere the mid-day sun hung over the rich undulating forest-land, we were thirty miles from our camp in the cotton-wood. Before noon, a lofty ridge rose before us; the trail wound up its long ascent. Rufus called it " the Look-out Mountain." The top was bare of forest, the day was bright with sunshine; not a cloud lay over the vast plateau of Middle New Caledonia.

Five hundred snowy peaks rose up along the horizon: the Nation Lake Mountains, the further ranges of the Ominica, the ridges which lie between the many tributaries of the Peace and the countless lakes of the North Frazer. Babine, Tatla, Pinkley, Stuart's, and far off to the west the old monarchs of the Rocky Mountains rose up to look a last farewell to the wanderer, who now carried away to distant lands a hundred memories of their lonely beauty. On the south slope of the Look-out Mountain, a gigantic pine-tree first attracts the traveller's eye; its seamed trunk is dusky red, its dark and sombre head is lifted high above all other trees, and the music which the winds make through its branches seems to come from a great distance. It is the Douglas Pine of the Pacific coast, the monarch of Columbian forests, a tree which Turner must have seen in his dreams.

A few miles south of the mountain, the country opened out into pleasant prairies fringed with groves of cotton-wood; the grass was growing thick and green, the meadows were bright with flowers. Three fat horses were feeding upon one of these meadows; they were the property of Rufus.

We caught them with some little difficulty, and turned our two poor thin animals adrift in peace and plenty; then mounting the fresh steeds, Rufus and I hurried on to Fort St. James.

The saddle was a pleasant change after the hard marching of the last few days. Mud and dust and stones, alternating with the snow of the mountains, had told heavily against our moccassined feet; but the worst was now over, and henceforth we would have horses to Quesnelle.

It was yet some time before sun-down when we cantered down the sloping trail which leads to the Fort St. James. Of course the Untiring was at his usual post—well to the front. Be it dog-train, or march on foot, or march with horses, the Untiring led the van, his tail like the plume of Henry of Navarre at Ivry, ever waving his followers to renewed exertions. It would be no easy matter for me to enumerate all the Hudson's Bay forts which the Untiring had entered at the head of his train. Long and varied experience had made him familiar with every description of post, from the imposing array of wooden buildings which marked the residence of a chief factor, down to the little isolated hut wherein some half-breed servant carries on his winter traffic on the shore of a nameless lake.

Cerf-vola knew them all. Freed from his

harness in the square of a fort—an event which he usually accelerated by dragging his sled and three other dogs to the doorway of the principal house—he at once made himself master of the situation, paying particular attention to two objective points. First, the intimidation of resident dogs; second, the topography of the provision store. Ten minutes after his entry into a previously unexplored fort, he knew to a nicety where the white fish were kept, and where the dry meat and pemmican lay. But on this occasion at Fort St. James a woful disaster awaited him.

With the memory of many triumphal entries full upon him, he now led the way into the square of the fort, totally forgetting that he was no longer a hauling-dog, but a free lance or a rover on his own account. In an instant four huge haulers espied him, and charging from every side ere I could force in upon the conflict to balance sides a little, they completely prostrated the hitherto invincible Esquimaux, and at his last Hudson Bay post, near the close of his 2500 mile march, he experienced his first defeat. We rescued him from his enemies before he had suffered much bodily hurt, but he looked considerably tail-fallen at this unlooked-for reception, and passed the remainder of the day in strict seclusion underneath my bed.

Stuart's Lake is a very beautiful sheet of water. Tall mountains rise along its western and northern shores, and forest promontories stretch far into its deep blue waters. It is the favourite home of the salmon, when late in summer he has worked his long, toilsome way up the innumerable rapids of the Frazer, 500 miles from the Pacific.

Colossal sturgeon are also found in its waters, sometimes weighing as much as 800 pounds. With the exception of rabbits, game is scarce along the shores, but at certain times rabbits are found in incredible numbers; the Indian women snare them by sacksful, and every one lives on rabbit, for when rabbits are numerous, salmon are scarce.

The daily rations of a man in the wide domain of the Hudson's Bay Company are singularly varied.

On the south shores of Hudson's Bay a *voyageur* receives every day one wild goose; in the Saskatchewan he gets ten pounds of buffalo-meat; in Athabasca eight pounds of moose-meat; in English River three large white fish; in the North, half fish and reindeer; and here in New Caledonia he receives for his day's food eight rabbits or one salmon. Start not, reader, at the last item! The salmon is a dried one, and does not weigh more than a pound and a half in its reduced form.

After a day's delay at Fort St. James, we started again on our southern road. A canoe carried us to a point some five and twenty miles lower down the Stuart's River—a rapid stream of considerable size, which bears the out-flow of the lake and of the long line of lakes lying north of Stuart's, into the main Frazer River.

I here said good-bye to Kalder, who was to return to Peace River on the following day. A whisky saloon in the neighbourhood of the fort had proved too much for this hot-tempered half-breed, and he was in a state of hilarious grief when we parted. "He had been very hasty," he said, "would I squeeze him, as he was sorry; he would always go with this master again if he ever came back to Peace River;" and then the dog caught his eye, and overpowered by his feelings he vanished into the saloon.

Guided by an old carrier Indian chief, the canoe swept out of the beautiful lake and ran swiftly down the Stuart's River. By sun-down we had reached the spot where the trail crosses the stream, and here we camped for the night; our horses had arrived before us under convoy of Tom the Indian.

On the following morning, the 31st of May, we reached the banks of the Nacharcole River, a large stream flowing from the west; open prairies of rich land fringed the banks of this river, and far as the eye could reach to the west no mountain ridge barred the way to the Western Ocean.

This river has its source within twenty miles of the Pacific, and is without doubt the true line to the sea for a northern railroad, whenever Canada shall earnestly take in hand the work of riveting together the now widely-severed portions of her vast dominion; but to this subject I hope to have time to devote a special chapter in the Appendix to this book, now my long journey is drawing to a close, and these latter pages of its story are written amid stormy waves, where a southward-steering ship reels on beneath the shadow of Madeira's mountains.

Crossing the wide Nacharcole River, and continuing south for a few miles, we reached a broadly cut trail which bore curious traces of past civilization. Old telegraph poles stood at intervals along the forest-cleared opening, and rusted wire hung in loose festoons down from their tops, or lay tangled amid the growing brushwood of the cleared space. A telegraph in the wilderness! What did it mean?

When civilization once grasps the wild, lone spaces of the earth it seldom releases its hold; yet here civilization had once advanced her footsteps, and apparently shrunk back again frightened at her boldness. It was even so; this trail, with its ruined wire, told of the wreck of a great enterprise. While yet the Atlantic cable was an unsettled question, a bold idea sprung to life in the brain of an American. It was to connect the Old World and the New, by a wire stretched through the vast forests of British Columbia and Alaska, to the Straits of Behring; thence across the Tundras of Kamtschatka, and around the shores of Okhotsk the wires would run to the Amoor River, to meet a line which the Russian Government would lay from Moscow to the Pacific.

It was a grand scheme, but it lacked the elements of success, because of ill-judged route and faulty execution. The great Telegraph Company of the United States entered warmly into the plan. Exploring parties were sent out; one pierced these silent forests; another surveyed the long line of the Yukon; another followed the wintry shores of the Sea of Okhotsk, and passed the Tundras of the black Gulf of Anadir.

Four millions of dollars were spent in these expeditions. Suddenly news came that the Atlantic cable was an accomplished fact. Brunel had died of a broken heart; but the New World and the Old had welded their thoughts together, with the same blow that broke his heart.

Europe spoke to America beneath the ocean, and the voice which men had sought to waft through the vast forests of the Wild North Land, and over the Tundras of Siberia, died away in utter desolation.

So the great enterprise was abandoned, and to-day from the lonely shores of Lake Babine to the bend of the Frazer at Quesnelle, the ruined wire hangs loosely through the forest.

During the first two days of June we journeyed through a wild, undulating country, filled with lakes and rolling hills; grassy openings were numerous, and many small streams stocked with fish intersected the land.

The lakes of this northern plateau are singularly beautiful. Many isles lie upon their surface; from tiny promontories the huge Douglas pine lifts his motionless head. The great northern diver, the loon, dips his white breast in the blue wavelets, and sounds his melancholy cry through the solitude. I do not think that I have ever listened to a sound which conveys a sense of indescribable loneliness so completely as this wail, which the loon sends at night over the forest shores. The man who wrote

"And on the mere the wailing died away"

must have heard it in his dreams.

We passed the noisy Indian village of Lake Noola and the silent Indian graves on the grassy shore of Lake Noolkai, and the evening of the 2nd of June found us camped in the green meadows of the West Road River, up which a white man first penetrated to the Pacific Ocean just eighty years ago.

A stray Indian came along with news of disaster. A canoe had upset near the cotton-wood cañon of the Frazer, and the Hudson's Bay officer at Fort George had gone down beneath a pile of driftwood, in the whirlpools of the treacherous river. The Indian had been with him, but he had reached the shore with difficulty, and was now making his way to Fort St. James, carrying news of the catastrophe.

Forty more miles brought us to the summit of a ridge, from which a large river was seen flowing in the centre of a deep valley far into the south. Beyond, on the further shore, a few scattered wooden houses stood grouped upon a level bank; the wild rose-trees were in blossom; it was summer in the forest, and the evening air was fragrant with the scent of flowers.

I drew rein a moment on the ridge, and looked wistfully back along the forest trail.

Before me spread civilization and the waters of the Pacific; behind me, vague and vast, lay a hundred memories of the Wild North Land.

For many reasons it is fitting to end this story here. Between the ridge on the west shore of the Frazer and those scattered wooden houses on the east, lies a gulf wider than a score of valleys. On one side man—on the other the wilderness; on one side noise of steam and hammer—on the other voice of wild things and the silence of the solitude.

It is still many hundred miles ere I can hope to reach anything save a border civilization. The road which runs from Quesnelle to Victoria is 400 miles in length. Washington territory, Oregon, and California have yet to be traversed ere, 1500 miles from here, the golden gate of San Francisco opens on the sunset of the Pacific Ocean.

Many scenes of beauty lie in that long track hidden in the bosom of the Sierras. The Cascadel Ramier, Hood, and Shasta will throw their shadows across my path as the Untiring dog and his now tired master, wander south towards the grim Yosemite; but to link these things into the story of a winter journey across the yet untamed wilds of the Great North would be an impossible task.

z

One evening I stood in a muddy street of New York. A crowd had gathered before the door of one of those immense buildings which our cousins rear along their city thoroughfares and call hotels. The door opened, and half a dozen dusky men came forth.

"Who are they?" I asked.

"They are the Sioux chiefs from the Yellowstone," answered a bystander; "they're a taking them to the the-a-ter, to see Lester Wallick."

Out on the Great Prairie I had often seen the red man in his boundless home; savage if you will, but still a power in the land, and fitting in every way the wilds in which he dwells. The names of Red Cloud and his brother chiefs from the Yellowstone were household words to me. It was this same Red Cloud who led his 500 whooping warriors on Fetterman's troops, when not one soldier escaped to tell the story of the fight in the foot-hills of the Wyoming Mountains; and here was Red Cloud now in semi-civilized dress, but still a giant 'midst the puny rabble that thronged to see him come forth; with the gaslight falling on his dusky features and his eyes staring in bewildered vacancy at the crowd around him.

Captain Jack was right: better, poor hunted savage, thy grave in the lava-beds, than this burlesque union of street and wilderness! But there was one denizen of the wilds who followed my footsteps into southern lands, and of him the reader might ask, " What more ?"

Well, the Untiring took readily to civilization; he looked at Shasta, he sailed on the Columbia River, he climbed the dizzy ledges of the Yosemite, he gazed at the Golden Gate, and saw the sun sink beyond the blue waves of the great Salt Lake, but none of these scenes seemed to affect him in the slightest degree.

He journeyed in the boot or on the roof of a stage-coach for more than 800 miles; he was weighed once as extra baggage, and classified and charged as such; he conducted himself with all possible decorum in the rooms and corridors of the grand hotel at San Francisco; he crossed the continent in a railway carriage to Montreal and Boston, as though he had been a first-class passenger since childhood; he thought no more of the reception-room of Brigham Young in Utah, than had he been standing on a snow-drift in Athabasca Lake; he was duly photographed and petted and pampered, but he took it all as a matter of course.

There were, however, two facts in civilization which caused him unutterable astonishment—a brass band, and a butcher's stall. He fled from the one; he howled with delight before the other.

I frequently endeavoured to find out the cause

of his aversion to music. Although he was popularly supposed to belong to the species of savage beast, music had anything but a soothing effect upon him. Whenever he heard a band, he fled to my hotel; and once, when they were burying a renowned general of volunteers in San Francisco with full military honours, he caused no small confusion amidst the mournful cortêge by charging full tilt through the entire crowd.

But the butcher's stall was something to be long remembered. Six or eight sheep, and half as many fat oxen hung up by the heels, apparently all for his benefit, was something that no dog could understand. Planting himself full before it, he howled hilariously for some moments, and when with difficulty I succeeded in conducting him to the seclusion of my room, he took advantage of my absence to remove with the aid of his teeth the obnoxious door-panel which intervened between him and this paradise of mutton.

On the Atlantic shore I bid my old friend a long good-bye. It was night; and as the ship sailed away from the land, and I found myself separated for the first time during so many long months from the friend and servant and partner who

> Thro' every swift vicissitude
> Of cheerful time, unchanged had stood,

I strung together these few rhymes, which were not the less true because they were only

MORE DOGGEREL.

Old dog, good-bye, the parting time has come,
    Here on the verge of wild Atlantic foam;
He who would follow, when fast beats the drum,
    Must have no place of rest, no dog, no home.

And yet I cannot leave thee even here,
    Where toil and cold in peace and rest shall end,
Poor faithful partner of a wild career,
    Through icy leagues my sole unceasing friend,

Without one word to mark our long good-bye,
    Without a line to paint that wintry dream,
When day by day, old Husky, thou, and I,
    Toiled o'er the great Unchagah's frozen stream.

For now, when it is time to go, strange sights
    Rise from the ocean of the vanish'd year,
And wail of pines, and sheen of northern lights,
    Flash o'er the sight and float on mem'ry's ear.

We cross again the lone, dim shrouded lake,
    Where stunted cedars bend before the blast ;
Again the camp is made amidst the brake,
    The pine-log's light upon thy face is cast.

We talk together, yes—we often spent
    An hour in converse, while my bit thou shared.
One eye, a friendly one, on me was bent ;
    The other, on some comrade fiercely glared.

Deep slept the night, the owl had ceased his cry,
    Unbroken stillness o'er the earth was shed ;
And crouch'd beside me thou wert sure to lie,
    Thy rest a watching, snow thy only bed.

The miles went on, the tens 'neath twenties lay;
   The scores to hundreds slowly, slowly, roll'd;
And ere the winter won itself away,
   The hundreds turn'd to thousands doubly told.

But still thou wert the leader of the band,
   And still thy step went on thro' toil and pain;
Until like giants in the Wild North Land,
   A thousand glittering peaks frown'd o'er the plain.

And yet we did not part; beside me still
   Was seen thy bushy tail, thy well-known face;
Through cañon dark, and by the snow-clad hill,
   Thou kept unchanged thy old familiar pace.

Why tell it all? through fifty scenes we went,
   Where Shasta's peak its lonely shadows cast;
Till now for Afric's shore my steps are bent,
   And thou and I, old friend, must part at last.

Thou wilt not miss me, home and care are thine,
   And peace and rest will lull thee to the end;
But still, perchance with low and wistful whine,
   Thou'lt sometimes scan the landscape for thy friend.

Or when the drowsy summer noon is nigh,
   Or wintry moon upon the white snow shines,
From dreamy sleep will rise a muffled cry,
   For him who led thee through the land of pines.

APPENDIX.

ON THE PASSES THROUGH THE ROCKY MOUNTAINS
IN BRITISH TERRITORY,

AND

THE BEST ROUTE FOR A CANADIAN RAILROAD TO
THE PACIFIC OCEAN.

APPENDIX.

NEARLY twenty years ago we began to talk of building a railroad across the continent of North America to lie wholly within British territory, and we are still talking about it.

Meantime our cousins have built their inter-oceanic road, and having opened it and run upon it for six years: they are also talking much about their work. But of such things it is, perhaps, better to speak after the work has been accomplished than before it has been begun.

The line which thus connects the Pacific and Atlantic Oceans bears the name of the Union Pacific Railroad. It crosses the continent nearly through the centre of the United States, following, with slight deviation, the 42nd parallel of latitude. Two other lines have been projected south, and one north of this Union Pacific road, all lying within the United States; but all have come to untimely ends, stopping midway in their career across the sandy plains of the West.

There was the Southern Pacific Railroad to follow the 30th parallel; there was the Kansas Pacific line following the Republican valley, and stopping short at the city of Denver in Colorado; and there was the Northern Pacific Railroad, the most ambitious of all the later lines, which, starting from the city of Duluth on the western extremity of Lake Superior, traversed the northern half of the State of Minnesota, crossed the sandy wastes of Dakota, and has just now come heavily to grief at the Big Bend of the Missouri River, on the borders of the " Bad Lands " of the Yellowstone.

In an early chapter of this book it has been remarked that the continent of North America, east of the Rocky Mountains, sloped from south to north. This slope, which is observable from Mexico to the Arctic Ocean, has an important bearing on the practical working of railroad lines across the continent. The Union Pacific road, taken in connexion with the Central Pacific, attains at its maximum elevation an altitude of over 8000 feet above the sea-level, and runs far over 900 miles at an average height of about 4500 feet; the Northern Pacific reaches over 6000 feet, and fully half its projected course lies through a country 3000 to 4000 feet above ocean-level; the line of the Kansas Pacific is still more elevated, and the great plateau of the Colorado River is more than 7000 feet above the sea. Continuing northward, into British territory, the next projected line is that of the Canadian Pacific Railway, and it is with this road that our business chiefly lies in these few pages of Appendix.

The depression, or slope, of the prairie level towards the north continues, with marked regularity, throughout the whole of British America; thus at the 49th parallel (the boundary-line between the United States), the mean elevation of the plains is about 4000 feet. Two hundred and fifty miles north, or in the 53rd parallel, it is about 3000 feet; and 300 miles still farther north, or about the entrance to the Peace River Pass, it has fallen to something like 1700 feet above the sea-level.

But these elevations have reference only to the prairies at the eastern base of the Rocky Mountains. We must now glance at the mountains themselves, which form the real obstacle to inter-oceanic lines of railroad.

It might be inferred from this gradual slope of the plains northwards, that the mountain-ranges followed the same law, and decreased in a corresponding degree after they passed the 49th parallel, but such is not the case; so far from it, they only attain their maximum elevation in 52° N. latitude, where, from an altitude of 16,000 feet, the summits of Mounts Brown and Hooker look down on the fertile plains at the sources of the Saskatchewan River.

As may be supposed, it is only here that the Rocky Mountains present themselves in their grandest form. Rising from a base only 3000 feet above the ocean, their full magnitude strikes at once upon the eye of the beholder; whereas, when looked at in the American States from a standpoint already elevated 6000 or 7000 feet above the sea, and rising only to an altitude of 10,000 or 12,000 feet, they appear insignificant, and the traveller experiences a sense of disappointment as he looks at their peaks thus slightly elevated above the plain. But though the summits of the range increase in height as we go north, the levels of the valleys or passes, decrease in a most remarkable degree.

Let us look for a moment at these gaps which Nature has formed through this mighty barrier. Twenty miles north of the boundary-line the Kootanie Pass traverses the Rocky Mountains.

The waters of the Belly River upon the east, and those of the Wigwam River on the west, have their sources in this valley, the highest point of which is more than 6000 feet above sea-level.

Fifty miles north of the Kootanie, the Kananaskiss Pass cuts the three parallel ranges which here form the Rocky Mountains; the height of land is here 5700 feet. Thirty miles more to the north the Vermilion Pass finds its highest level at 4903; twenty miles again to the north the Kicking Horse Pass reaches 5210 feet; then comes the House Pass, 4500 feet; and, lastly, the pass variously known by the names of Jasper's House, Tête Jeune, and Leather Pass, the highest point of which is 3400 feet.

From the House Pass to the Tête Jeune is a little more than sixty miles, and it is a singular fact that these two lowest passes in the range have lying between them the loftiest summits of the Rocky Mountains from Mexico to the Arctic Ocean.

The outflow from all these passes, with the exception of the one last named, seeks on the east the river systems of the Saskatchewan, and on the west the Columbia and its tributaries. The Tête Jeune, on the other hand, sheds its dividing waters into the Athabasca River on the east, and into the Frazer River on the west.

So far we have followed the mountains to the 53° of N. latitude, and here we must pause a moment to glance back at the long-projected line of the Canadian Pacific Railroad. As we have already stated, it is now nearly twenty years since the idea of a railroad through British America was first entertained. A few years later a well-equipped expedition was sent out by the British Government for the purpose of thoroughly exploring the prairie region lying between Red River and the Rocky Mountains, and also reporting upon the nature of the passes traversing the range, with a view to the practicability of running a railroad across the continent. Of this expedition it will be sufficient to observe, that while the details of survey were carried out with minute attention and much labour, the graver question, whether it was possible to carry a railroad through British territory to the Pacific, appears to have been imperfectly examined, and, after a survey extending

APPENDIX. 349

as far north as the Jasper's House Pass, but not including that remarkable valley, the project was unfavourably reported upon by the leader of the expedition.

The reasons adduced in support of this view were strong ones. Not only had the unfortunate selection of an astronomical boundary-line (the 49th parallel) shut us out from the western extreme of Lake Superior, and left us the Laurentian wilderness lying north of that lake, as a threshold to the fertile lands of the Saskatchewan and the Red River; but far away to the west of the Rocky Mountains, and extending to the very shores of the Pacific, there lay a land of rugged mountains almost insurmountable to railroad enterprise.

Such was the substance of the Report of the expedition. It would be a long, long story now to enter into the details involved in this question; but one fact connected with "this unfortunate selection of an astronomical line" may here be pertinently alluded to, as evincing the spirit of candour, and the tendency to sharp practice which the Great Republic early developed in its dealings with its discarded mother. By the treaty of 1783, the northern limit of the United States was defined as running from the north-west angle of the Lake of the Woods to the river Mississippi along the 49th parallel; but as we have before stated, the 49th parallel did not touch the north-west angle of the Lake of the Woods or the river Mississippi; the former lay north of it, the latter south. Here was clearly a case for a new arrangement. As matters stood we had unquestionably the best of the mistake; for, whereas the angle of the Lake of the Woods lay only a few miles north of the parallel, the extreme source of the Mississippi lay a long, long way south of it: so that if we lost ten miles at the beginning of the line, we would gain 100 or more at the end of it.

All this did not escape the eyes of the fur-hunters in the

early days of the century. Mackenzie and Thompson both noticed it and both concluded that the objective point being the river Mississippi, the line would eventually be run with a view to its terminal definitions, the Lake of the Woods and the Mississippi. In 1806, the United States Government sent out two Exploring Expeditions into its newly-acquired territory of Louisiana; one of them, in charge of a Mr. Zebulon Pike of the American army, ascended the Mississippi, and crossed from thence to Lake Superior. Here are his remarks upon the boundary-line. "The admission of this pretension" (the terminal point at the river Mississippi) "will throw out of our territory the upper portion of Red River, and nearly two-fifths of the territory of Louisiana; whereas if the line is run due west from the head of the Lake of the Woods, it will cross Red River nearly at the centre, and strike the Western Ocean at Queen Charlotte's Sound. This difference of opinion, it is presumed, might be easily adjusted between the two Governments at the present day; but delay, *by unfolding the true value of the country*, may produce difficulties which do not now exist."

The italics are mine.

Zebulon Pike has long passed to his Puritan fathers. Twelve years after he had visited the shores of Lake Superior, and long before our Government knew "the value of the country" of which it was discoursing, the matter was arranged to the entire satisfaction of Pike and his countrymen. They held tenaciously to their end, the Lake of the Woods; we hastened to abandon ours, the Mississippi River. All this is past and gone; but if to-day we write Fish, or Sumner, or any other of the many names which figure in boundary commissions or consequential claims, instead of that of Zebulon Pike, the change of signature will but slightly affect the character of the document.

But we must return to the Rocky Mountains. It has ever been the habit of explorers in the north-west of America, to imagine that beyond the farthest extreme to which they penetrate, there lay a region of utter worthlessness. One hundred years ago, Niagara lay on the confines of the habitable earth; fifty years ago a man travelling in what are now the States of Wisconsin and Minnesota, would have been far beyond the faintest echo of civilization. So each one thought, as in after-time fresh regions were brought within the limits of the settler. The Government Exploring Expedition of sixteen years since, deemed that it had exhausted the regions fit for settlement when it reached the northern boundary of the Saskatchewan valley. The project of a railroad through British territory was judged upon the merits of the mountains lying west of the sources of the Saskatchewan, and the labyrinth of rock and peak stretching between the Rocky Mountains and the Pacific. Even to-day, with the knowledge of further exploration in its possessions, the Government of the Dominion of Canada seems bent upon making a similar error. A line has been projected across the continent, which, if followed, must entail ruin upon the persons who would attempt to settle along it upon the bleak treeless prairies east of the mountains, and lead to an expenditure west of the range, in crossing the multitudinous ranges of Middle and Southern British Columbia, which must ever prevent its being a remunerative enterprise.

The Tête Jeune Pass is at present the one selected for the passage of the Rocky Mountains. This pass has many things to recommend it, so far as it is immediately connected with the range which it traverses; but unfortunately the real obstacles become only apparent when its western extremity is reached, and the impassable "divide" between the Frazer, the Columbia, and the Thompson Rivers looms up before the traveller. It is true that the cañon valley of the North Thompson lies open, but to follow this outlet, is to face still more imposing obstacles where the Thompson River unites with the Frazer at Lytton, some 250 miles nearer to the south-west; here, along the Frazer, the Cascade Mountains lift their rugged heads, and the river for full sixty miles flows at the bottom of a vast tangle cut by nature through the heart of the mountains, whose steep sides rise abruptly from the water's edge: in many places a wall of rock.

In fact, it is useless to disguise that the Frazer River affords the sole outlet from that portion of the Rocky Mountains lying between the boundary-line, the 53rd parallel of latitude and the Pacific Ocean; and that the Frazer River valley is one so singularly formed, that it would seem as though some superhuman sword had at a single stroke cut through a labyrinth of mountains for 300 miles, down deep into the bowels of the land.

Let us suppose that the mass of mountains lying west of the Tête Jeune has been found practicable for a line, and that the Frazer River has been finally reached on any part of its course between Quesnelle and the Cascade range at Lytton.

What then would be the result?

Simply this: to turn south along the valley of the river, would be to face the cañons of the Cascades, between Lytton and Yale. To hold west, would be to cross the Frazer River itself, and by following the Chilcotin River, reach the Pacific Ocean at a point about 200 miles north of the estuary of the Frazer. But to cross this Frazer River would be a work of enormous magnitude,—a work greater, I believe, than any at present existing on the earth; for at no point of its course from Quesnelle to Lytton is the Frazer River less than 1200 feet below the level of the land lying at either side of it, and from one steep scarped bank to the other is a distance of a mile or more than a mile.

How, I ask, is this mighty fissure, extending right down the country from north to south, to be crossed, and a passage gained to the Pacific? I answer *that the true passage to the Pacific lies far north of the Frazer River*, and that *the true passage of the Rocky Mountains lies far north of the Tête Jeune Pass.*

And now it will be necessary to travel north from this Tête Jeune Pass, along the range of the Rocky Mountains.

One hundred miles north of the Tête Jeune, on the east, or Saskatchewan side of the Rocky Mountains, there lies a beautiful land. It is some of the richest prairie land in the entire range of the north-west. It has wood and water in abundance. On its western side the mountains rise with an ascent so gradual that horses can be ridden to the summits of the outer range, and into the valley lying between that range and the Central Mountain.

To the north of this prairie country, lies the Peace River; south, the Lesser Slave Lake; east, a land of wood and musky and trackless forest. The Smoking River flows almost through its centre, rising near Jasper's House, and flowing north and east until it passes into the Peace River, fifty miles below Dunveyan. From the most northerly point of the fertile land of the Saskatchewan, to the most southerly point of this Smoking River country, is about 100 or 120 miles. The intervening land is forest or musky, and partly open.

The average elevation of this prairie above sea level would be under 2000 feet. In the mountains lying west and north-west there are two passes; one is the Peace River, with which we are already acquainted; the other is a pass lying some thirty or forty miles south of the Peace River, known at present only to the Indians, but well worth the trouble and expense of a thorough exploration, ere Canada hastily decides upon the best route across its wide Dominion.

And here I may allude to the exploratory surveys which the Canadian Government has already inaugurated. A great amount of work has without doubt been accomplished, by the several parties sent out over the long line from Ottawa to New Westminster; but the results have not been, so far, equal to the expenditure of the surveys, or to the means placed at the disposal of the various parties. In all these matters, the strength of an Executive Government resting for a term of years independent of political parties, as in the case of the United States, becomes vividly apparent; and it is not necessary for us in England to seek in Canada for an exemplification of the evils which militate against a great national undertaking, where an Executive has to frame a budget, or produce a report, to suit the delicate digestions of evenly balanced parties.

It would be invidious to particularize individuals, where many men have worked well and earnestly; but I cannot refrain from paying a passing tribute to the energy and earnestness displayed by the gentlemen who, during the close of the summer of 1872, crossed the mountains by the Peace River Pass, and reached the coast at Fort Simpson, near the mouth of the Skeena River.

But to return to the Indian Pass, lying west of the Smoking River prairies. As I have already stated, this pass is known only to the Indians; yet their report of it is one of great moment. They say (and who has found an Indian wrong in matters of practical engineering?) that they can go in three or four days' journey from the Hope of Hudson to the fort on Lake Macleod, across the Rocky Mountains; they further assert that they can in summer take horses to the central range, and that they could take them all the way across to the west side, but for the fallen timber which encumbers the western slope.

Now when it is borne in mind that this Lake Macleod is situated near the height of land between the Arctic and Pacific Oceans; that it stands at the head of the Parsnip River (the south branch of the Peace); and that further, a level or rolling plateau extends from the fort to the coast range of mountains at Dean's Inlet, or the Bentinck arm on the coast of British Columbia, nearly opposite the northern extreme of Vancouver's Island; the full importance of this Indian Pass, as a highway to the Pacific through the Rocky Mountains, will be easily understood.

But should this Indian Pass at the head of the Pine River prove to be, on examination, unfit to carry a railroad across, I am still of opinion that in that case the Peace River affords a passage to the Western Ocean vastly superior to any of the known passes lying south of it. What are the advantages which I claim for it? They can be briefly stated.

It is level throughout its entire course; it has a wide, deep, and navigable river flowing through it; its highest elevation in the main range of the Rocky Mountains is about 1800 feet; the average depth of its winter fall of snow is about *three feet;* by the first week of May this year the snow (unusually deep during the winter) had entirely disappeared from the north shore of the river, and vegetation was already forward in the woods along the mountain base.

But though these are important advantages for this mountain pass, the most important of all remains to be stated. From the western end of the pass to the coast range of mountains, a distance of 300 miles across British Columbia, there does not exist one single formidable impediment to a railroad. By following the valley of the

Parsnip River from "the Forks" to Lake Macleod, the Ominica range is left to the north, and the rolling plateau land of Stuart's Lake is reached without a single mountain intervening; from thence the valley of the Nacharcole can be attained, as we have seen in my story, without the slightest difficulty, and a line of country followed to within twenty miles of the ocean, at the head of Dean's Inlet.

I claim, moreover, for this route that it is shorter than any projected line at present under consideration; that it would develope a land as rich, if not richer, than any portion of the Saskatchewan territory; that it altogether avoids the tremendous mountain ranges of Southern British Columbia, and the great gorge of the Frazer River; and, finally, that along the Nacharcole River there will be found a country admirably suited to settlement, and possessing prairie land of a kind nowhere else to be found in British Columbia.

With regard to the climate of the country lying east of the mountains, those who have followed me through my journey will remember the state in which I found the prairies of Chimeroo on the 22nd and 23rd of April, snow all gone and mosquitoes already at work. Canadians will understand these items. I have looked from the ramparts of Quebec on the second last day of April, and seen the wide landscape still white with the winter's snow.

In the foregoing sentences I have briefly pointed out the advantages of the Peace River Pass, the absence of mountain-ranges in the valleys of the Parsnip and Nacharcole Rivers, and the fertile nature of the country between the Lesser Slave Lake and the eastern base of the Rocky Mountains. It only remains to speak of the connecting line between the Saskatchewan territory and the Smoking River prairies.

The present projected line through the Saskatchewan is eminently unsuited to the settlement; it crosses the bleak, poor prairies of the Eagle Hills, the country where, as described in an earlier chapter, we hunted the buffalo during the month of November in the preceding year. For all purposes of settlement it may be said to lie fully 80 miles too far south during a course of some 300 or 400 miles.

The experience of those most intimately acquainted with the territory points to a line *north* of the North Saskatchewan as one best calculated to reach the country really fitted for immediate settlement; a country where rich soil, good water, and abundant wood for fuel and building can be easily obtained. All of these essentials are almost wholly wanting along the present projected route throughout some 350 miles of its course.

Now if we take a line from the neighbourhood of the Mission of Prince Albert, and continue it through the very rich and fertile country lying 20 or 30 miles to the north of Carlton, and follow it still further to a point 15 or 20 miles north of Fort Pitt, we will be about the centre of the *true* Fertile Belt of this portion of the continent. Continuing north-west for another 60 miles, we would reach the neighbourhood of the Lac la Biche (a French mission, where all crops have been most successfully cultivated for many years), and be on the water-shed of the Northern Ocean.

Crossing the Athabasca, near the point where it receives the Rivière la Biche, a region of *presumed* musky or swamp would be encountered, but one neither so extensive nor of as serious a character as that which occurs on the line at present projected between the Saskatchewan and Jasper's House.

The opinions thus briefly stated regarding the best

route for a Canadian-Pacific Railroad across the continent result from no inconsiderable experience in the North-West Territory, nor are they held solely by myself. I could quote, if necessary, very much evidence in support of them from the testimony of those who have seen portions of the route indicated.

In the deed of surrender, by which the Hudson's Bay Company transferred to the Government of Canada the territory of the North-West, the Fertile Belt was defined as being bounded on the north by the North Saskatchewan River. It will yet be found that there are ten acres of fertile land lying *north* of the North Saskatchewan for every one acre lying south of it.

These few pages of Appendix must here end. There yet remain many subjects connected with the settlement of Indian tribes of the West and their protection against the inevitable injustice of the incoming settler, and to these I would like to call attention, but there is not time to do so.

Already the low surf-beat shores of West Africa have been visible for days, and 'midst the sultry atmosphere of the Tropics it has become no easy task to fling back one's thoughts into the cold solitudes of the northern wilds.

SIERRA LEONE, *October* 15*th,* 1873.

GILBERT AND RIVINGTON, PRINTERS, ST. JOHN'S SQUARE, LONDON.

www.ingramcontent.com/pod-product-compliance
Lightning Source LLC
Chambersburg PA
CBHW030425300426
44112CB00009B/862